Paul Stenhouse MSC:
A Life of Rare Wisdom,
Compassion and Inspiration

Paul Stenhouse MSC:
A Life of Rare Wisdom, Compassion and Inspiration

Wanda Skowronska

Connor Court Publishing Pty Ltd

Connor Court Publishing Pty Ltd

Copyright © Wanda Skowronska 2021

ALL RIGHTS RESERVED. This book contains material protected under International and Federal Copyright Laws and Treaties. Any unauthorised reprint or use of this material is prohibited. No part of this book may be reproduced or transmitted in any form or by any means, electronic or mechanical, including photocopying, recording, or by any information storage and retrieval system without express written permission from the publisher.

PO Box 7257
Redland Bay QLD 4165
sales@connorcourt.com
www.connorcourt.com

ISBN: 9781922449443

Cover design by Janusz Tydda

Printed in Australia

*Dedicated to the Missionaries of the Sacred Heart,
who never cease reaching out,
and quietly change the world.*

Note

Given the various ways people referred to Father Stenhouse, and the frequency with which his name is used, this book will mostly refer to him as 'Fr Stenhouse', although some reference to him is made as 'Paul', when he was a young man, and Father Stenhouse or Fr Paul, as some used to say. Similarly the term 'Brother' in the MSC order is at times referred to as 'Br'. Also, as *Annals* underwent several name changes, the journal will be referred to simply as *Annals* as that is what most people called it, while the longer relevant title will be given in the references: e.g. *Annals Australasia: Journal of Australian Catholic Culture*. The editions of *Annals* are mostly referred to by month and year and sometimes by volume and year. The manner of giving dates varies slightly within the book but does not, I hope, impede clarity. There are many ways of writing Phd (Ph.D and PhD) and PhD is used in this text. There will be some differences in Australian and American spelling, especially if American friends of Fr Stenhouse are quoted or direct quotations yield an idiosyncratic spelling. In addition, if there were errors in quotations, some minor editing was done to aid matters. As regards the friends of Fr Stenhouse, the text and date of interviews is acknowledged in the references. While most photos are mine, several come from his friends and others from my photos of Fr Stenhouse's photos in his office at the Sacred Heart Monastery in Kensington, Sydney. Every effort has been made to verify quotations and events and copies of original interviews are with the author.

Acknowledgements

I am grateful to so many for assistance in the preparation of this book that all the acknowledgments would in themselves create a new book. Among them all, I express particular deep gratitude to: Professor James Franklin who suggested I put my fingers on the keyboard to write this biography and helped in many ways, with practical suggestions, proof-reading and moral support: Richard Stenhouse and Jamie Stenhouse who kindly shared their stories and memories with me; Peter Macinante who regaled me with accounts of the Stenhousian decades and who disappeared into alcoves and climbed incredibly high ladders, risking life and limb to find old *Annals* articles I had requested; his wonderful wife Gloria who came up with quick answers to seemingly insoluble problems; John Madden who assisted with matters legal and historical; Fr Chris McPhee who generously allowed me to view the office papers of Fr Stenhouse which were such a help in filling in some gaps; the MSC priests and brothers who recounted their stories of friendship spanning many years; Karl Schmude whose perceptive comments and suggestions were truly invaluable; Irene Drizulis who was very helpful in many ways; to all who knew Fr Stenhouse and who shared many unique, rich and poignant memories of their spiritual, wise, witty and compassionate friend; Janusz Tydda, who helped in abstruse cyber matters; and friends Maureen and Roger Goodwill, who never ceased enthusing about it all the way.

Contents

Introduction — xi

1 Childhood, books and Camden — 1

2 Early studies, ordination and Dubrovnik — 18

3 *Annals* surges ahead — 47

4 Writing on just about any subject — 82

5 Some Islamic themes from *Annals* — 108

6 Reaching out to the world, universities, and Cardinal Pell — 139

7 The people he knew — 163

8 More people he knew — 195

9 Sowing courtesy and kindness in communities everywhere — 227

10 Andiamo! And on to eternity — 261

Endnotes — 281

Introduction

On a late spring day in 2019, a large group of people crowded into the church of Our Lady of the Rosary in Kensington, Sydney. They were there to farewell Fr Paul Stenhouse, a recently deceased priest of the Missionaries of the Sacred Heart (MSC), about whom people used the terms "legendary", "distinguished", "extraordinary" and "kind." How could anyone describe this scholar, writer, publisher, historian, witty conversationalist, editor and friend? In a *Catholic Weekly* tribute published on 5 December, which stated that his gifts were "beyond summing up in any normal sense", Greg Sheridan called him "a cosmopolite of astonishing diversity and virtuosity, a prodigious reader, a knower of infinite facts and theories and a deeply wise, friendly, good, pastoral priest." In the same article Archbishop Fisher observed that Fr Stenhouse "was a missionary through and through ... His missionary vocation took him all over the world and allowed him to collect exotic languages, stories and friends along the way."

Fr Stenhouse had made a deep impression on a multitude of people who could not quite believe that he was gone, or as Archbishop Anthony Fisher put it at his funeral, had changed addresses. Frank Sheed once said that every Christian lives in the neighbourhood of eternity, and now the ever-present Fr Stenhouse, ambassador for Christ on earth, had gone there forever.

It was not only that Fr Stenhouse lived in the MSC monastery, to which belonged the renowned 'Doc' Rumble, Fr 'Paddy' Ryan and many other wonderful MSC missionaries and priests. It was not only that he was a ground-breaking scholar, accomplished linguist and acute thinker. It was not only that he had reached out to many communities – the Armenian, Lebanese, Malaysian, Chinese, Assyrian, Indonesian, Tobagan, Trinidadian, Jewish, Polish and Vietnamese – to name some. It was not only that he had sailed through the turbulence of modernity and post-modernity seemingly unscathed, albeit with skeptical, lambasting, 'Stenhousian' observations. It was even more. It was that he was a constant presence in the universe, an anchor of wisdom, a planet in the solar system – and planets do not disappear, do they?

Even if they do, larger than life figures like Fr Paul Stenhouse leave a strong spiritual legacy after they have gone. One of the mourners, Quinney Chau, told me that she made it through the riots in Hong Kong just to get a plane in order to make it to the funeral in Sydney! With tears in her eyes, she told me of her family's deep friendship with the departed priest (they had lived in Sydney for some years). Vony Sugiarto, of Indonesian background, told me how Fr Stenhouse used to visit and help her family. Chris Lim from Malaysia recalled so many students who had received his help. Members of the Trinidad/Tobago community, for whom Fr Stenhouse said Mass at the monastery each year, had come out of respect for their beloved friend.

After the funeral, driving down to St Mary's Towers at Douglas Park for the burial with *Annals* co-workers Hendrikus Wong and Peter Macinante, I heard stories of frantic, late-night drives to publishers to get *Annals* printed, and continual visits to students and families all over Sydney. Dramatic tales and memories hovered around all of us.

A few days later, some friends of Fr Stenhouse contacted me and suggested that, as I had written for *Annals* in recent times, I should try to put something down in print. I was very hesitant. It was clear to me that it was well-nigh impossible to write such a biography,

Introduction

for several volumes would not be enough. As *Annals* writer Robert Stove observed, quoting Sydney Smith, "'[t]he meaning of an extraordinary man is that he is eight men, not one man."

As the days went by, however, I felt that filaments of a deeply rich life were swirling around me. How to stem this rapid flow of memories, to prevent them from disappearing into the ether forever? At the very least some of us could try recording some of them. And so it happened that what I thought well-nigh impossible started to take form, even if I felt I was a tiny sparrow fluttering around trying to describe an eagle. I could see that people wanted to remember this fervent follower of Christ, this assiduous helper and hero for God, seeking some anchor for their memories within the passing of time. This book is the result – a general narrative told in broad brushstrokes by one who met Fr Stenhouse in the latter part of his life. May it be a gateway to wider reflection on this wonderful priest.

Having written for *Annals* for over fifteen years, that longest lived Catholic publication in Australian history, whose circulation outdid the *Bulletin* at one stage, it was a privilege, as it was for all who met Fr Stenhouse, to sense something of that ceaselessly enquiring mind and spirit dedicated to his religious order – the Missionaries of the Sacred Heart. It was a privilege to encounter a soul so focused on what is meaningful and true, burning with endless zeal, seeking God in every crevice, mountain, every hidden shadow and in all corners of the universe.

فَلْيَكُن
مَحْبُوبًا
فِي كَلِ مَكَان
قَلْبُ يَسُوعِ
الأَقْدَس

'May the Sacred Heart of Jesus be everywhere loved'

Written by Father Stenhouse and kept in his office at the Monastery of the Sacred Heart Kensington, among other comments and Biblical passages in several languages.

1
CHILDHOOD, BOOKS AND CAMDEN

He in our childhood with us walks,
And with our thoughts mysteriously He talks.

'The Approach', Thomas Traherne.

There are some souls who enter this world quietly, yet are like blazing comets, infused by extraordinary wisdom and light. Despite our sad world, they seek its goodness and find it. They create oases of kindness, and draw many to see what they see, a vision of the world within and beyond. And then, after their earthly stay, they fly to eternity with many gazing on at the fiery trails that their words and deeds have left behind. This is the story of such a person – Father Paul Stenhouse – who by his gifts of mind and soul, graced his religious order, his country and countless friends, with wisdom, compassion and inspiration. What follows here are the outlines of some of the heights, depths, and spiritual lights of his life.

Paul Francis Lester Stenhouse was born on 9 December 1935, in Casino, 726 km north of Sydney, Australia. His father, Richard, was born in New Zealand but later moved to Australia.[1] He met Paul's mother, May Kathleen Huntley Skinner (known as May), and in 1933 married her in Camden, NSW. Soon afterwards, the young Stenhouses moved to Casino. This was around the time of the Depression and people moved to wherever they could find employment. Paul's father actually had obtained work as a journalist in Casino, as related to me by his friend Margaret Fisher who had heard it from Paul himself.[2] Not long after this, Paul's father was forced to change his line of work to do painting, doubtless due to the economic crises of the time. Paul was born during this time in Casino but in his first year tragedy struck the family and affected their lives forever. As related to me by Richard Stenhouse (junior), his brother, their father died from complications of pneumonia. So Paul and Richard, (Paul's elder brother by 18 months), never had the chance to know their father. Shortly after the funeral in Casino, Mrs Stenhouse moved back to Camden, to the area where she had lived and where many of her family lived.

Camden was a familiar world to return to – everybody knew everybody. The young Stenhouse family was surrounded by closer and more distant relations, by great-aunts and great-uncles and cousins who owned land, many of whom kept peacocks on their farms and grew muscatel grapes.[3] The young Paul saw it all and took in myriad scenes of those times, a true budding observer of nature and people. This old world Camden had a sawmill, milk-works, and even an old saddlery, with saddles, bridles and stirrups showing in the front windows! There were still horses on the road. May Stenhouse and her young children initially lived at the Coaching Inn in Argyle Street Camden (the young Paul's first memory of Camden is of this Inn) before moving to a house in Oxley Street in the same area. As related by Paul Stenhouse himself, in an memoir of his childhood which he wrote in the final edition of *Annals* (November, 2019), the house had been previously owned by the wife of an Anglican Bishop, Edward Wilton. When the Stenhouses moved in, they lived with other family and boarders, as well as having a passing parade of people staying at various times. Brother Richard Stenhouse told me that his grandmother (his mother's mother, to whom he was close) lived with them and helped financially as "the widow's pension was not much."

Childhood, books and Camden

As anyone who met Fr Stenhouse will recall, he was extraordinarily observant for piquant and 'human' details around him – and this applies to the memories of his childhood. He listened keenly to stories of his family's history. Not everyone can trace their ancestry back several generations, but if anyone could do it, it was Paul. On his paternal side he was descended from John Farrell who was a gifted journalist, social reformer, poet and editor, who was much admired by contemporaries such as Henry Lawson.[4] On his mother's side he was a descendant of Thomas Huntley, a farmer from Tenterden in Kent, whose son, George Huntley, came to Australia in 1839 on the *Cornwall* and married Eliza Willis from Crookwell in 1843. From this marriage came many branches of the family whom the future priest met and knew.

The very first memory of Paul Stenhouse was related in a 2014 *Annals* article:

> My first clear individual memory is of my brother Richard, aged about three, walking past me, or more accurately, walking underneath me, one day in the mid-1930s as I was sitting in an old-fashioned high chair, placed on large flagstones near the front entrance of an old Coaching Inn – long since demolished in the name of progress – that was our grandmother's home in Argyle Street Camden. My brother was strolling past the chair wearing a brightly coloured cap. I must have been around eighteen-months-old. My extra height, thanks to the chair, seems somehow to have gone to my head, or perhaps I wanted Richard to notice me. Whatever the case I distinctly remember leaning over and trying to grab his cap. Naturally he clung on to it, and in the tussle that ensued my high chair and I toppled over. I have no idea what happened to the chair, and I suppose that I must have been hurt, but I have no memory of any of that. I do remember stretching for the cap, and certainly remember falling. My brother recalls the

incident too, though I've never thought to apologise to him for trying to grab his cap ... I blame no one but me.[5]

Though this article is about the "unique Treasury of Memories and Mystery" within the Catholic Church and within all of us, Fr Stenhouse's focus turns to his "foolishness" here and the strange nature of memory itself, that enigmatic realm where some things stay and from which some things are lost. What was evident in this reflection on young Paul's life, along with his keen sense of observation, was an unflinching sense of realism and a reluctance to sentimentalise the past or, indeed, anything. So Stenhousian one might say! And that word 'Stenhousian' will crop up at times in the following pages to describe various aspects of his life, as there was something unexpected and striking about them. His brother Richard shows a similar intense realism, especially when remembering the overriding shadow of World War II which was not far from the family's thoughts at that time in Camden. In fact, as he related to me, the Stenhouses prayed every night for their mother's brother, Amos Skinner, who fought the Japanese in Papua New Guinea and who was captured there. His name is recorded on the Australian ex-Prisoners of War Memorial site as: "Skinner, Amos, Richard, NX24832, 2/30 infbn, Private, Japanese, Held Fukuoka Japan."[6] Richard told me that while his uncle Amos survived, he told horrific stories of how the prisoners had had to do back-breaking work for the Japanese. Many of his fellow Australians ended up at the earthly hell of the Burma Railway. As children, Paul and Richard heard about it and would have been rapt listeners and observers of the brave airmen coming and going to the town. As one Camden historical site says:

> There were thousands of servicemen who passed through the Camden area between 1939 and 1946 at the various defence facilities. Many of those who enlisted in the Camden district probably had little to do with the area

except for the fact that they came here to enlist and most likely had their initial training for the Army and Air force at one of the training establishments. That they were here is ample reason to honour them ... The major military establishments were the Narellan Military Camp on the Northern Road at Narellan, and the Eastern Command Training School at Studley Park, Narellan.[7]

As the Air Force personnel were allowed some visits from their families, the latter needed rooms to rent in Camden. Thus the Oxley Street rooms where the Stenhouses lived were very sought after.

This house was near the war-time camp, also not far from the saddlery in Argyle street – a strong contrast of old and new – horses and planes! It was also close to Mrs Stenhouse's childhood home called *Matavai*, in Cobbitty. *Matavai* is a place whose name resonated with deep significance. May Stenhouse wrote a detailed account of her childhood there saying, "it was my spiritual home until I was received into the Catholic church."[8] She said this place "conjures up many, many memories – some nostalgic, some delightful and some with a sadness that can hurt even now."[9] She remembers the kerosene lamps, the visiting remittance men, the fruit picking, the dances, fireplaces and a homestead filled with people – a true kaleidoscope of Australiana. This part of the world was more rural compared to its highly built-up appearance and modern infrastructure nowadays. And, yet, it was his mother's childhood home which engraved itself, with a deep, almost mythic significance into the mind and hearts of the Stenhouses over the years. People with whom Fr Stenhouse corresponded over the years would have perhaps been puzzled by the word '*Matavai*' in his email address. I imagined it was some exotic Polynesian village which he might have visited once, as he had been to so many places. But no. The reason he used it was simple – it was the lively, colourful, quintessentially Australian place where his mother had lived. One can only imagine, despite his lack of sentimentalism, the deep emotion behind the choice of word the priest-son took as his 'permanent' cyber address when the digital world took over.

Fr Stenhouse recalls that growing up in Camden, from the late 1930s till 1953, yielded memories which were, "on the whole happy ones."[10] While Paul's mother had been born and raised in Cobbitty as an Anglican, in 1924 when she was in her twenty-first year, she read widely on many subjects and found herself poring over the history of Christianity. Having a questioning nature, one thing led to another, and she found her way into the Catholic Church believing it to be the church Christ founded, which has happened to many converts. One would not be understating it to say this had a profound effect on the lives of her children.

Despite this life-changing conversion, May Stenhouse maintained her contact and friendship with Anglicans and in this lies the seed of that characteristic reaching out to people of all faiths and backgrounds in the future priest. As priest and author Fr Michael Fallon states of him: "He picked up from his mother a deep respect for people", adding that her "influence on Paul was immense."[11] This influence extended from matters of the faith to the world of reading and engendered a love for books. This love of books included such things as French Fairy Tales – old volumes of *contes et legendes*. His aptitude for French would have been sparked in these early years (he called it his favourite language) though no-one, not even the future priest, would have had an inkling of the extraordinary aptitude for languages, ancient and modern, which was to reveal itself in due course. Rob Marden, a friend from Camden, recalls his mother saying that May Stenhouse was "lively, happy and chatty", teaching all "to discover and inspect" a person interested in everything. Does this remind us of someone?

Photo of the old St Paul's Church in Camden, reprinted with permission of the Camden Historical Society.

Aerial photo of Camden circa 1950, reprinted with permission of the Camden Historical Society.

Paul Stenhouse (left) stands with his brother Richard circa 1940 and (right) Annie Stenhouse, grandmother of Richard and Paul Stenhouse. Undated.

Back row: Richard Stenhouse (left), father of Paul and Richard; Richard Stenhouse senior (right), their grandfather. Written on the back of the photo are the following names from left to right: Grandmother Farrell, Aunty Alice Anderson, Aunty Olivia Macinante and Aunt Moya O'Brien. In front is Betty O'Brien.

Richard (left) and Paul (right) on a Sydney street in 1943 with a family relation; on right, a teenage Paul Stenhouse (centre) with his mother (right) and grandmother shortly before entering the Apostolic School, a minor seminary, at Douglas Park.

The house called 'Matavai' (sometimes written Matavoi) in Cobbitty, where Paul and Richard Stenhouse's mother, May Huntley Skinner, spent her childhood years with memories of swagmen, dances, fruit picking and social occasions. She wrote a memoir of this time and a copy was among Fr Stenhouse's papers in his Sacred Heart Monastery office in Kensington, Sydney.

Fr Stenhouse's uncle (his mother's brother), Private Amos Skinner (front row, first on the left) with fellow Australian soldiers, in Osaka, Japan, 1945. These Australian prisoners-of-war were released on Kyusai, Southern Japan and hitchhiked 200 miles to reach Allied occupation troops, living off the land and asking food from Japanese civilians. https://www.awm.gov.au/collection/C243875.

Fr Stenhouse's brother Richard (right) and nephew Jamie Stenhouse (left) at the memorial evening to Fr Stenhouse held at the Monastery of the Sacred Heart chapel, just before his funeral, on 26 November 2019. In later years, Richard (left) with his brother Paul share a light moment with their mother May Stenhouse.

Childhood, books and Camden

Early education at home

Many may be surprised to learn that the young Paul did not attend school in his early years as he was home-schooled by his mother due to his sicknesses and from her he imbibed his faith and early learning. In his own reflection on this time he states:

> I had various illnesses that stopped my getting what you could call a normal schooling but gave me a unique opportunity to be educated by my mother. I am a product of home schooling more than anything else.[12]

Regarding these illnesses, Paul's brother Richard told me that Paul had an "enlarged heart" and problems with breathing due to asthma. He had the continual care of the local GP, Doctor Gregory, and evidently was not thought healthy enough to attend school. Mrs Stenhouse had not had the chance of a formal education herself but was very much self-taught, knowledgeable and very well-read. Young Paul was read to and taught languages at an early age and quickly became proficient in literacy and language. Instead of receiving toys as presents, the children mostly got books at Christmas and on birthdays. Being read to by various members of the household was a precious memory for Paul and the basis of a continual theme of his educational advice in later years. He even talks of 'exploiting' others to read to him:

> All the things that are said these days about the advantages of children being read to by parents and siblings are true from my experience ... And being read to is a wonderful aid to bonding between adults and children. I loved being read to. My mother and grandmother and my brother Richard would read to me until they discovered that I knew perfectly well how to read, and was exploiting their kind natures.[13]

Conversations, some schooling in Camden

Also significant as a means of learning and a conduit to the world beyond was the fact that the household was full of people, not only airmen, who told stories of all kinds. According to Fr Stenhouse's account, in their Oxley Street house lived Mrs Stenhouse, her two sons, their uncles Frank and Roy and two guests, Bessie O'Dwyer and one whom Paul Stenhouse called the "tall, refined old gentleman whose name escapes me."[14] As well, the house welcomed various tramps who would turn up at the door and there would always be a meal for them and their clothes would be washed – and all had their stories. As Fr Stenhouse recalls:

> Tramps could come to Camden from Cobbitty and stay with us. They had been accustomed to hospitality at Matavai, where my grandmother would never turn them away. So they continued to stay with us when the family moved to Camden. They lived in the house, ate with us and used the time to get their few clothes cleaned and ironed and then would set out again on their travels. They were proud men and would always find some work to do around the house while they were with us. [15]

Those who knew Fr Stenhouse, witnessed his facility for getting on with a wide variety of people throughout his life, from distinguished scholars, soldiers, shopkeepers, students, wandering salesmen and homeless people. Again, so typically Stenhousian. His early experience with the people at Oxley Street doubtless contributed to his future facility as a priest in getting on with Labor and Liberal politicians, not to mention Orthodox priests, Rabbis, Imams, Buddhists, and ministers of various Protestant denominations. He later learned to converse with people in various languages about current issues, to tune into what they needed and to help them if required. This is a rare quality, to penetrate the surface of what a person says and understand what lies within – a capacity for social and spiritual empathy. He always found common human ground with others and listened to what they said. When he was silent, he was not aloof, but thinking, turning things over in his mind, with his unique ability to assess the complexities of the situation. It all started in Oxley Street!

Of the time that young Paul did later spend in school, when he recovered from his illnesses, he recalls the teaching of the Sisters of St Joseph at St Paul's Convent School in Camden with gratitude and affection, noting their example of generosity and self-sacrifice. In previous times, John Macarthur had provided a building in that area and a Catholic teacher to instruct the children of the employees who worked on his estate.[16]

The Parish of Camden was established in 1859 while Archbishop Polding was still in office as the Archbishop of Sydney. When a Fr Sheridan arrived in 1879 he began the task of finding suitable teachers for the school. He wrote to none other than Mother Mary MacKillop and the Sisters of St Joseph requesting them to establish a school similar to St. Anthony's at Picton. Finally, in January of 1883, two Josephite nuns arrived and began classes there. In 1900, it became clear that the school wasn't large enough and a new school was begun. As the school's website recounts, the children helped to clean the bricks for re-use and the new, expanded school was opened on 3 March 1901.[17]

Richard Stenhouse recalls the fact that by the time his brother Paul started school, he was easily the "smartest kid in the class", which did not always endear him to everyone. He remembers occasions where Paul's intelligence and defence of what he thought to be true upset other children, as can happen in any school, such is human nature. Richard said occasionally some helpful students told him, "You'd better get him out of here or he'll get killed" and Richard would intervene and get Paul out of harm's way.

The local ambience of Camden made a deep impression on the young Paul. He recalls the parish priest of Camden, Father O'Dea and the people of Burragorang Valley, the Oaks, Menangle and Teresa Park. In particular, he recalls that a Mr Carlon from Burragorang Valley enchanted the children with tales of hidden caves in the valley.[18] The great hope to explore these caves, which in Paul's mind had been transformed into mysterious caverns, was dashed by the building of Warragamba Dam which flooded the Burragorang Valley and its surrounds. This flooding of the nearby valley did not impede his adventurous spirit, however, as his later life showed.

Meantime in the midst of exploring the environs of Camden, the memories of the future priest are of "summer days, unvaryingly and often unbearably hot" and swimming in the Nepean River. Alongside these hot summers are memories of the harder side of life, hauling large "blocks of ice back home with his brother from the ice-works just up from the railway stations", the "black frosts of winter", and "reading by lamp-light" which may have affected his vision.[19]

Leaving school and finding work

While Camden and its surrounding towns and farms were the setting for young Paul's activities and learning, this did not have the effect of limiting him to provincial interests alone – quite the opposite. Within the ambience of saddleries, tales of mysterious caves, ice-boxes, a large interesting household and endless reading, there was the conviction that not only this world but the world beyond was of profound interest. In particular, the Catholic Church provided a stable moral universe that threaded it all together. Through the influence of a mother very devoted to the Catholic faith, the sisters of St Joseph, the parish priest Father O'Dea, and Camden's Catholic milieu, he clearly came to understand that the Catholic church was his Western cultural heritage. Whether it was because of his illness or some other reason, the young Paul was not an altar boy, unlike his older brother Richard who remained one until he was 18 so that everyone thought that Richard would become a priest. There was no indication from young Paul as yet that he wanted to be one. Nevertheless, he understood that his Catholic faith was an all embracing world, one in which all persons were included, that life was threaded with suffering, that there was always much to be seen, observed and learned from all humanity – and part of that learning came from regularly reading *Annals*! Richard recalls their reading this publication, enjoying its children's section and, in particular, seeing Paul read the articles of Father 'Doc' Rumble and absorbing the Catholic universe in this way. However, the honour of mentioning the name of Paul Stenhouse for the first time in print must go to the *Catholic Weekly* of 5 December 1946, where birthday greetings are listed on the Children's Page, among the names being that of 11-year-old Paul Stenhouse.[20]

In the meantime, the future priest left the world of formal schooling at age 15, as the school only went up to Intermediate level. Why did he leave school at such a young age? His brother Richard and cousin Trish Kavanagh think that, given the financial difficulties of the household, there was no possibility of paying the fees for any higher education at the nearest Catholic School, St Gregory's at Campbelltown. So Paul had no option at the time but to start work. In addition, he had an inherent interest in journalism, for his father and great-grandfather had engaged in it, not to mention the evident facility with words on the part of his mother. The first long-term job was with the *Camden News* where he learned, as did most budding journalists of the time, how to be a machinist, compositor and linotypist. It was a way of combining his interest in stories, facts and figures with a necessary job. As Richard relates, Paul also worked as an usher at the local cinema on

Saturday afternoons, at one stage having the job of keeping children who bought 'Stalls' tickets within the Stalls, to stop them sneaking into 'better' sections like the 'Dress Circle'. As a young boy, while writing his stories, he was enacting justice at the local cinema!

Once he started earning money, as brother Richard relates, Paul handed his paypacket over to his mother, as he did himself. Meantime Paul had enduring memories of his early days in journalism: "I have fond memories of Mr George Sidman, who gave me my first job on the *Camden News*, and taught me much," and goes on to say that "Sidman gave me a little book that I still treasure entitled *The Law of Libel and the Press* along with advice about writing that still stands me in good stead."[21] Along with the Bible, this would have been a constant in his life. When you think of it, in an age of growing litigation, Fr Stenhouse managed to walk through the libel minefield all his life and, as far as I know, was never sued, though some vented their anti-Catholic spleen on him in poison pen letters which he read in an unfazed way and responded to with a welter of facts. Even enemies of the Church would eventually find a good word to say about him in the end. Perhaps because he would always find a good word to say about them.

The future editor of *Annals* worked on the *Camden News*, *Campbelltown News*, the *Picton Post*, and at the same time produced the *Warragamba Times* as an extra task. He certainly learned how to set out an entire newspaper by learning the technical aspects of journalism. This would have been of immense benefit later as he could set out the various sections of *Annals* with great skill. Later, he also showed aptitude in adapting to the digital world, as related by Greg Quinn, friend and computer programmer who worked with Fr Stenhouse in the days to come.

In the meantime, the teenage Paul looked with gratitude on the world around him. He mentions a Mr Gordon Thomas "who reported Camden Council Meetings for the *Campbelltown News*, and on numerous occasions steered me safely around hidden and dangerous journalistic reefs."[22] Gordon's vast experience of Canadian journalism, and his varied life experiences on the Klondike and riding out the Depression, left a lasting impression on the fledgling writer. Gordon Thomas died in 1952, however, as did George Sidman not long after. While reporting the news in Camden, the young Paul Stenhouse must have wondered what on earth he would do for the rest of his life.

2

EARLY STUDIES, ORDINATION AND DUBROVNIK

*I will pass my life in the presence of Yahweh,
in the land of the living.*

Psalm 116

In one of those ironies that resonated long throughout his life, the young Paul Stenhouse decided to become a priest when he saw an advertisement for the Apostolic School (a minor seminary) in the *Annals*! He himself attests to this. The Missionaries of the Sacred Heart (MSC) ran an Apostolic School for young men at St Mary's Towers Douglas Park, south of Camden. In his own words, Fr Stenhouse says that an advertisement "caught the eye of a 17-year-old linotypist and compositor/reporter working at the time for *The Camden News*."[1] No-one could add to such a prophetic moment – a calling to the priesthood from a journal he was to edit. Perhaps had there been someone around speaking Samaritan, Hebrew or Ugaritic at the time, that would have provided an extra prophetic sign. There is no evidence, however, that anyone was speaking Ugaritic in the environs of Camden on that day.

Some describe their journey to the religious life as a long, complex route. It was not so with young Paul, who seems to have sped like an arrow shot from a strong bow, to his spiritual destination. Who can say, nevertheless, what deep thoughts transpired in his soul when the divine call came? It is safe to say that having received his interior inspiration, he did not look to the left or the right but just saw his future path as one leading to the priesthood. He got in touch with the MSCs and, as his brother Richard recalls, Paul told his family without much fanfare that he was going to be a priest and was going to Douglas Park. The seventeen-year-old Paul would have packed his bags one day in 1953 and said good-bye to his mother, brother and other family. His older brother Richard (a mechanic by then) drove them all to St Mary's Towers Douglas Park in his Plymouth car. In fact Douglas Park was not too far from Camden. Paul was duly enrolled in the Apostolic School and began boarding there to tackle his senior high school years which he had missed out on by leaving school early and going to work as a journalist. A great adventure in spiritual growth and learning had begun.

In his book *Monastery on the Hill: A History of the Sacred Heart Monastery Kensington: 1907-1997* (2000), Anthony Caruana states of Paul Stenhouse that "at the age of seventeen he was required to join fifteen year olds in third year high school to learn Latin and Greek."[2] This must have been the only time he was behind other students in any class, for his future studies were to show his dazzling proficiency in learning. Fr Jim Littleton MSC taught the future priest Ancient History and recalled that "he was obviously a gifted student" and who knows what soaring inspiration this teacher gave him. One can only imagine the future linguist and historian absorbing these early lessons concerning the ancient world and how he must have been inspired to delve further into it all. Fr Littleton became good friends with his student in later years and they travelled to many places together.[3] Paul passed his Leaving Certificate, as the final exam at school was called then, and did so with Honours, then proceeding to the Novitiate, also at Douglas Park.

The minor seminary – a path to religious life

It is of interest that the young Paul did these high school studies at what was called at an Apostolic School. The terms 'Apostolic School', 'minor seminary' or 'Juniorate' are used interchangeably for this – though 'minor seminary' is more customary nowadays. It is apt to say a few words about this kind of education. Minor seminaries may have disappeared in Australia, but can still be found in other parts of the world, notably in developing countries. In Paul's youth, minor seminaries could be day or boarding schools which especially trained young men spiritually and academically for a future life as a priest. There was no compulsion, as those without understanding of the Catholic Church might imagine. While the boys followed a strict routine, they were free to leave if they did not wish to pursue this course of study. They had a balanced program with plenty of sports and could receive visitors at appointed times. A few years ago, I had the chance to visit a minor seminary in Vanimo, in north west Papua New Guinea, and the boys seemed very keen on their education and some went on to the major seminary there. For those who did not, it provided a high quality education infused with a Catholic heritage which equipped them for many kinds of work in PNG, including the civil service and even politics.

The Australian MSC website notes the following concerning the minor seminary at Douglas Park – though its preferred terms are 'juniorate' and 'Apostolic School':

> The Provincial Chapter of 1910 decided to open a juniorate at Douglas Park. This was called the Apostolic School, where boys from the ages of 14 to 18 would undertake preparatory studies before entering the novitiate to begin their journey to the priesthood. When it began in 1912, Fr Nouyoux was in charge, and Fathers Fleming, Vandel, Frank Tyler, Power and Donovan and scholastics Tom O'Loughlin and Vincent Tyler made up the teaching staff.

Fr Linckens, visitor from the Roman superiors with powers to regulate the Australian Province, drew up the rule for them, based on the model already existing in Europe. Its purpose was to train young men in priestly, missionary and religious life.[4]

In fact the Apostolic School was established not long after the purchase of the property at Douglas Park, situated on land which is very beautiful and eye-catching, as anyone who has been there will testify. On 7 December 1904, Brother Robert South MSC received the keys of Nepean Towers, as it was called them. It was located near Wilton, and had been the mansion which Sir Thomas Mitchell built in 1842. And in a great historical touch, a few days later the great Bishop Alain-Marie Guynot de Boismenu (now Venerable), renowned MSC missionary of Papua New Guinea, said the first Catholic Mass within its beautiful old chapel. Thus fifty years after the foundation of the order in France (1854), and a bit over twenty years after their arrival in Sydney to care for the Pacific missions entrusted to them (1885), the Missionaries of the Sacred Heart order took possession of this rural property which was to be a significant part of its history. It was at various times a training centre for the order's Australian members through its school, novitiate seminary, farm, parish centre, retreat centre and renewal centre.[5] Many people go there nowadays to stay at its peaceful retreat centre and recount wonderful memories of staying there.

At the time Fr Stenhouse came to Douglas Park in 1953, Fr Littleton remembers there being about 50 students in residence. During the 1960s decade such minor seminaries were still in their heyday and Fr Littleton remembers the numbers exceeding 80 at one stage. Though they were soon on the cusp of their disappearance forever in Australia (Douglas Park closed in 1966), Fr Stenhouse was one who took to the type of educational and spiritual formation minor seminaries offered.[6] Naturally it would not suit everyone but many bishops and priests have benefited from entering religious life this way. Paul's brother Richard remembers that "Paul found his niche there", adding "he was as happy as anything."[7] The long experience of the Church had shown that a priestly vocation often grew in such minor seminaries. Sometimes we hear of callings to the religious life at an even earlier stage. One priest I knew, the late Fr Peter Little SJ, related that he received his vocation at age 5 (!) when hearing the words: "You are a priest forever, according to the order of Melchizedek" (Hebrews 7:17). And, yes, he became a priest, a learned and wise Jesuit.

With minor seminaries the idea was that the religious inclination of such students was worth nurturing, especially in a world increasingly secularised and hostile to the existence of any spiritual dimension.[8] The *Decree on Priestly Formation* from the Second Vatican Council (1962-65) praised such schools:

> In minor seminaries erected to develop the seeds of vocations, the students should be prepared by special religious formation, particularly through appropriate spiritual direction, to follow Christ the Redeemer with generosity of spirit and purity of heart. Under the fatherly direction of the superiors, and with the proper cooperation of the parents, their daily routine should be in accord with the age, the character and the stage of development of adolescence and fully adapted to the norms of a healthy psychology. Nor should the fitting opportunity be lacking for social and cultural contacts and for contact with one's own family. Moreover, whatever is decreed ... about major seminaries is also to be adapted to the minor seminary to the extent that it is in accord with its purpose and structure. Also, studies undertaken by the students should be so arranged that they can easily continue them elsewhere should they choose a different state of life. (Par. 3)

The minor seminary transmitted an entire culture, and who is to say how deeply their existence has spiritually influenced societies around them. During his years at Douglas Park, Paul was drawn to learning and religious growth – his spirit was truly sparked, but not so much by sport! Robert Brian, a contemporary of Fr Stenhouse in the Apostolic School, recalls that those not inclined to sport at Douglas Park were permitted to do gardening. Rob and Paul carried hoes over their shoulders on many occasions, tending the gardens, while discussing a multitude of topics.[9]

From 1955 till 1957, young Paul finished his high school studies and then attended the novitiate on the same site. While, as brother Richard recalls, Paul's mother "missed him", she wrote Paul letters and told others about her son who was going to be a priest. In fact May Stenhouse was "thrilled to bits" that her son was going to be a priest.[10] Knowledge of Paul's studies was transmitted in the 1954 *Camden News*, the paper for which he had written:

> Paul Stenhouse, of Oxley Street, is at present enjoying a vacation at home from his studies at St. Mary's Towers, Douglas Park.[11]

Rob Marden, younger than Paul Stenhouse by 15 years and an Anglican living nearby in Camden, walked past the Stenhouse home in Oxley Street each day to school and often heard a running commentary from May Stenhouse about how Paul was going at school, novitiate and the seminary.[12] Rob's mother was a lifelong friend of the Stenhouses, as was Rob himself, and he vividly recalls May Stenhouse's energetic nature. He relates that she taught children with learning disabilities in Camden, a task at which she shone, and spoke about this to Rob. On 'Open Days' at Douglas Park, when families and friends could visit, Paul was a great tour guide, showing family and friends all around the buildings, chapel and dormitory. This was a hint of his future role as a tour guide in Rome, to which many gave testimony as we shall see.

Douglas Park must have been quite a thriving, busy if not crowded place in those years.[13]

There were students from the minor seminary, novices and MSC priests coming and going to chapel, classes and meals. The beauty of the buildings, the stillness of the surrounding countryside and the focus on prayer and study would have drawn all to quietness, to the interior life. The day was regulated as follows:

> ... rising at 5.00am, morning prayer, an hour of meditation, after breakfast in silence some study of spiritual writers or a talk from the novice master or study of the MSC constitutions and rules, perhaps some study of Latin, examination of conscience, meals usually in silence with reading from an uplifting book such as the life of some holy person, Rosary, visit to the Blessed Sacrament, a period of manual work, perhaps a bush walk or a swim, spiritual reading in common, a couple of short periods of recreation, night prayer and early bed. The novices donned the black religious habit, usually a much patched one, at the beginning of the year, and received a fine new tailored one at the end when they pronounced their first commitment to the society.[14]

During this time, the young Paul's liking for words and their etymology manifested themselves. One of his fellow MSCs told me that one day during a break, the novice Paul explained the origin of the word 'window' to a group of them, saying something along the lines of its coming from the Old Norse 'vindauga', from 'vindr', meaning 'wind' and 'auga' meaning 'eye', thus 'wind eye' and 'window'. Again one might say – so Stenhousian! Whatever the effect on the listeners, this revealed a mind which delved ceaselessly into words, their meanings, into the meanings of their meanings, and all else in a very precise way.

MSC origins and expansion to the Antipodes

After completing the novitiate, the young Paul took vows on 26 February 1957. It is apt to say something here of the religious order Paul Stenhouse had joined, for it was the source of his life and work, his *raison d'etre*. How could one understand him without it? Cousin Trish Kavanagh said of her cousin that "[h]e really loved the MSCs." This order not only inspired his entire life but without doubt played a significant role in Australian Catholic history, the history of Australia itself and Oceania with its priests, brothers and helpers giving so much to evangelisation, the missions, welfare, education and writing.

The religious order of the Missionaries of the Sacred Heart (MSCs), known originally as *La Société des Missionnaires du Sacré-Cœur*, was founded in Issoudun France on 8 December 1854, by Fr Jules Chevalier (now a Servant of God). Issoudun, 300 kilometres south of Paris, was also the site of a new basilica, dedicated to Our Lady of the Sacred Heart, to become one of the major Marian shrines in France. The first apostolic school opened in Chezal-Benoît in 1867, which educated young boys from Catholic villages who could not otherwise have afforded an education and who were recruited by visiting missionaries who sought to inspire them for religious life and Catholic education. The prevailing political drive of *Kulturkampf* in Europe meant the suppression of many religious houses, in France as well as Germany, and, as historian Regina Ganter observes, taking the Church beyond Europe seemed the best way of ensuring its long-term survival.[15] In this context, along with its missionary zeal, the MSC order spread to other parts of the world. The first overseas foundation was among French Canadians in Watertown in the United States. In 1881 Pope Leo XIII devolved to Chevalier the Vicariate Apostolic of Melanesia and Micronesia, and therefore "the MSC took on responsibility for the Catholic missions in Oceania, which included the Philippines and Australia."[16]

This new religious congregation of priests and lay brothers was formed to promote understanding of the devotion to the Heart of Jesus as embodied in the revelations of Jesus to the seventeenth century French nun, Saint Margaret Mary Alacoque, and of offering personal reparation to the Divine Heart. The society's motto is: *Ametur ubique terrarum Cor Jesu Sacratissimum* ("May the most Sacred Heart of Jesus be everywhere loved").[17] So the missionaries spread to many parts of the globe and were inspired "[t]o be on earth the heart of God." This drew generations of men to reach out to bring the Gospel to far flung places, to help a suffering world, to enact justice in whatever way possible. In addition, a Convent of Our Lady of the Sacred Heart (OLSH) was established by Jules Chevalier in 1874, also in Issoudun. The OLSH sisters were to be pioneering missionaries in many parts of the world. French Mother Superior Marie Louise Hartzer was instrumental in sending five Sisters to the Oceanic Missions. They left France in 1884 and landed in Sydney on 31 January 1885, taking on the parish of Botany. As they themselves relate, the sisters began in Sydney in 1885 and then in 1886 went to Thursday Island.[18]

Afterwards, there followed more foundations in NSW. In 1905, four sisters left for Mathinna in Tasmania, also establishing foundations there. In 1908 the first five Daughters left for Darwin. In 1916, a foundation was made in Queensland, in 1929 in Victoria, and in 1947 in South Australia.[19] Meantime a school for girls had been established in Kensington in Sydney. When the first section of the new convent was completed in 1897, a small combined primary and secondary college was conducted in the convent premises. The continual growth of student numbers led to an expanded college in 1913. As their website states, the sisters were also inspired to engage in missions without limits, leading to great work among the indigenous people. One among many was the renowned Sister Anne Gardiner OLSH, who helped record the

Tiwi culture and language and whom the Australian ABC referred to in glowing terms.[20]

There are many people, even Catholics, who do not know the great history of these early pioneering missionary orders in the Antipodes. They made a significant impact on the history of many countries of Oceania. In order to counteract such prevalent cultural amnesia, it would be apt for every Catholic school to include a course in 'History of Mission Orders', telling of their extraordinary work in education and welfare. For this is our family history, our own ancestry.com. Whatever views one may hold of the missions, at least it is useful to know some facts about them.

The MSCs, along with the Daughters of Our Lady of the Sacred Heart and the Marist Order, were to become part of the great success stories of Australia, sending missionaries to Papua New Guinea, the Marshall Islands and the Gilbert Islands. In an *Annals* article Fr Stenhouse explains, in a brief historical outline, how the MSC missionaries came to the Antipodes and went to Papua New Guinea via Botany Parish as this supply base had been active in Sydney from 1885 onwards.[21] Many *Annals* articles focus on missionary activities and in a 1936 article entitled "Eastern Papua Mission Club", Fr P. Fleming invites readers, for one shilling a year, to help missionaries "spread ... Christ's Kingdom in Papua especially in that portion so recently committed by the Holy Father to the care of Australia, Eastern Papua." He points out that "into the entire area of Papua and its islands one might pack Denmark, Holland, Belgium, Portugal and Switzerland, and still have a considerable space to spare."[22]

The young Paul entered a religious order with decades of past experience. The formal Australian Province of the MSC order was established in 1905. The MSCs were to become active in missionary work not only in PNG but also within Australia. There are many Indigenous people who testify happily to have been educated by them, contrary to the post-modern, anti-Christian rhetoric that all Christian missions resulted in torture and degradation. This is far from the truth. Some bad things happened in some places but this does not describe the overall reality. Most Indigenous Australians, those in PNG and surrounding islands, attest to the great value of their education by members of religious orders.[23]

From the late nineteenth century onwards, the MSC Congregation continued to grow and established provinces in the Netherlands (1894), the United States (1939), Spain (1946), Ireland (1952), Indonesia (1971) and the Dominican Republic (1986). When they reached Australia, the MSCs originally settled in the eastern suburbs of the expanding city of Sydney. The congregation began to accept local Australian vocations and a mission seminary was established in Kensington (it opened in 1897). If you can imagine huge tracts of undeveloped land at Kensington, with one big building there, you can imagine these early years (captured in photos displayed on the monastery walls). The French order put down deep roots in Australian soil and the MSC Australian Province was erected (in 1905) with Father Pierre Marie Tréand as the first Provincial.[24]

Within a short time, both the monastery in Kensington and developments at Douglas Park were in full swing. There were some memorable MSC predecessors of Fr Stenhouse. It would be impossible to list all those amazing souls who went to the missions for each gave generously to church and country. But a few names spring to mind whenever the MSCs are mentioned. One is Fr Frank Flynn (Fr Francis Stanislaus Flynn, 1906-2000), born in Sydney, one of nine children. He studied medicine at Sydney University and later at the Royal Ophthalmic Hospital in London. He did original research, introducing a new drug, Mydricaine, to enable the maximum dilation of pupils. He also designed and patented a machine used in detached retinal operations, becoming known as a leading surgeon. While in London, he mixed with figures such as G. K. Chesterton and Hilaire Belloc, regaling others with vivid memories of their conversations. It was in London that he took the decision to become an MSC priest. On his return to Australia he entered the Missionaries of the Sacred Heart (where he met Bishop Gsell) and was both ophthalmologist and chaplain, helping during the war and on many Aboriginal missions. Two of his three sisters entered the Brigidine Convent. Few know that Fr Flynn became a Wing Commander in the Australian Air Force, a missionary in Papua New Guinea, as well as a pioneer ophthalmologist who treated, as he put it, the body and the soul. He was also parish priest of St Mary's Darwin, a parish covering 300 square miles. Nor do many know that the renowned Australian ophthalmologist Fred Hollows regarded Father Frank Flynn as his inspiration and mentor. In fact, the two men formed a strong friendship that lasted to the end of their lives.[25]

Also of great renown was missionary Bishop Francis Xavier Gsell (1872-1960), familiarly known as 'the Bishop with 150 wives' who joined the MSCs at age 20 and studied in Rome alongside Eugene Pacelli (later to become Pope Pius XII). Gsell's desire was always to join the missions, the MSC site stating that "Francis Xavier Gsell became the founding stone on what some consider to be one of the most successful and enduring Aboriginal missions in Australian history."[26] In 1900 his active missionary work began in Papua New Guinea. In 1906, he was appointed Apostolic Administrator of the Northern Territory but "his heart yearned to continue missionary work among the Aboriginal people" and he applied to the Government Administrator in Adelaide to establish a mission on the Tiwi Islands, north of Darwin.[27] Fr Gsell was granted 10,000 acres and thus began a long association with the Tiwi people on Bathurst Island (where Sister Gardiner was to work). Immensely respectful of the Tiwi culture the bishop did intervene, however, on one occasion when he saw a Tiwi girl with a spear through her leg, as she did not want to go through with an arranged marriage with an older man as custom dictated. James Franklin describes this well:

> Martina was one of the young girls about the mission. A "hairy anonymous man" comes to fetch her, his promised wife according to tribal custom. Martina refuses to go but Gsell accepts that tribal law is final and nothing can be done ... Five days later she is back, speared in the leg but determined to stay at the mission. In the evening an angry mob of tribesmen arrive and demand her back. Not forgetting to call on God's help, Gsell welcomes them with flour and tobacco and suggests a good sleep before talking in the morning. Overnight he lays out calico, tobacco, a mirror, pots of meat and tins of treacle. When the tribesmen have woken up and had a good look, he names the price: Martina is to stay. After an interminable council, they agree. Martina is brought up by the nuns and contracts a free Christian marriage with a mission youth. Over the following decades, Gsell "bought" in similar fashion a hundred and fifty promised girls, all of them, according to tribal law, his wives.[28]

These 'wives' were all offered safety and an education by Bishop Gsell. One can read more about the fascinating story in the book *The Bishop with 150 Wives* (1954). There is much more one could relate about these two renowned MSCs as one could of other missionaries within this order. It is not overstating it to say the MSCs changed the course of history in Australia and its environs in the scope of their outreach in education, welfare, health and communication and still does so to this day. Its current activities are listed as follows:

> In Australia we work in Parishes, among youth in Colleges, in Spirituality and Retreat Centres, among urban and traditional aboriginal Australians, in Tertiary Institutions, in Media, in hospital chaplaincies and among people

Left: From *Annals*, April 1953, inspiring young men like Paul to the religious life. Right: From Annals, September 1953, Fr Docherty, who worked on Aboriginal Missions for 25 years, talks to boys from the Apostolic School of the Missionaries of the Sacred Heart at Douglas Park.

Left: Some buildings at Douglas Park, in a peaceful rural setting about 75 kms south of Sydney. Right: A photo of Douglas Park in the *Annals* of October 1953. It was quite a crowded place at times, as some of its previous novices recall.

Clockwise from top left: Paul Stenhouse, during his early years of study; Basilica of Our Lady of the Sacred Heart in Issoudun, France, where the order of the Missionaries of the Sacred Heart was founded, which Fr Stenhouse visited several times; MSC priest, Father Stanislaus Francis ("Frank") Flynn, renowned ophthalmologist (1906-2000), who performed many eye operations at Aboriginal missions and was the inspiration for Fred Hollows; Fr Jules Chevalier, Servant of God, founder of the Missionaries of the Sacred Heart.

Clockwise from top left: Paul Stenhouse on the right at Croydon Seminary with fellow seminarians in Melbourne; Fr Stenhouse in the early years of his priesthood; MSC missionary, Bishop Francis Xavier Gsell (1872-1960). From the family archives of Benoît Gsell (Benfeld) and Dominique Thirion (Strasbourg), in Regina Ganter's book: *German Missionaries in Australia – A web-directory of intercultural encounter* (Griffith University, 2009-2018); A very proud May Stenhouse with her son, the young priest in Croydon, after his taking of final vows.

At dinner when a young priest (centre left). On the front right is Father Ted Collins, a long-time friend.

Left: Buildings of the Missionaries of the Sacred Heart, Kensington Sydney where, apart from his travels, Fr Stenhouse lived for 53 years. Right: While Father Stenhouse studied in Croatia he visited many churches in nearby countries also under Soviet rule, saying Masses there. Here is Ključarovci pri Ljutomeru, a village in the Municipality of Krizevci in north-eastern Slovenia among Fr Stenhouse's photos of that time.

suffering with HIV/AIDS, as well as in Justice and Peace ministries. Overseas, there are Australian MSCs working for the development of the local churches of Papua New Guinea and the Islands of the Pacific, in China, Japan, India and Vietnam, as well as in Media and communication.[29]

Then there is the work you rarely hear of, lesser known stories of spiritual influence and everyday kindnesses to the physically and mentally ill, refugees, the lonely and the abandoned. I know such stories from those not wanting their names printed. There are many and they exist. It was into this furnace of good work and kindness that Fr Stenhouse entered.

Priestly ordination and further studies

After absorbing the spirituality and rich history of his order at Douglas Park, and after taking vows in 1957, Paul Stenhouse was transferred to Victoria for the seven years of seminary study at Croydon in Melbourne. If, as his brother Richard says, he was happy in the minor seminary and Novitiate, he found his niche ever more deeply in the studies of theology, philosophy and church history. Fellow seminarian Fr Pat Austin recalls Paul as "a voracious reader."[30] The seminarians would take turns to make copies of notes (on old gestetners!) for other students, and when it was Fr Austin's turn to do copying, he always found large piles to be done for Paul. Fr Michael Fallon, two years ahead of Paul at the seminary, remembers him as a serious student. While he was not sporty, Paul had the duty of bee keeping and, as with everything he took on, he learned as much as he could about bees.

The seminary years progressed smoothly by all accounts and then came the day of ordination to the priesthood on 20 July 1963. Richard remembers the day well, with many being present in a packed St Mary's Cathedral and Cardinal Gilroy saying Mass. The family were proud of the new priest. Fr Stenhouse said his first Mass at St Paul's Church Camden. Reflecting on his ordination later in a 2015 *Annals* Article, he stated:

> By my ordination as a Catholic priest, I undertook to be a true servant of the Church which, as St Paul stresses, is the Body of Christ ... We priests are the unworthy custodians of this Catholic Faith. We were not ordained to redesign the Church but to hand on the Deposit of Faith, loyal to future generations.[31]

In the years of priesthood, he was to echo the spirituality of the MSC founder, Jules Chevalier, of whom it is written:

> From the beginning of his clerical life Father Chevalier had the highest idea of the priestly dignity. He repeated often to himself and to us, his young fellow students that the priest should be another Christ. It is necessary then that he shows forth in his life the great virtues of which Christ has left us such sublime examples. Like Christ, he should be meek and humble of heart; like Him, the priest should love poverty, practice penance, be sympathetic to the weak, be helpful to sinners and bring back the lost sheep on his shoulders to the divine fold. Like his Divine Model, the priest should be ready to suffer all things for the salvation of souls. Neither trials nor sufferings nor persecutions nor the fear of death itself should deter the priest in his service of God ... [32]

Fr Stenhouse lived out his priestly vocation modelled on these qualities. After ordination, he was not sent to a parish for pastoral work. Given his previous experience as a journalist, it was not long before he was appointed to *Annals*, first as business manager in 1964 and then as editor in 1966. And one could say 'the rest is history' except that, no, there are many more strands to this story.

Studies, the 60s, calls for revolution

John McMahon MSC records that in 1968 Paul Stenhouse was made a member of the Provincial Council of the Missionaries of the Sacred Heart. He also records that it was in this year that Fr Stenhouse also began a Bachelor of Arts course at the University of Sydney, majoring in Modern Hebrew and Arabic and graduating with Honours in 1972.[33] Thus began a new journey for the young priest that would continue throughout his life, that of a scholar in various fields – languages, Biblical studies, history and literature.

Meantime, Fr Stenhouse lived in an era clamouring for change, breaking at the seams. The *soixante-huitards* (or 1968-ers), as writer Peter Seewald recalls (as he was one of them), were trying to foment revolution and change Western society, influenced by Marcuse, Jean Paul Sartre, Gramsci and their peers. Seewald recalled those heady days:

> During the student rebellions of 1968 I began to engage with politics. Christianity seemed something of a relic from the past then. I felt that its mixture of power and madness had to be overcome in order finally to build a genuinely progressive society. So one day I withdrew myself from the Church. I felt liberated, and I fought for the ideas of Marx and Lenin.[34]

Seewald later returned to the Church after what he saw as torrid attempts to tear down the Western legacy of history and ideas. Yet in the 1960s and 70s, while many revolutionaries focused on deconstruction of the past, Fr Stenhouse looked to the past to understand the present. He spent hours studying ancient history and practising Hebrew at the Department of Semitic Studies at the University of Sydney. I recall him telling me once that he would talk to the Jewish students studying Hebrew in the break times, after intensive sessions in the 'language lab' where they repeated words and phrases till they got it right. He did not elaborate on what they talked about, but I think it was an example of that 'Stenhousian' outreach, a feature which permeated his whole life. He ended up speaking Hebrew so well that he taught it at tertiary level. Friend Joseph Assaf recalled him marking Hebrew exam papers at Sydney University. Jim Giltinan, another friend, who supported *Annals* for many years, says Fr Stenhouse also marked Hebrew exam papers for the HSC (Higher School Certificate) in NSW for a long time.[35] Jim related to me that Fr Stenhouse went to the Board of Studies one year to complain that "the final Hebrew exam paper was too easy."

There were other languages he was learning in the late 1960s and early 70s. One can only guess at the intense focus in mastering ancient languages at the same time. Fr John Conroy MSC related to me that, while at the University of Sydney, Fr Stenhouse would rise very early (around 3-4 am) to study. In fact, he asked to be woken early with a knock on the door by none other than 'Doc' Rumble who was still alive then and apparently also an early riser. After hours of prayer and study came Mass and the other duties of each day.

Growing interest in the Samaritans and more

While enmeshed in his studies of Hebrew and Arabic Fr Stenhouse had become fascinated by the Samaritans. His Honours thesis was entitled "A Critical Edition of the historical sections of the Samaritan Hebrew Hilukh." For those not aware of who the Samaritans are, apart from the parable of the Good Samaritan, it is necessary to know a little about them to understand what Fr Stenhouse was doing and why. To put it briefly, when the Israelites were deported by the Assyrians in 772 BC, not all were taken. Many remained and claimed, and still claim, to be the descendants of the Northern Israelite tribes of Ephraim and Manasseh, and are now known as the Samaritans. The Samaritans hold differing beliefs from the Jews in that they only follow the first five books of the Bible, what we know as the Pentateuch. Also the sacred mountain on which they worshipped was Mount Gerizim, referred to in the biblical account of Jesus speaking to the Samaritan woman at the well (John 4: 1-42).

While the Samaritans are of immense historical interest, it is not so easy for scholars to read their writings and Fr Stenhouse had to study several ancient languages in order to do so. He had to contend with the fact that there was not only Samaritan Hebrew, but also Samaritan Aramaic and later Samaritan Arabic. Another important fact is that one of the research areas of Professor Alan Crown who taught Fr Stenhouse in the Semitic Studies Department at Sydney University, was that of Samaritan studies. One can safely surmise that Fr Stenhouse was inspired by this renowned scholar to pursue Samaritan studies. So inspiring was Professor Crown, that he became a lifelong mentor and friend, of whom Fr Stenhouse writes:

> He genuinely made a difference to the lives of many as a mentor, a source of great knowledge, a father figure ... He was an acclaimed international expert on the Samaritans, and has published widely on this topic and many others, including the Dead Sea Scrolls, Yiddish language and culture, Jewish education, Zionism and Australian Jewry.[36]

Professor Crown pointed to the need to translate hitherto little known, untranslated manuscripts. When Fr Stenhouse began an Honours M.A. at Sydney University, he began translating the Samaritan Arabic text: *History of the Samaritans* of Abu'l-Fath. The relevant manuscripts were in such poor condition, however, (according to his cousin Trish Kavanagh, who saw them at the monastery in Kensington), it became clear that ongoing work was needed. Thus the proposed M.A. thesis was upgraded to a PhD consisting of a critical edition of thirty or so manuscripts of the Samaritan medieval Arabic text.[37]

In the meantime, while undertaking his Samaritan studies, Fr Stenhouse temporarily left the *Annals* in 1976 as he was invited to be the Private Secretary to the Father General (later Auxiliary Bishop) Eugene Cuskelly (1924-1999) in Rome, staying at the General House of the MSC order. He also enrolled in St Catherine's College Oxford for a D.Phil. in 1976 but did not continue and left the course in the same year. He continued as Private Secretary to the Father General, holding that position until 1979.

Rome, Communists and doctoral studies

While in Rome, things took an interesting turn. While Fr Stenhouse was Private Secretary and worked on his PhD at the same time, he had incessant interruptions due to his wide circle of friends who called on him constantly. He was always 'there' for them and gave wonderfully detailed spiritual and historical tours of the ancient city and, of course, this meant less time for his thesis. So where did he go in 1979 to finish his PhD on medieval Samaritan texts? Where else but Communist-ruled Yugoslavia under Tito. Staying mostly in Dubrovnik (Croatia), he was able to complete his thesis entitled: "A Critical Edition of the Kitab al-Tarikh of Abu'l-Fath." (Abu'l-Fath was a Samaritan priest and the Kitab al-Tarikh was the title of one of his works).

Who would have thought Communist Croatia was the perfect place to write a PhD? Whether Fr Stenhouse decided on Dubrovnik himself, or whether he met someone who arranged for him to go there, it turned out to be the perfect place to complete his doctorate. It is understandable that few friends journeyed to this Communist country to meet him. But one who did go to that part of the world to see him was friend Rob Marden. As previously mentioned, Rob hailed from Camden, was younger than Fr Stenhouse and had become a good friend.[38] His mother had known Fr Stenhouse's mother well from their days in *Matavai*.

Rob recalls that while he and his wife Judy were travelling in Europe, they made a plan to meet Fr Stenhouse in Venice, just before Fr Stenhouse headed to Dubrovnik. Rob recalls waiting on the station in 1979 as the train pulled in and being concerned at not seeing Fr Stenhouse emerge. After some time, his anxiety was relieved at seeing his priest friend emerge with two very heavy suitcases weighing 26 kilos each. As he stepped out of the train, Fr Stenhouse yelled out, "I got the manuscripts", meaning some of the old manuscripts in Samaritan Arabic that he needed to work on. Rob recalls that Fr Stenhouse mentioned receiving some from Moscow, and remembers the mention of the 'Russia State Library.' Exactly how Fr Stenhouse obtained these manuscripts is unclear. What was clear was that he was delighted that he had them as they helped with his PhD. Rob recalls helping to carry the heavy suitcases filled with Samaritan Arabic manuscripts as they travelled to Trieste and other places. This was but one of several meetings that Rob, Judy and Fr Stenhouse had in then Yugoslavia for Fr Stenhouse also travelled up to Slovenia to visit Rob and Judy who were staying with Judy's Slovenian parents. Fr Stenhouse became fascinated with Slovenia and its local Catholic churches trying to survive Communist 'paradise.' He visited churches, presbyteries and priests absorbing its culture and history, saying Masses wherever possible. Rob recalls Fr Stenhouse having two passports, one with no Israeli visas, another with no Lebanese visas, using whichever was most appropriate.

While working on his doctorate, Fr Stenhouse also began learning Croatian, so he could speak with his new countrymen, no doubt saying Mass in Croatian within a short time.[39] Among his books were several Serbo-Croat dictionaries and readers. Needless to say, he was not enamoured of the regime, nor of anything Communist. Of his time in Tito's Communist Yugoslavia, Fr Stenhouse wrote in a 2010 *Annals* article:

I am not one of those who hold the view that Tito's regime was benevolent. Those who do must never have lived under it, or if they did, they must have belonged to the Nomenklatura or privileged caste; or they benefited, as 'ordinary' Communists from the proceeds of the brutality and fear that was widespread throughout that beautiful country.⁴⁰

He notes the immense suffering that accompanied the arrival of the Tito regime: "Rarely in the course of history had the arrival of a new regime been preceded by a bloodbath on a scale of the one seen in Jugoslavia", and then asks if anyone "remembers or sheds a tear for the more than one million anti-Communist Jugoslavs butchered at the end of World War II by the Communist partisans of Tito?"⁴¹

Sarajevo operations, Slovenian hunting boots, doctorate

Sydney businessman and friend of Fr Stenhouse, Joseph Assaf, introduced me to his Croatian friend Marko Franovic, who related an interesting story to me via telephone.⁴² Not long after he arrived in Dubrovnik, Fr Stenhouse was ousted from the hotel he was staying in at 11 pm. Marko said this was "some kind of Sarajevo operation" meaning it was a typical secret police operation. Not that Fr Stenhouse was being chased by the secret police or anything like that. He was rather the victim of one of their typical night time 'actions' which involved kicking out everyone from various hotels for whatever reason they had at the time. One can imagine the ejected people on the street wondering what they would do next, among them a Catholic priest writing a doctorate about Abu'l-Fath! People who have lived in Communist countries have not a whit of trouble understanding this type of raid. Needless to say it was not easy to find a place to stay at nearly midnight. It turns out, however, that Fr Stenhouse knew of a small place on 'an island' near the coast, a guest house with 20-30 rooms. Whether he went that day or later, whether he slept in the street or not, Fr Stenhouse soon ended up at the guest house for a while.

When Joseph first told Marko of his friendship with Fr Stenhouse, Marko was amazed to hear how this Australian priest had lived and studied in Communist Yugoslavia. Once further into the story, when Marko heard of the particular 'island' on which Fr Stenhouse lived for a while, he was ever more curious and wanted to meet Fr Stenhouse. Joseph organised a dinner for them at his place in Sydney and here it was that they met. After some exchange of details, it turns out that it was Marko's family who ran the guest house where Fr Stenhouse had ended up staying after he was kicked out of his Dubrovnik hotel years ago. The conversation blazed on for a long time and Fr Stenhouse recalled how cold the Croatian winters had been. In fact when he visited what is now known as Slovenia, he bought some bigger, better boots to curtail frostbite – boots which Giles Auty called his "Slovenian hunting boots", mingling admiration with mirth.

In later years, writer and friend of Fr Stenhouse, Robert Stove, was to recall what his priest-friend had told him of this time in Croatia, then in Tito's Yugoslavia:

> ... what about Fr Stenhouse's description of the preferred Titoist method for temporarily rounding up stray peasants so that the latter wouldn't disturb the consciousness of idiotic Western tourists visiting Dubrovnik? The local jail network wasn't big enough to accommodate all such peasants, so for several days they were consigned to ... packing cases. Oh it wasn't too bad, the packing cases had holes punched in them, so that the captives didn't actually asphyxiate. But after a few days of that treatment, it was amazing how docile a Tito supporter even the stroppiest Ustashi nostalgic became.[43]

Fr Stenhouse learned to live with the depredations of a Communist country and made his way by public transport, recalling to Joseph that sometimes he did not have the right bus fare. Once a kind bus driver said, "Give me whatever you can", and Fr Stenhouse would give him some coins, replying in Croatian, "Thank you, oh well, we have to learn to get by", a typical colloquial comment by the citizens of Tito's Yugoslavia in many situations.

Meantime work proceeded on his PhD thesis in Dubrovnik (during 1979-1980). Fr Stenhouse's accommodation arrangements changed several times and friend John Madden recalls that at one stage his priest-friend "lived and worked on his thesis in the roof cavity above a church close to the sea wall and run by the Jesuits in Dubrovnik."[44] He lived simply, and whatever the situation, Fr Stenhouse always adapted and made good progress with his doctorate.

Graduation and back to *Annals*

In 1980 he returned to Australia with the doctorate finally completed and waited for it to be assessed and, when it was, he obtained his PhD from the University of Sydney, graduating in 1982.[45] His thesis was in three volumes and, according to Fr Michael Fallon, it took some time to find an examiner for it as Fr Stenhouse was the only person in the world at that stage who understood its content. Not only did Fr Stenhouse produce a critical edition of the middle Arabic Samaritan text, but had provided dictionaries so scholars (and examiners!) could read it. An entry on the University of Sydney site in the Mandelbaum publishing section refers to Fr Stenhouse's pioneering work, stating:

> Based on an analysis of all the important MSS and accompanied by copious notes on the Arabic original, this work is the first translation of the whole of this most important of the Samaritan chronicles into English.[46]

Meantime, as previously mentioned, Fr Stenhouse had become good friends with Alan Crown. Cousin Trish Kavanagh speaks of the immense respect of Fr Stenhouse for him and Stuart Rowland recalls visits to the professor's house with his priest friend. On the day of his graduation, brother Richard remembers the Stenhouse family going to the North Shore home of Professor Crown afterwards and how "very nice and polite" the professor was to them.[47] Interestingly, Professor Crown was to write for *Annals* in the future, another indication of the scholarly reach of this publication. Some titles were: "The Dead Sea Scrolls Part 1" and "The Dead Sea Scrolls – Part 2" (1990); "God's Word or the word of the Bible translators? Which Bible Do You Read?" (1997); "Eyes, Teeth And Tunnels In The Bible" (1999).[48]

After the completion of his PhD and ensuing research, Fr Stenhouse taught at Sydney University for over a decade and, as mentioned earlier, marked Hebrew papers there.[49] He became a foundation member of the Council of the *Société d'Études Samaritaines* within the *Collège de France* (the latter, a prestigious higher education and research establishment founded in 1530). With his fluency in French derived from childhood, along with his several other languages, he would have had no difficulty in contributing to the many conferences he was invited to. For example he gave a lecture in 1986 in Paris on "The Reliability of the Chronicle of Abu'l-Fath and the dating of Baba Rabba."[50] In the years to come he delivered scholarly papers not only in Paris but also in Tel Aviv, Jerusalem, Oxford, Venice, Helsinki, Budapest, Zürich and more recently in Tartu, Estonia. Fr Stenhouse also wrote the entry on the 'Samaritans' for the *Encyclopaedia of the Qur'ān* in June 2002.

Amidst the ongoing research, Fr Stenhouse had taken up the reins of *Annals* again in 1981 on his return from overseas. While some may have pronounced autopsies on the journal, due to a temporary declining circulation, rumours of its death were premature. The journal revived with gusto, rising in circulation and influence. From this humble but resilient publication, the new doctoral editor was able to transmit the depth and breadth of his knowledge on Biblical history and theology, Catholic heroes, saints, art, music and controversies. He embarked on journalistic expeditions all over the world, gathering writers on a multitude of subjects, and on occasion even wrote about the Samaritans![51]

3

ANNALS SURGES AHEAD

*Wise speech is rarer and more valuable
than gold and rubies.*
Proverbs 20:15

*Wonder is dead, you say!
Wonder can never die.
Not while within a shining pool
A man can see the sky*
'By the Roadside', Dame Mary Gilmore.

If there is anything that came to be increasingly associated with the name Father Stenhouse, it was the *Annals*, although this journal underwent several minor changes of name throughout the years of its publication. Here, in a few lines, is a list of its titles. It was originally *The Australian Annals of Our Lady to the Sacred Heart*; then it changed to *Annals 68* from the first issue of 1968; it then became *Annals Australia: Journal of Catholic Culture* in 1981; and then finally *Annals Australasia: Journal of Catholic Culture* from the first issue of 2000. The popular name by which it was known, *Annals*, will be mostly used throughout the following chapters.

Fr Stenhouse, no doubt due to his prior experience in journalism, was appointed the business manager of this journal in 1964 and then in 1966, he took over its editorship from Fr Aloysius English. While he was not appointed to a parish, Fr Stenhouse, from the outset of his priestly life, was also always intensely pastoral, reaching out to people of all nationalities and religious backgrounds – politicians, poets, students, artists and musicians. He could talk to the world and the world talked to him. And he brought it all to *Annals*.

Who could have predicted that Fr Stenhouse would chart the course for this journal for over 53 years? Despite some breaks he remained its editor until 2019, when he signed off on the last edition in November 2019, shortly before his death. The long existence of *Annals* was nothing short of extraordinary, it being the longest lasting journal in Australian history. This remains one of the great intellectual and missionary achievements of the MSC order, for it reached out to a wide public – religious, layman and scholar alike.

Fr Stenhouse assumed editorship during a period of great cultural upheaval in the post-Vatican II years. Fr Stenhouse provided a rational, reflective counterbalance to the growing post-modern fragmentation in the decades to come. In the continued editions of this 'miracle' journal lay Fr Stenhouse's ability to draw writers from varied fields – church history, modern and ancient history, art, music, literature, philosophy, linguistics, education, travel, and humour. And underlying this was a sense of 'wonder' at the world, in all its forms, because such perennial wonder was a quintessential aspect of Fr Stenhouse's nature. He was not a pedant, rather always alive to the myriad phenomena and hidden things of the world. It is not by chance that he quoted from poet Dame Mary Gilmore's poetry, saying 'Wonder can never die', in his final comment about his work with *Annals*.[1]

The *Annals* – surpassing expectations of sceptics

Annals surprised many from the beginnings of its publication. The *Little Blue Book*, as the *Annals* was at times affectionately known, surpassed the expectations of sceptics who saw little future for it. In a later overview, Fr Stenhouse records that it is other publications that "have returned to the pulp, lead and dust out of which they were produced":

> How many today have even heard of *The Boomerang*, *The Illustrated Sydney News*, *The Picturesque Atlas of Australasia*, the *Australian Standard*, the *Lone Hand*, the *Stockwhip and Satirist*, the *Express*, the *Melbourne Star* or the *Sydney Evening News*? [2]

Australians love a story that is threaded with survival against the odds and the history of *Annals* is just such a story. As Fr Stenhouse notes, *Annals* first appeared in 1889, amidst a ferment of literary, political and religious newspapers and journals that sprang to life in the 1870s and 1880s. This was nine years after the renowned publication *The Bulletin* hit the streets, hot off the presses of the *Freeman's Journal* which had started in 1850 changed names in 1932 to *Catholic Freeman's Journal* and later merged into the *Catholic Weekly*. It was a time when "[a]lmost everyone who had something to say and could write, was either editing, publishing or writing for some new paper" and Australia was on the eve of nationhood with its air permeated with excitement.[3] He observes that people did not shrink from discussing social, political and religious issues in an era of journalism when things really mattered and were discussed with more rationality than by the current one-liner twitterati:

> ... in the 1880s truth and integrity were catchcries, fiercely, if at times inadvisedly, pursued: not a lot of thought was given to libel laws, so-called sacred cows or others' feelings.[4]

Despite the nineteenth century's predilection for frank discussion of issues, no one could have foreseen the long survival of the religiously and culturally inclined *Annals* (1889-2019), outlasting even the *Bulletin* (1880-2008), least of all, Fr

Stenhouse's own paternal great-grandfather, John Farrell. Farrell was a poet, journalist, patriot and social reformer in this hub of nineteenth century literary ferment. He wrote for *The Bulletin*, contributing verse, and was one time editor and leader writer for the *Daily Telegraph*. He, like many of his literary contemporaries, would have had "little patience for clerical journals and would not have approved of yet another religious voice being heard around Sydney."[5] That is not to say that Farrell did not have a strong moral sense and passion for justice, which he focused on the single tax campaigns. He was just not overtly religious. Yet he was revered as a poet: Henry Lawson idolised him. He was a friend to Mary Cameron (later, Dame Mary Gilmore) and he met Mark Twain on the occasion of the American author's visit to Australia.

Wishing to rescue Farrell from relative obscurity, his great-grandson Fr Paul Stenhouse wrote a literary and personal biography about him entitled *John Farrell: Poet, Journalist and Social Reformer, 1851-1904*, publishing it in 2018.[6] This work is nothing less than fascinating and a landmark scholarly work about nineteenth century literature and society. Australian Emeritus Professor of English literature Michael Wilding noted that it was "an important, scholarly account of a major figure. Here was a major contribution to the literary and political history of the 1890s."[7] Fr Stenhouse captured the journalistic and literary ambience of the times as well as the enigma of his ancestor and one might ask whether he saw something of himself in Farrell? Despite different worldviews, John Farrell and Fr Stenhouse had a certain similar 'X' factor, a journalistic, literary gift, an expansive openness to the world alongside an avoidance of the limelight, and a humility in the midst of the great cosmos.

No apparent relation (but surely distantly related) is Australian Nicol Drysdale Stenhouse who was a great collector of books and literary patron of the nineteenth century who also happened to be a great linguist, about whom Ann-Mari Jordens has written in *The Stenhouse Circle* (1979). This mysterious figure appears to have had many of Fr Stenhouse's scholarly gifts, generosity to others, encouragement of writers and a constant presence: perhaps one day, further explorations will discover if there is direct genealogical link.

Interestingly, when Fr Stenhouse took on the editorship of *Annals* another friend, politician and writer Peter Coleman (1928-2019) was editor of *The Bulletin* (from 1964 to 1967). Both editors became good friends, both acute analysts of the cultural shifts of the times, both witty and superb masters of the written word. Fr Stenhouse was to learn much of *The Bulletin's* life from the earliest days because of Farrell's involvement in it and ongoing conversations with Peter Coleman. While both editors wrote for different publications, they came to have very similar views on cultural and political issues. Fr Stenhouse had works by Peter Coleman on his bookshelves with inscriptions by his friend. In the end, none would have been happier than Coleman to see *Annals* outlast other Australian contenders for its marathon longevity of 131 years. *The Bulletin* had lasted 128 years.

The Origins of *Annals* in Australia

In *Monastery on the Hill* (1998), Fr Caruana said of the first appearance of *Annals* in 1889 in Australia:

> [T]he monastery was the centre for the production of the *Annals of Our Lady of the Sacred Heart*, a thirty-two page monthly magazine, with a circulation of 20,000 per month. The editor, Fr Matthew Smith, with the assistance of Mary Agnes Finn, a parishioner of Randwick who actually was the first editor of the *Annals* in 1889, made sure that the magazine had a balance of spiritual, devotional, missionary and topical articles.[8]

Fr Stenhouse, in his account of the early years of *Annals*, also notes that the first editor of the publication was Mary Agnes Finn, a devout member of an old established Randwick Catholic family. He writes that she was assisted by Father Emil Merg, MSC, a priest from Alsace-Lorraine, whose English at the time was poor, though on paper at least, he was seen as responsible for the production of the magazine. Without making any campaign about it, Fr Stenhouse adds that because of the prevailing attitudes of the time, "Mary Agnes Finn was never given the recognition that was her due. Her role as editor was never publicised, and apart from the occasional piece of pious fiction carrying her by-line, she worked in relative obscurity." [9]

The next editor of *Annals* was none other than Provincial Fr Tréand himself and he too was helped in editorial work by local teacher and writer Agatha le Breton.[10] Among other early editors were Fathers Davitt Forrest and Eric Dignam. The latter was very musical and literary and transformed the content and appearance of the publication and greatly increased its circulation.

> During these years the circulation actually reached 50,000 subscribers and it was due in no small part to the spectacular "drives" he organised among school children in which he offered a prize for the one who obtained the most new subscribers (two dead-heated with 500 new subscribers each!), in addition there were regular minor prizes (cricket bat or a book) for every 5 new subscriptions obtained. In the period of two months there were 4,000 new names added to the subscription lists.[11]

Annals and its French origins

Yet even before this first appearance in Australia in 1889 of *The Annals of Our Lady of the Sacred Heart* (as it was then known), the journal had earlier French origins no doubt unknown to many Australian readers. It hailed from the town of Issoudun in the diocese of Bourges in central France, which as we noted, was where the MSC order was founded.

In content and design, *Les Annales de Notre-Dame du Sacré-Coeur* was based on its old-world French prototype which was so successful that by 1889 editions had appeared in Flemish, German, Spanish, Hungarian and American English. So its appearance in Australian English was part of this spectacular rise. Though the Australian editions were mainly mission orientated, focusing on the MSC missions in PNG and nearby islands, the devotional articles on the Sacred Heart and Our Lady of the Sacred heart reached out to those isolated in country areas within Australia, who eagerly looked forward to each edition as a connection with the world of Christendom. Thus in the midst of the expansion of MSC missionary activity *outside* Australia, this new publication had a missionary quality to it *within* Australia, reaching out to all to transmit the essence of the MSC's focus on love of God in times which did not reflect them, a world which rather extolled the anti-Christian thrusts of Marx, Feuerbach and Darwin, and which echoed social ferment and moral unease.

The early editions had an elaborate engraving of Our Lady of the Sacred Heart on the front cover and its first Australian edition in 1889 came not long after the MSC took on the parish of Randwick, whose church was dedicated to Our Lady of the Sacred Heart, which was "built in the French style."[12] These early editions transmitted Catholic news, hefty doses of mainly French piety, even down to citations from French Bishops, and reports on the missions in what were known then as Papua and New Guinea. This, observes Fr Stenhouse, would not have enthralled "the liberal-minded Sydney Bohemians!"[13]

Some memorable early contributors

The new journal included articles on the *Irish Question*, the Great War, the canonisation of St Thérèse of Lisieux in 1925, and several topical Australian issues. It included the work of internationally known Catholic writers such as Hilaire Belloc, C.C. Martindale SJ, along with local writers Dame Mary Gilmore, Agatha le Brereton, Susan Gavan Duffy, Beatrice Grimshaw, Fr 'Doc' Leslie Rumble MSC, Fr Pat 'Paddy' Ryan MSC and Frank Sheed (who made his debut as a writer in *Annals*). James McAuley had his "Poems of Papua" published in a March 1956 edition of *Annals*, dedicating his poem "New Guinea" to MSC Archbishop Alain-Marie Guynot de Boismenu, who had been influential in McAuley's conversion to Catholicism. Bishop de Boismenu had inspired many religious and lay missionaries.[14]

A great predecessor of Fr Stenhouse, who used the media to further the horizons of the Catholic church, was known familiarly as 'Doc Rumble' (1892-1975), whose full name was Rev. Dr. Leslie Audoen Rumble, MSC, and who was born in Enmore in Sydney in 1892 into an Anglican family. Torn between Anglicanism and his interest in Catholicism in his youth, he decided on Catholicism, entered the MSC Minor Seminary in 1913 and was ordained to the priesthood on 26 July 1924. He taught theology and, having a gift for oratory, spoke on various issues on 2UE from 1928 onwards, answering queries about Catholicism in a most eloquent manner. This show became very popular and Dr Rumble's 'Question Box' was transferred to the Catholic station 2SM and continued until 1968. Interstate Catholic papers carried this material to those outside the range of the radio signal. Four collections of his questions and answers (the first in 1934) sold seven million copies, principally in America, making him a much-quoted spokesman. The originals and reprinted versions are a prized possession of many Catholics up to the present day. They are reprinted on the *Annals* website which includes articles, pamphlets and magazine articles by the 'Doc' preserved for posterity as a great MSC treasure.[15] His knowledge of the Bible, his rationality, wit and calm attracted people of all faiths to ask him questions about the

Catholic Church. The 'Doc' collated a final book, *Questions People Ask About the Catholic Church* (1972), of which it is said:

> [It] read like a temperature chart of the Church after the Second Vatican Council. Dr Rumble, although loyal, was not comfortable in that era. [16]

He died on 9 November 1975 in Lewisham Hospital and was buried in the Sacred Heart cemetery, Douglas Park. Fr Stenhouse knew him and exuded his predecessor's great legacy of knowledge, clarity and depth, having a photo of him in the *Annals* office and several of his books on his shelves.

Another renowned MSC priest who contributed to *Annals* was the learned Fr Paddy Ryan. He promoted the work of the Catholic Evidence Guild, and 'examined' the expositions of Catholic faith by Catholic High School students, as here described in 1937:

> Rev. Dr. P. J. Ryan, M.S.C., examined at the Dominican Convent, Santa Sabina, Strathfield, on Thursday, 28th ult., and expressed the highest satisfaction with the lectures given by the girls. The subjects chosen were: 'The Divinity of Christ,' 'Christ, the Modern,' ' The Redemption, "The Fall of Man,' 'Baptism' and 'Penance.' [17]

Fr Ryan was not always met with great enthusiasm by those with whom he debated controversies of the day. Of him, Australian Catholic historian James Franklin writes:

> In Sydney, Catholic philosophy, apologetics and controversy in the 1930s and early 1940s was almost a one-man show. The man was Father Paddy Ryan. If it was a question of attacking Communists, or replying to objections on radio, or debating philosophers, or setting up Catholic adult education, or writing a pamphlet to prove the existence of God, one contacted the Sacred Heart fathers at Kensington and got Father Ryan on the job.[18]

Fr Ryan collected signatures in 1939 to protest the inordinate influence of the deterministic views of John Anderson, atheist Professor of Philosophy at Sydney Teachers' College, whose views were taught by others at the College. Ryan stated:

> I personally have argued for hours with graduates of Sydney University in a futile endeavour to convince them of their own existence – so deeply had their very reason been undermined by scepticism and sophistry.[i.e. taught by Anderson]. In condemning things of this sort, we are not condemning critical or progressive thought. We are condemning a perverse negation which spells the suicide of thought and makes all progress impossible. In defending self-evident truths like one's own existence and personality, or easily demonstrable truths like the existence of God, we are merely defending the foundations without which all talk of justice and injustice is so much meaningless twaddle.[19]

Fr Ryan not only debated the determinists of the day but also involved himself in the actions of the Movement, a Catholic group dedicated to fighting the increasing Communist influence in Australian society. In 1942 he railed against those spreading Communist views in Australia:

> Communists or fellow-travellers like Ernie Thornton, Adam Ogston, Sid Jordan, John Dease, Rupert Lockwood, and Mrs. Diana Gould are regular speakers ... No criticism of Communism is allowed. As a result, Communist propaganda has increased a hundredfold in extent and volume, without in the least becoming more trustworthy.[20]

Particularly memorable was his public debate with a Communist on 23 September 1948 where a group of Catholic nuns booed the Communist speaker's assertions. While Fr Ryan wrote on various subjects in *Annals*, a persistent theme was his critique of Communism as expressed in "The Bolshevik War on Religion" (May, 1934) and "Is Peace Possible?" (March, 1956). In the latter he writes:

> The Communist plea for peace is nothing more than a propaganda device calculated to undermine the will to resist aggression and to lull the peoples of the democratic countries into a false feeling of security which will make their destruction so much easier to accomplish. Acceptance of this propaganda at its face value would hasten the coming not of peace but of war.[21]

Fr Ryan's forebodings came to pass with the Soviet Union's invasion of Hungary which did convince a few Australian Communists of the Soviet Union's deceptions and nefarious game-plan.

Taking over *Annals* in the 60s

Fr John McMahon notes that Fr Stenhouse took on *Annals* not long after a milestone event in Australian Catholic history. A 1963 article published the speech given by Fr. J. McMahon, on the occasion of the Pontifical High Mass celebrating the golden jubilee of Eileen O'Connor's religious group 'Our Lady's Nurses for the Poor' (also known as 'The Brown Nurses'), which had been given the canonical statute of a Pious Association of the Catholic Church in 1949 and was thriving.[22] Interestingly Fr Stenhouse was to say Masses at their Coogee centre, as his 2019 diary records, up to the last months of his life.[23]

Though many gifted editors had preceded Fr Stenhouse, Fr McMahon states that when he came on the scene "*Annals* took on a new lease of life."[24] Not only did he raise a sagging circulation, here was someone who had had first-hand experience as a journalist *before* he entered the priesthood and acquired a means of transport, thus fulfilling the dream of a former editor. As Fr McMahon observed:

For the first time *Annals* had an editor who had had practical experience of the publishing business – as a journalist and apprentice printer with a country paper while still in his teens. Also, for the first time in its history *Annals* had a vehicle – a second-hand, somewhat broken-down blue Morris Van – and thus were realised all the hopes of Eric Dignam who in the 1920's (forty years previously!) tried manfully time and again to persuade his Superiors that *Annals* needed some sort of transport.[25]

With his blue Morris van, Fr Stenhouse got around and noted the moral and cultural upheaval around him. What a time to become editor! Those who lived through it would have differing memories, though all would remember it as a time of cultural upheaval. During the 1960s and 70s Joyce Milton, in her book, *The Road to Malpsychia* (2003), explained that what seemed like innocent calls for 'progress' were really the promotion of a hyper-individualist creed that became hell bent on rejecting Western civilisation as authoritarian and patriarchal. From this arose the wars between the sexes, the imbibing of Marxism's various forms of Kool-Aid, while referring to the 'free secular liberal West'.[26]

From the outset, Fr Stenhouse seems to have had an inbuilt 'barometer of equanimity' guiding him while polemics and deconstruction raged around him. This equanimity is an uncommon quality. Who can say where it comes from? Is it a gift, or is it acquired through years of observation or analysis – or perhaps all of these? It certainly bespeaks a moral depth arising from understanding and wisdom. It requires a vision and knowledge in reading the times, in its positive and destructive features, an ability to maintain exquisite balance, restating perennial truths of the Catholic faith within the boundaries and cultural understanding of the contemporary mind. Fr Stenhouse did it; he saw the need for speaking to his age, in the manner that the Second Vatican Council had exhorted us all to do, to reach out to the times without losing any of the substance of the inherited legacy of the church.

When I asked Cardinal Pell in an interview how Fr Stenhouse had retained his calm in a time of Western cultural decay, he pointed without hesitation to his friend's deep knowledge of Church history. This gave clear perspective, balance, and a solid anchor to Fr Stenhouse as it did for the Cardinal himself who said that many of their discussions referred to earlier conflicts and events in the Church and history in general.[27]

With his balanced vision, Fr Stenhouse could restate in short syntheses the enduring truths buried beneath the debris of increasing deconstructionism. While he was sympathetic to the Vietnam war protestors, offering counsel and support, even being their chaplain for a while, he always tried to see things in a wider historical perspective. In a 1966 *Annals* article, he writes in an editorial, "[l]et us pray for peace, work for peace, but let us also assess realistically the enemy's tactics and prepare our deterrence accordingly." [28]

Tuning in to the current age took form in producing materials for religious education that appealed to students and teachers: these were called the *Catechetical Supplements*. From 1967 to 1976, the *Annals*, then called *Annals Australia*, featured a catechetical supplement every month, comprising eight pages of quotations, questions, photos, illustrations, alongside comments on contemporary, social and religious issues. Members of religious orders in Sydney, brothers and nuns, formed a committee to supervise the content of the *Supplements*. Of these teaching materials Fr Peter Malone states:

> He [Fr Stenhouse] went to North Sydney, met a Josephite sister called Sister Peter and she opened up the whole world of religious education to him. He got inspired then to have catechetical supplements in the *Annals* on all

the topics of the time that were important, especially for secondary school students. It also had catechetical guides which he didn't write, which some others of us spent a lot of time on interpreting that material ... it was quite extraordinary ...[29]

Soon there were extensive 'Guides' to the Supplements. It was a heyday in circulation before so many other magazines and booklets were produced and the photocopier became commonplace.

Fr Stenhouse himself recalls in his memoir of *Annals* that the period 1968-1974 "was one of phenomenal success for *Annals*", although "it wasn't all plain sailing as anyone growing up at that time will remember."[30] *Annals* had a growing circulation for it was bought by schools, even non-Catholic and State schools. He recalls: "Chaplains in non-Catholic schools also welcomed the religious education material that was thoroughly Australian in content and design, and while non-polemical, was still unashamedly Catholic."[31] During these years (1960s and 70s), Fr Pat Austin remembers Fr Stenhouse coming to the Vocations Office to speak with Fr Frank Fletcher, who was then Vocations Director (Fr Pat was his assistant) about the needs of young people. Fr Austin listened with fascination to the long discussions that developed between the two priests, each one asking the other to co-operate in various projects.[32] Fr Fletcher wrote articles on how to deal with young people. For example, his 1963 article, entitled "Understanding a Teenager", gave examples of how to deal with adolescent confusion.[33] Included in *Annals*, were articles on friendship, drug-taking, the search for meaning, the changing Church, war, where we are all heading, capital punishment and abortion. As regards the latter issue, *Annals* got publicly attacked for its trouble but did not resile from presenting the Catholic perspective.

Annals' circulation climbed from 25,000 in 1960s to 58,000 in 1972. Some months 70,000 copies sold. The supplements included references for teachers on the Church Fathers and documents; nothing was haphazard. At the beginning of the year, "teachers and priests were notified of the course that *Annals* was planning and the plan was followed" so the influence of *Annals* was not inconsiderable on the entire Catechetical program. *Annals* reviewer Trish Kavanagh, wondered why she was allocated the best seats in the house whenever she went to a cinema or theatre. One of the theatre staff informed her that if a play or film got a good review in *Annals*, then there was a guaranteed large audience each time. So it was very wise to treat *Annals* reviewers with great respect.

As the 1980s approached, there were rising sirens of new age thinking, an *ersatz* spirituality of increasingly anti-Christian and post-modernist views. There was a growing cultural amnesia about the historical bedrock of Western civilisation. When demand for the Catholic supplements waned in this decade, Fr Stenhouse perceived the need to break through this growing cultural amnesia, putting focus on the Church Fathers and reasoned explanations, going to the sources. He also focused on spiritual movements, encouraging membership of what was formerly known as the 'Archconfraternity of Our Lady of the Sacred Heart' and afterwards changed to the 'House of Mary: an Association of Our Lady of the Sacred Heart.' Fr Stenhouse noted in a 1983 *Annals* article that this lay movement had started in Australia in the same year that *Annals* did, 1889, now having "hundreds of thousands of members" and inviting anyone to join as soon as possible.[34] Sister Mary Ruth (OLSH), who had been a missionary in Papua New Guinea, met Fr Stenhouse on several occasions, and recalls his "extraordinary devotion" to Our Lady of the Sacred Heart, with holy cards and booklets published for the House of Mary Masses.

As well as promoting lay devotion to Our Lady of the Sacred Heart, *Annals* carried material on theology, Church history, philosophy, psychology and morality and also turned to critiques of the deceptions of the age. Fr Stenhouse had books on his shelves on engineering, linguistics, journalism, Biggles books, travel, poetry as well as large tomes of Biblical reference, the saints and the liturgy, not to mention his books in various languages, mainly French, Arabic, Hebrew, Italian, Spanish and Croatian, even a book on conversational Rumanian. He possessed books given by many friends and listened to what others said with great interest. Long-time friend Karl Schmude commented:

> *Annals* was notable for the quality of its writers from overseas as well as Australia. While it was published mainly for an Australian audience – and its editor had an intuitive sense of the cultural style and sensibility of Australians – it attracted many international contributors, in particular from the United States, such as the philosopher, Jude P. Dougherty, the editor and anthologist George J. Marlin, and the president of the Faith & Reason Institute, Robert Royal.[35]

Annals writers, Lawrence of Arabia, French villages, jazz bands and philosophers

Early in his journalistic forays, Fr Stenhouse travelled to France in the 1970s and spent many a night in the French village of Sury-en-Vaux, in the library of Richard Aldington, author of *Lawrence of Arabia* (1955). He went on occasion with Cyril Pearl of whom he was to say that he was "one of Australia's greatest writers and a fine journalist and editor and his wife Paddy."[36] It was during one of these stays in France, and after Aldington's death, that Fr Stenhouse met Alister Kershaw (1921-1995) who had been the ABC's Paris correspondent, as well as a renowned writer and satirist. Fr Stenhouse had admired Kershaw before he met him in the gardens surrounding the house of the author of *Lawrence of Arabia*.

Doorway to the *Annals* Office in the MSC Monastery in Kensington and Father Stenhouse with a young *Annals* reader.

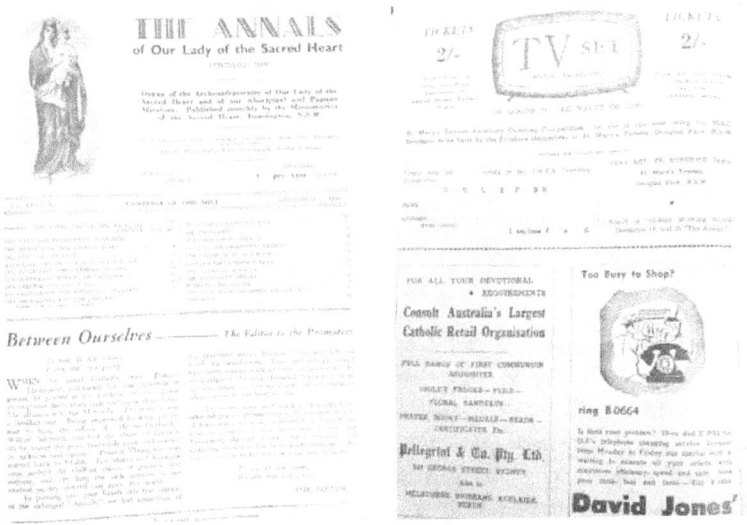

Left: Contents page from a December 1934 edition of *Annals*, with article titles such as "The National Eucharistic Congress", "New Aboriginal Missions", "Palm Island Aboriginal Mission" and "Doc Rumble's Question Box." Right: Advertisements from the December 1956 edition. Advertisers helped defray the costs of publishing the magazine.

Clockwise from top left: The renowned MSC priest, Fr "Doc" Rumble, who regularly wrote for *Annals*, answering questions on his regular 2SM radio show; Hal English, gifted illustrator and painter who did artwork for *Annals*; One of Fr Stenhouse's photos, taken in Papua New Guinea and used as a cover photo for *Annals*; A photo Fr Stenhouse had on the wall of his personal office for many years, showing the front of a shop called "Stenhouse Kosher Food Store"; Many articles in *Annals* were about the missions in Papua New Guinea. In later years many Papuans in Australia came to dance on special occasions in the gardens of the MSC Monastery in Kensington.

Some artwork for *Annals* by Hal English and an example of the artwork by Hal English's successor, Kevin Drumm, whose wit entertained Fr Stenhouse and *Annals* readers.

Left: Longtime friend of Fr Stenhouse, James (Jim) Waldersee (1926-1988), lecturer in history at the University of Sydney, whom Father Stenhouse befriended after meeting him in the University staffroom. Jim, a highly skilled musician, could play several instruments and wrote for *Annals* for many years. Right: John Colborne-Veel who was a regular *Annals* contributor on music, especially on Christmas carols.

On left: Some of the *Annals* team, Fr Stenhouse, Peter Macinante, who worked around 40 years for *Annals*, and Jennie Hiatt who worked for over 20 years in the *Annals* office; Fr Stenhouse, in his well-known jacket, with Colin Offord and another friend. Colin designed the new layout for *Annals* in the early 1980s. On right: Henry (Henryk) Skrzyński (1913-2008), officer, writer, diplomat, refugee, Australian of Polish background with a long *Annals* association; The multi-talented Robert James Stove, a regular contributor to *Annals*, who has written on a wide variety of subjects, including music and espionage. Here, playing the organ at St Michael's Uniting Church, Melbourne, 13 February 2020 (photo by Martin Houben; Fr Stenhouse was a friend of the Chaplain to the international Indy 500, Fr Phil de Rea. Here is a signed photo given to Fr Stenhouse by a racing car champion Emerson Fittipaldi.

Here Fr Stenhouse learned that it was in fact Alister Kershaw who encouraged Aldington to write the famous book and who was, in fact, his secretary for many years, and for whom Aldington provided a home nearby in a hamlet in the Loire valley, surrounded by vineyards and undulating hills. One can imagine the witty, informative conversations within picturesque gardens near the Loire. These were evidently forever engraved in the mind of Fr Stenhouse who was impressed with Kershaw's "sonorous voice and impeccable grammar" and to whom the beauty of language, its sound as well as meaning, gave immense pleasure.[37] Naturally, Fr Stenhouse invited Kershaw to write for *Annals* which he did for many years, his last piece being entitled "Guilty as Charged." (1995).[38] In a tribute to his friend, Fr Stenhouse wrote of "Alister's well-deserved place in the Australian literary and artistic tradition" and "a command and love of English that wrung from the language its last drop of beauty of sound and meaning."[39]

Another literary figure who was not only a friend of Fr Stenhouse but, unknown to many, also on the Board of *Annals* for several years, was Australian novelist Christopher Koch (1931-2013). Koch is well known for his book *The Year of Living Dangerously* (1978), which described the violent events that led to the fall of the Sukarno regime in Indonesia in 1967 and which was made into a popular film by Peter Weir in 1982. There were also other novels, which were also highly acclaimed, *The Doubleman* (1985) and *Highways to a War* (1996), both of which won the Miles Franklin Award. It was through the legendary journalist Frank Devine that Fr Stenhouse met Koch whereupon they became firm friends with Koch agreeing to be on the Board of *Annals*, eventually becoming its Chairman till his death in 2013.

Jim Waldersee contributed articles focusing on historical themes, though Fr Stenhouse was to say at his funeral Mass that he was "a true polymath – an all round genius of the kind that the modern education system will find it more and more difficult to produce."⁴⁰ As well as scientific qualifications (he topped the state in Maths and Physics in his final school year), Jim was a Jazz musician playing piano with the Riverside Jazz band, the Banksia Badmen and the 'Catholic contingent.' He lectured in history at Sydney University and met Fr Stenhouse in 1968 in the staff room there, initiating many series of conversations. Not long after, Jim started writing for *Annals*.

Philosopher Jude Dougherty was also a long time contributor to *Annals*. Having completed his PhD at the Catholic University of Washington, he became professor there in 1966 and dean of the School of Philosophy. He was editor-in-chief of *The Review of Metaphysics* for 44 years and became an emeritus member of the Pontifical Academy of St. Thomas Aquinas. He has published several works, including *The Logic of Religion* (CUA, 2002) and *Jacques Maritain: An Intellectual Profile* (CUA, 2003). His articles and reviews for *Annals* included acute analyses of philosophy and its trajectory over the past century.

Professor Dougherty related to me via email that his meeting with Fr Stenhouse began, as far as he could recall, when a "Patrick Quirk, who was visiting in the United States at the time, gave me some sample copies of *Annals*."

Clearly the professor was interested in the journal's content and style:

> .... Eventually I sent Fr. Stenhouse a piece of my own work when that piece seemed to transcend national boundaries because it addressed common issues confronting the U.S. and Australia.

He adds to this:

> There is another side of the story. In the sixties, [then Fr] Pell and I were both writing for the L'OSSERVATORE

ROMANO on priestly formation. Vatican II seemed to undercut the role of philosophy in priestly formation. I was not only a devotee of Leo XIII, but as Dean of the School of Philosophy, I was the lay head of a Pontifical faculty, apparently the first ever, at least in the States. Fr [later Bishop] Pell and I must have corresponded, for on a trip to the States he paid me a visit. The only time I met Fr. Stenhouse was when the three of us had dinner at Pell's club in Sydney. Stenhouse was everything I expected him to be, a kindred spirit to be sure.

Fr. Stenhouse and I, in our correspondence, mainly addressed social and political issues, although towards the end, he asked for prayers. I found him, by virtue of his uncommon learning, to be more than a correspondent, but a tutor to be emulated. When my son Thomas was living in Australia, at my request he visited Fr. Stenhouse. Thomas married an Aussie, so I have four Aussie grandchildren.

And the wide world of *Annals* contributors

Then there was also Sydney lecturer and writer Robert Tilley, who framed his reflective articles with wit and irony. Michael O'Connor contributed many fascinating articles on Australian history and its immediate political situation. There was also Susan Reibel Moore, long-time friend of Fr Stenhouse who wrote on literature and did engaging book reviews. There was Brian Pollard who focused on contemporary ethical issues in an age which preferred to forget them. There was Frances Hackney who wrote on pro-life issues, as did Steven Hitchings, and post-abortion counsellor Anne Lastman who reached out to those who were suffering. Another friend and writer Fr Stenhouse made in later years was professor Marek Jan Chodakiewicz, US Professor of History at the Institute of World Politics, a graduate school focusing on history and politics. Chodakiewicz was an expert on East-Central Europe's Three Seas region and author of *Intermarium: The Land Between The Baltic and Black Seas* (2012), among other books. My cousin, historian Janusz Tydda, had told me of his writings which I found most interesting, and as things turned out, I acted as go-between, introducing Fr Stenhouse to Professor Chodakiewicz in cyberspace. Chodakiewicz was delighted to meet this renowned priest scholar whose writings he had read for years. Fr Stenhouse similarly expressed his delight in meeting Professor Chodakiewicz and this led to several exchanges and in publishing some of the latter's articles.

Another friend, James Franklin, Professor of Mathematics at the University of New South Wales, as well as historian, recalls first seeing Fr Stenhouse in action in the 1980s when he gave a lunchtime talk at the University of New South Wales, where James was a young academic. The topic of the presentations concerned the threat to the Christian community in Lebanon posed by the war then in progress, which he said threatened to turn into a genocide.[41] This riveted James, who was to get to know Fr Stenhouse in the years to come and appreciated that he was "highly intelligent and well-informed" and "was telling truths at odds with the received ideas that constituted the 'progressive' narrative common to Australian universities and other cultural institutions." Fr Stenhouse encouraged James to write for *Annals* and from this ensued articles on Australian freemasonry, myths about the Middle Ages, the Grameen bank, the missions to Aboriginal Australians of Bishop Gsell and other Missionaries of the Sacred Heart, and Catholic philosophy. This led James to ask: "What other editor would cope with, or even understand, such diversity?" He referred to Fr Stenhouse's lightning quick mind on topics such as:

> ... the alphabeticity of Ugaritic and the survival of the Lollards are topics on which we hear all too little these days. The vast breadth of his understanding of virtually all subjects in the humanities made him a joy to talk to, provided

one could keep up. At our last meeting, a few months before he died, he reminisced about his considerable personal relationships with both Géza Vermes and Rupert Lockwood. I admit I was rather proud of myself to be able to show I knew who both of them were. (For the benefit of the young people of today who may be reading this, Vermes was one of the most celebrated and controversial scholars of the New Testament; Lockwood was possibly the best-known Australian Communist of the 1950s as the author of the notorious Document J that played a central role in the Petrov Royal Commission, later a Catholic and contributor to Annals).[42]

Fr Stenhouse understood what had to be culturally preserved and renewed to get us through threatening and degenerative times as did James Franklin. In the latter's book *Corrupting the Youth: A History of Philosophy in Australia* (2012) and in the *Journal of the Australian Catholic Historical Society,* James Franklin himself has given very penetrating and engaging accounts of the intellectual assaults on our times, and from where they come. He has continued the extraordinary task which Fr Stenhouse began and the website (www.australiancatholichistorical society.com.au) gives copies of past journals and a concise outline of some of the major figures and events of Australian Catholic history.

Polish diplomats, Katyn massacres and concentration camps

Another great friend of Fr Stenhouse was Henry (Henryk) Skrzyński (1913-2008), an Australian of Polish background who had an association with *Annals* for 25 years. Few know about his dramatic life. While Henry had a Polish background, he was born in Genoa as his father was Polish consul there. The family later moved back to their Polish family estate, 'Radlow' and Henry was educated by the Marian Fathers at Bielany and then graduated from the Law Faculty of Warsaw University in 1935. As his family were in the Diplomatic Service, he also did training at the Consular Academy in Vienna, completing this in 1937. He also did military service with the Polish Cavalry Reserve Officer Corps and then married Halina Jablonska in 1939, before the outbreak of the war. These latter facts have an immense bearing on his life for when Germany invaded Poland, along with many fellow officers fleeing the Germans, Henry planned to go east towards Russia to regroup. His wife Halina, however, had a premonition that Henry should not go east and he did not go. Thus he evaded the murderous fate of his fellow Reserve Officers which would have surely befallen him. Without doubt he would have been killed in the Katyn massacre (nearly 30,000 were killed by the Russians) and in fact all his officer friends were killed there.[43]

By not going east, however, Henry was arrested by the Germans and spent time in Auschwitz as political prisoner 88561, and then in Sachsenhausen north of Berlin. He was rescued by the Americans on 2 May 1945. Subsequently, his wife was smuggled out of Poland, joining him in the British sector of West Germany, where he lived as a displaced person. His two sons, Matthias and Joseph, were born in Germany before he came to Australia in 1950 and it is from them I learned of their father's fate. The family spent time in Bonegilla and Greta migrant and refugee camps. Henry worked at the Water Board and later in the Taxation Department. He was skilled in several languages, had many fields of knowledge, started a branch of a French cooking group called the Escoffier Society. At some point he also met Father Stenhouse and came to write for *Annals*. I was fortunate to be able to correspond with Henry's sons, one of whom, Matthias, had studied with the MSCs for some years, recalling:

> My father's observations on European history of the mid 20th century in particular were of great interest to Father, considering that my father had lived and suffered the destructive vagaries of Nazism and communism in his

native Poland. His fluency in several languages and wide reading gave depth to his comments. His love of the Church's magnificent and ancient history was an abiding topic they both shared and almost, one is tempted to say, they both reveled in it, like two ducks in a familiar and delightful pond.[44]

He adds:

> My own recollections of the scant meetings I had with Father are of a most patient and wise priest of God. His dedication to his vocation was what struck me most. Often he would cut short our meeting because he had to help some Asian students with their studies and in some cases his preparation for them to be received into the church.[45]

And Matthias points to the strange coincidences that led to meeting Fr Stenhouse:

> My Father had decided, in his retirement, to write a book about the socio/religious condition of Jewish women at the time of Christ. Initially he made contact with Professor Crown at Sydney University for help and advice, and was soon directed amongst others to see Father about publishing his book.[46]

Imagine the delight with which Professor Crown introduced Henryk to his good friend Fr Stenhouse. A deeply religious man, Henry told Fr Stenhouse that he attributed his survival during the war to his devotion to Our Lady and this sparked an extraordinary project. While suffering in the concentration camps, Henryk vowed he would write a book about the Virgin Mary, if he survived. And he did just that. He wrote *The Jewess Mary, Mother of Jesus* (Chevalier Press, 1993). Fr Stenhouse was eager to help and when the book was published it created much interest and still continues to do so.

Among the many memories was Fr Stenhouse's involvement in Henryk's funeral. Matthias recalls:

At my father's funeral at St. Joseph's Edgecliff on the 6th of April (which happened to be the transposed feast day of St. Joseph due to some clash with the Lenten liturgical calendar that year, most unusual) was con-celebrated with Father Stenhouse, Bishop Moore and Fr. Campion. Father Stenhouse sang the Dies Irae as requested by my father, but not in Latin, but in English as translated by Father Stenhouse himself. Wonderful. Then we had a couple of Polish singers sing the recessional Hymn which was my father's cavalry regiment's daily morning hymn… Bogurodzica. ["Mother of God"), the oldest Polish anthem composed somewhere between the 10th and 13th centuries.[47]

Colour, art, Hal English and Kevin Drumm

As much as Fr Stenhouse was attuned to the beauty of form in language, he was also acutely sensitive to the visual world. He was very drawn, aesthetically, psychologically and spiritually, to the work of the artist Hal English (1913-1986) whom he describes in *Annals* as a true friend of the "little people."[48] Hal was raised around Brewarrina in north western New South Wales and left school at the relatively young age of 12 to help support his mother and sisters. He worked on sheep stations, on a fishing trawler, a sausage factory, a printer, and at Goodyear Tyres. According to reports he could "turn a lathe, design and make his own tools, and was never happier than when he was creating something beautiful or useful, out of wood, metal or pen, ink and paper."[49] He had also drawn pictures from his childhood and a life-long friend Leslie Gray encouraged Hal to enter the field of commercial art. With time, his talent was recognised and he worked for publishing houses, such as Cleveland Publishing, John Sands and numerous advertising agencies. He became a master of pen and ink, line and wash, water colour and oils and his paintings evoked the natural colours of the bush. He could conjure up Australian outback scenes, eucalypts, water, sheep, native flora and fauna. *Annals* carried much of his art work. While he exhibited the true artistic spirit that sees reality more clearly beneath its appearances, Fr Stenhouse observed that he did not possess that 'business' acumen that may have raised his life out of the relative poverty that threaded it. But as "a real artist, with unusual gifts, Hal spent a life-time submitting himself to whatever it was that led him to paint ... Behind all was the beckoning hand and finger of God."[50] When Fr Stenhouse met Hal, he instantly recognised a rare talent and included his artwork in *Annals* for years beyond Hal's death. In a tribute to Hal, Fr Stenhouse reflected:

> It is to the poets, the artists, sculptors and actors that we turn most confidently in search of insights into Mystery: and especially the Mystery of God: the mystery of life and the mystery of death ... the poet, the artist – these deal not in finality of absolution, but with tentative glimpses, snatch glances at the real, translated into sound, colour and shape...[51]

Following the death of Hal in 1986, an artist with more comic leanings came on the scene. Kevin Drumm (1943-2006) originally came from Walkworth, a country town north of Auckland, New Zealand. He was recommended to Fr Stenhouse by journalist Cliff Baxter and, far from being a stopgap illustrator, the priest-editor recalled that Kevin illustrated for 18 years and "stayed on with *Annals* until a few weeks before his death."[52] Fr Stenhouse greatly valued the sense of whimsy, of the "incongruous and the bizarre" of this illustrator cum caricaturist. Pointing out some of these illustrations to me, Fr Stenhouse used them to accompany some articles I wrote on psychology.

Fr Stenhouse had a very original artist in Kevin, one whose illustrations suited a number of differing political, philosophical, psychological and literary contexts. In Fr Stenhouse's words, he:

... managed effortlessly to slip into that impish mode when drawing human being. Combined with his inclination to comic-irony was a gentle, almost reverential touch and loving attention to detail ... This ever present whimsy of his softened his caricatures and delighted the eye.

Carols and John Colbourne-Veel

Many readers of *Annals* will recall the regular contributions of composer John Colborne-Veel (1945-2012), particularly in the Christmas music collections put together each year. Colborne-Veel was at home with a wide range of musical styles, from jazz, film, TV, as well as liturgical music, and arrangements for stage, ballet and theatre. He presented a monthly Australian music program on 2MBS FM from 1990 to 2000. A Vietnam war veteran, he attended the NSW Conservatorium of Music on his return, studying composition in the mid-1970s with Dallas Haslem. He was a skilled jazz trombonist, working with Graeme Bell's band and the Ray Price Quintet in the mid-to-late 1970s. From 1980 onwards, Colborne-Veel increasingly dedicated his time to composing. Out of his several liturgical masses, *St Mary – A Festival Mass with Jazz Soloists* (1984) had numerous public performances in Sydney's Catholic churches. Richard Hughes, a highly skilled jazz pianist (and writer and friend of Fr Stenhouse) played for several of these performances.

Perhaps Colborne-Veel has been especially remembered by *Annals* readers for his transcriptions of traditional carols and Gregorian chants specific to liturgical feasts. In the "Annals History of Carols" he notes that:

> St Francis of Assisi is credited with introducing religious carols into the Liturgy at Grecchio in 1223, when he set up the first crib of the infant Saviour ... Carols for Christmas and other seasons became very effective catechetical tools.

Ten percent of the surviving Mediaeval English carols come from sources associated with the Franciscan order.[53]

Through Colborne-Veel's well researched account we learn that there was a rich cultural history of English carols between 1223 and 1533, until the renunciation of Papal supremacy by Henry VIII. After this the singing of carols was attacked by the Puritans, who in *The Anatomie of Abuses*, published in 1583, also condemned Mayday singing: "... young men and maides, olde men wives, gadding over night into the woods, groves, hills and mountains, where they spend all night in pleasant pastimes." Christmas Day was not celebrated in 1644 and denounced in the English Parliament as a day "much abused in superstition and profaneness."[54] It was abolished altogether, along with other Catholic festivals in 1647.

Many Catholics are unaware of this suppression of Catholic liturgical music and that the publication of surviving English carols did not revive till the nineteenth century, many collected by Davies Gilbert in 1882 and then William Sandys in 1883, to whom we owe such carols as "The First Nowell" and "I saw Three ships." Colborne-Veel certainly puts into perspective the immense value of those that did survive, including the virtually unknown "Cloverdale's Carol" and "Pleasure it is", giving the musical transcriptions to any *Annals* readers who wanted to revive them.

Music, wit and Sir Charles Villiers Stanford

Another friend of Fr Stenhouse, who particularly brought the world of music and hymnody to life for *Annals*, was Robert James Stove, Melbourne author, scholar, composer and organist.

Despite thinking Catholicism to be "the greatest racket in human history" when very young, Robert's conversion to the Catholic faith followed a long, fascinating path, which not many follow in our times when confronted with meaning-of-life dilemmas. He did it through questioning and persistent seeking. This took him to realms of philosophy, theology, literature and, in particular, music. Sharing the story of his conversion with others, he described the 'atmosphere' of his upbringing:

> It was a compound of introverted heathenism, dusty second-hand books, long dignified silences, the smell of dry sherry, and a perpetual fog of tobacco smoke. When I read a biography of Sir Leslie Stephen, Virginia Woolf's father, I found the mental climate of Stephen's existence so similar to my own nonage as to be positively scary. It was as if the author was describing my own home life, quite as much as Stephen's.[55]

When Robert did convert he immersed himself in sacred music. In his book about Palestrina, Robert says in his preface: "Here we have a master whose pre-eminence not even the most deranged iconoclast disputes, yet whose music has over the last few centuries had the reputation of being Good For You rather like spinach." As reviewer Christopher Connolly observes, "Robert Stove's book brings Palestrina to life and places him in our midst" and proceeds to explain how he does it for an audience brought up on post Vatican II rhythm and blues. Not only does Robert talk the talk, he walks the walk. A gifted organist, he also has given many artful performances of sacred music in various churches around Melbourne.

For his doctorate Robert chose to write on the Dublin born, Cambridge educated composer, Sir Charles Villiers Stanford (1852-1926). Bringing this relatively unknown composer to life, Robert conveys irrepressible joy in the discovery of hidden treasures, and more significantly, the injustice of such "forgetting" of great talent. For example in a public talk, interweaving history with musicology, Robert said of Stanford's second (one of five) organ sonata:

When Stanford came to write his Second Organ Sonata in August 1917, he deliberately [gave]... to his sonata's first movement the title 'Rheims.' The city of Rheims was, historically, associated with French kings' coronations. But Stanford in 1917 had in mind a much more recent event than any monarchical enthronement: namely, the German army's shelling of the city's cathedral, which became a gift to Allied propagandists, along with the army's destruction of Louvain's university library in Belgium at the same period.[56]

Robert's writing in *Annals* covered not only music and musicology but also espionage and book reviews. There were many emails, phone conversations and hand written letters which threaded the years of friendship with Fr Stenhouse with whom he shared an aversion for many so-called intellectuals of the past century. Apropos this theme, in one of his reviews critiquing a book on Bertrand Russell, he includes a comment on Russell by Illinois' Classics Professor R.P. Oliver, to make his deadly point that the ultimate dishonesty of such supposed intellectuals is, "lying by persons who have been trained as scholars and who use their expert knowledge not only to swindle the uneducated but to destroy the very civilisation that made scholarship possible."[57] Robert, like so many other *Annals* writers, was out to expose the intellectual swindlers who strove to misguide the innocent.

A unique editorial sensibility

Fr Stenhouse had a unique ability to attract writers on all kinds of subjects, from the world of literature, history, theology, art and music, to experts on food and car-racing on occasion! He went along with the way in which they wanted to write, taking account of the varied sensibilities of his writers. On occasion he rang to clarify some point, or some plays on words – he was quite indulgent in this way. He allowed the writers to transmit their vision, wit and style – there was no template to follow.

Clearly, this approach to editing had a positive effect and readers largely enjoyed the broad spectrum of interest and writing styles. Fr Stenhouse's decades long correspondence with *Annals* readers is preserved in separate folders, some of which I had the privilege to peruse. Readers were filled with praise for Fr Stenhouse and the journal. One reader writes that he is, "dazzled" by your width and depth of vision"; another praises an "unforgettable ... stellar edition"; another declares it is "highly inspirational"; another states "we are avid readers of the *Annals* and are great admirers of your articles", adding they are of "exceptional intelligence" in "building a Catholic culture"; another encloses a donation, "in appreciation for a top class magazine'; yet another praises "Robert Tilley's articles ... always a highlight for us" adding "[c]ongratulations on such a gem of a magazine."[58]

Karl Schmude grasped this unique wide-ranging editorial sensibility, a fine touch which:

> ... blended to a marked degree the "high" and the "low" traditions of religion and culture. He was immersed in the tradition of intellectual probing and aesthetic appreciation – in philosophy and theology, art and architecture, literature and music – but he did not allow this to form a barrier to the experience of private prayer and popular devotion. He knew that the life of intellectual penetration needed to strengthen and validate the spiritual intuitions and habits of ordinary people, and he would publish excerpts from early and later authors – from the Church Fathers to John Henry Newman and G.K. Chesterton – who fused these traditions of insight and experience in illuminating ways.[59]

Annals articles were interspersed with quotations from Catholic authors, using that superb psychological technique of 'the throwaway line.' Fr Stenhouse used excerpts from G.K. Chesterton, Christopher Dawson, Theodore Dalrymple, not to mention apt quotes from saints and theologians. I once heard a psychiatrist speak about the effectiveness of the 'throwaway line', saying that one of the best ways of having a point remembered was to give a spontaneous remark, as if you did not really mean to say it. He said the listeners are often likely to remember it more than a scholarly point. That is not to say the main focus of *Annals* articles themselves did not generate great immense interest, but sideline comments had their own peculiar punch too. For example, a tangential reflection on 'magnanimity' springs out in the midst of an article on Kashmir:

> Magnanimity is ... not so much the pursuit of Olympic gold, or musical stardom, or financial success, much less fame and international repute, as it is the pursuit of great moral achievement.[60]

Through these incidental comments, one often encountered a new name or a new thought, inspiring one to delve further. Along with the articles, art, and film reviews, there was always something for everybody, except that some special topics stood out, as we shall see in the next chapter.

4

WRITING ON JUST ABOUT ANY SUBJECT

As long as words a different sense will bear,
And each may be his own interpreter
Our airy faith will no foundation find
The Word's a weathercock for ev'ry wind.
'The Hind and the Panther', John Dryden

Your word is a lamp to my feet
and a light to my path.
Psalm 119: 105-106

Annals covered just about any subject of interest to the modern Catholic reader. As Fr John McMahon observed:

> Along with the very striking artwork of Hal English and historical articles by Dr James Waldersee and others, the Editorials and articles on just about any subject of interest to the modern Catholic reader, saw the *Annals* approach the celebration of its Centenary in December 1989 with confidence.[1]

Fr Stenhouse had realised that the era in which he lived was one of which the seventeenth century poet Dryden might well say "each may be his own interpreter." Hearing the plethora of viewpoints on everything, he challenged the cultural confusion and strident anti-Christian animus growing from the 1960s onwards, and kept reminding Catholics of their remarkable heritage. As reason and religion were replaced by rejection of the transcendent, Western secular society slid into an 'anything goes' type of moral relativism. Michael Novak warned:

> The greatest danger of secularism is that it steadily undercuts natural law, moral reason, and religion – in the name of privileging personal preference, taste, and selection. It tends first toward moral relativism and then begins sliding toward moral nihilism.[2]

Like a lighthouse in a storm, Fr Stenhouse kept bringing the perennial truths and great deeds of Christendom and human nature to his readers with constant clarity, pithy 'Stenhousian' observations. In Professor Marek Chodakiewicz's words, "[h]e made the *Annals* a powerhouse of Catholic intellectual prowess."[3] He took readers on remarkable journeys of Biblical significance to Jerusalem, Petra and Damascus and infused *Annals* with stories of the suffering Catholics in Kashmir, Syria, Uzbekistan, Lebanon, not to mention the fate of East European countries. The reader could feel he or she was an Indiana Jones, along with Fr Stenhouse, travelling with him along lesser-known, historically fascinating pathways. The intrepid traveller regaled them with current affairs in Papua New Guinea, East Timor, Africa, Kashmir and Albania. Wherever he went, like Orwell, he unmasked fake political and religious analyses of Christendom and the West and continued to do so right up to his death.

Fr Stenhouse understood clearly that the rise in perpetual critique of the West which permeated many humanities departments from the 1970s onwards (and I am a witness to that) aimed at opposing what Antonio Gramsci called the 'cultural superstructure' of Western civilisation – religion, marriage, notions of democracy and individualism. Vocal critical theorists of last century, such as

Herbert Marcuse, declared the West did not need to be transformed, it had to be eliminated. Therefore its historical and spiritual heritage had to be destroyed. Any cursory reading of his books published in the 1950s and 60s, such as *Eros and Civilisation* (1953) and *One Dimensional Man* (1964), will testify to this. Yet, at the same time as these books were influencing university students, Fr Stenhouse was walking past such students, to give lectures on and write about the historical legacy of the West. If ever there was an antidote in human form to post-modernism and cultural Marxism, it was Fr Stenhouse.

Many would not have picked up the new post-modern narrative at that time. Who knew where things were going in the 1960s and 70s? Nevertheless, the view that all the West is irredeemably bad because it is racist, sexist, misogynistic, homophobic, xenophobic, unfair, transphobic and so on was soon to hit Western culture big-time. The wrongs of some racists were foisted on everyone; the wrongs of some colonialists were foisted on *all* Christian missionaries and philanthropists; and the undeniable evils of *some* people were cast onto *all* Western civilisation This ideological fanfare, this attempt to 'cancel culture', obliterating the past, tried to silence core Christian beliefs and its battering ram aimed to attack Christianity, to discard metaphysics and reject the notion of the human person as a spiritual seeker. The more the core beliefs were shouted down, the more Fr Stenhouse reminded people of them and ceaselessly recounted artistic, philosophical, scientific or religious glories of the past.

Not everyone may see things in the same way and Fr Stenhouse would always welcome discussion of varying viewpoints. He did, however, see the long march of the cultural Marxists through the institutions. For example, in a 2003 *Annals* article entitled "Cambridge Spies and Marxism's Post-Modernist Front", he gives a pungent commentary on post-modernism's attempts to erase the history and culture of the West. Digging for deeper roots, he goes back to the inter-war years, to the rise of the anti-West Cambridge spies, who turned against their own country and became Soviet agents. They certainly wished to 'cancel' their culture, joining the Communist cause while students in the 1930s. They saw in Marxism a bright utopian future which totally eliminated the Judeo-Christian past from any worldview.[4] Fr Stenhouse could see through such past and present revolutionary messianism in a lightning flash. He quotes from Michael Straight, who almost joined the 'Cambridge Apostles', the source of many 1930s and 40s pro-Soviet agents, but who got out in time:

> We were among the last of the Utopians ... we repudiated all versions of original sin ... we were not aware that civilization was a thin and precarious trust ... only maintained by rules and conventions skilfully put across and guilefully preserved. We had no respect for traditional wisdom and the restraints of custom. We lacked reverence ...[5]

Fr Stenhouse goes on to reflect on how naive these 1930s political neophytes proved to be in their assessment of the world-scene. And he notes how long their influence has lasted into our times, in spawning post-modernism and its loathing for Western culture. He writes of the new millennium university ambience:

> New recruits for a hypothetical 21st century post-modernist university dining-club at a university near you, would be bombarded with scepticism about the past and the present. 'The truth is unknowable and beyond the reach of us all,' they will be told. 'Historical research is impossible, because history is "fiction". The difference between historical "fact" and "falsehood" is ideological.' As we can't know anything about the past, it's better to ignore it; or to dismiss it as ideologically distorted by those who recorded it.[6]

Fr Stenhouse noted that while the Soviet Union might have 'fallen', its anti-spiritual notions had seeped into Western society for decades in a new toxic form of political correctness, 'woke' thinking, and further rejection of its past and beliefs. He was anti 'woke' long before the word 'woke' was used.

Reviving Catholic culture – the memory of what it means to be human

In the cultural wars who would have thought that *Annals* would become a tenacious bulwark against such ideological 'all or nothing' thinking and resist the post-modern miasma for decades? It did so because its editor recognised the ideological toxins seeping into the public square from the 60s onwards. He also, as Cardinal Pell put it, had found his anchor in "deep reading of early church history and the church Fathers."[7] With such reading and an extensive perspective, Fr Stenhouse could describe the ideological storms but not fall prey to them. It is not overstating it to say that *Annals* became a spiritual guerilla force in continually advocating for what is good and true in Catholic culture. Fr Stenhouse was enacting what Pope Benedict XVI envisioned:

> The Church represents the memory of what it means to be human in the face of a civilization of forgetfulness, which knows only itself and its own criteria. Yet just as an individual without memory has lost his identity, so too a human race without memory would lose its identity.[8]

The memory of what it means to be human in the face of forgetfulness became the constant *leitmotif* – historical, philosophical, Patristic and papal works focusing on the genealogy, memory of the saints and culture were regularly quoted. This was not just 'looking back', this was counteracting cultural amnesia in regular doses. In his last book which drew on previous *Annals* articles, Fr Stenhouse stressed the need for the West to *rediscover* its core, quoting Pope John Paul II:

> European culture gives the impression of 'silent apostasy' on the part of people who have all that they need and who live as if God does not exist.[9]

Fr Stenhouse took on the challenge of the 'silent apostasy'. He not only reminded people of their Catholic heritage, he boosted the morale of Catholics who felt beleaguered in the public square. He often wrote of the catacombs in Roman times and the growing new catacombs of our era, where saying simple things like 'marriage is between a man and a woman' became offensive, leading to a court case. He supported Archbishop Porteous when he was threatened with conviction in 2015 for saying just this. His use of the short article/essay form was as brilliant and effective a method as one could devise, in an age where human beings could not face too much reality at once. Short bursts of truth, irony, humour, putting things in historical context and reasonable explanations were the go.

The cultural smelling-salts approach

A good example of *Annals*' cultural smelling-salts approach was in the 1997 article where Fr Stenhouse commented on the new fad for non-Christian Baptismal names pervading not only mainstream society but the Catholic world. Instead of hand-wringing, he takes on the tone of trustworthy Catholic friend and amiable persuader.[10] He recalls that there was a time when parents naming children "Venus", Lennon' or 'X-files" for Baptism, would be met with a 'stoney look' from the priest and "the child would leave with "Mary, Margaret or Michael."[11] He goes on to say that the priest cannot assume that the parents understand "that baptismal names are a symbol of one's belonging to Christ."[12] In his serene Stenhousian manner, he then gives some salient facts about the past, namely that in the first three centuries people yearned to give Christian names to their children but could not under pain of death. It was not until the Edict of Milan in 313 AD, which ended the persecution of the Christians, that the latter were free to appropriate Christian names at their Baptism. And they did so with joy. Of course, Fr Stenhouse throws in some extra facts, as he often did, with typical linguistic panache, explaining that many words are derived from saints' names. For example he explains that Sydney is "an English corruption of St Denis, first bishop and patron saint of Paris" and then informs us that each of the 14 bells of St Mary's Cathedral have saintly names and that we would do well to think of them when passing the Cathedral.[13] By the end of the article the reader has learned a lot.

This way of reviving the culturally amnesic patient is very astute – no psychologist could do better. Confronted with such a person, a psychologist might ask 'What is your name?', 'Where do you come from?', and so on, giving the answers if they had forgotten. Fr Stenhouse just kept repeating stories and historical facts in short doses, reminding readers of their identity, their lives, and encouraging those who knew their identity to go out and remind other culturally amnesic family and friends. His amiable tone was a kind of pedagogy, a teaching method modelling to his readers how to transmit our Catholic heritage without anger or angst. This is also a very 'Stenhousian' quality. He knew when to give the witty epigram and when to give a more structured explanation. This is decidedly a higher order skill, a kind of insight reserved to the wise, who have knowledge, patience and a superb sense of timing and who know in an instant how to reply to a person's questions in an appropriate manner.

Fr Stenhouse covered many topics, such as why bishops have croziers, why churches are dedicated, why Catholics have Confraternities, why haloes are used for holy people, why Catholics have Viaticum, ring bells and so much more.[14] He had an uncanny gift for explaining myriad subjects in a succinct way as when he put together a highly useful summary of Catholic cultural 'facts' in *Annals Alamanac of Catholic Curiosities* (Chevalier Press, 1992, with illustrations by Hal English and Kevin Drumm). In addition, when explaining what happened to the relics of the Cross or what happened to the twelve apostles, he chose the form of monograph, a short book with several short sections within, to get across what others have taken 10 volumes to explain.[15]

Thus, while Christians were typecast as unoriginal, rigid and anti-progress by the new hostile, secular elites, *Annals* kept producing a relentless alternate narrative of inconvenient truths of the extraordinary legacy of Christianity. It had continual articles about its pioneering works in schools, hospitals, women's refuges, AIDS clinics, helping the homeless, refugees, the abandoned and countless organisations relevant to each age in which it existed. As Walter McEntee pointed out in a 1983 *Annals* article, the Christian legacy of helping others went back a long way:

> The Christians within the Roman Empire ran an internal welfare state. They looked after widows and orphans and shared their belongings according to the pattern of the Acts of the Apostles (2:42ff.)[16]

In continually regaling readers with modern day organisations (Aid to the Church in Need, Caritas, Family Life International, Knights of Malta, Catholic hospitals, homes for the elderly and countless religious organisations), Fr Stenhouse reminded others that the contemporary life of the Church had long roots, always adapting to the needs of the age and in fact was heir to the largest welfare network in the world.

Early church history and ongoing martyrdom

Along with other *Annals* writers, Fr Stenhouse never ceased referring to the early years of the Church, the martyrs and the entire history of Christianity. If anyone ever wished to have a quick course in early Church history it is possible to access articles on the *Annals Archive*.[17] In McEntee's articles, for example, readers are transported back to the early years of Christianity, and invited to see how the Romans must have viewed Christ's crucifixion. They were stunned that "the god of the Christians should have allowed this to happen to himself."[18] These multinational Christians engendered a true fear of the unknown in speaking Aramaic, Greek, Hebrew, Latin and Syriac. Wild rumours spread about Christians who were mocked and Nero had no trouble blaming them for the fire of Rome in 64 AD. McEntee quotes from Tacitus' *Annals* to make his point:

> Mockery of every sort was added to their deaths. Covered with the skins of beasts, they were torn by dogs or were nailed to crosses, or were doomed to the flames. These served to illuminate the night when daylight faded. Nero had thrown open his gardens for the spectacle.[19]

McEntee reminds his readers of the inspiration of St Polycarp, and how he continues to inspire Christians today:

> Christians took courage from the death of their martyr-confessors. For example, they could look to the witness of the aged bishop Polycarp, who was urged by the Proconsul: "Swear and I will release you; curse the Christ," to whom he answered: "Eighty-six years I have served him and he has done me no wrong. How can I then blaspheme my king who saved me?" [20]

In a 2014 *Annals* article Fr Stenhouse recalls the later martyrs of Tyburn Tree in England, pitching the narrative at a level all could understand:

> The 'Tree,' as you've probably guessed, was not a real tree. The term is a euphemism for the wooden gallows built in such a way that up to 24 persons could be hanged at

once. It was erected in 1571. Our Mass was offered in Tyburn Convent's crypt which teemed with memories. The convent is dedicated to the memory of the martyrs whose horrific deaths took place only a few hundred metres from where the Mass was being offered. All of the martyrs were hanged – some until they were dead, and others until they were almost dead. The latter were then taken down, 'drawn' [a euphemism for 'emasculated' and 'disembowelled'] and quartered [another euphemism for their body's being cut into four parts], and beheaded. Their heads were displayed on spears set up on the Tower, or on London Bridge. The Tyburn martyrs who, as the words of the Mass keep reminding us, were 'joined to Jesus in a death like His,' have never been forgotten.

Later martyrs and post Soviet times

Of special interest to Fr Stenhouse were the innumerable and mostly forgotten martyrs of the more recent Soviet empire. With the 'end' of the Soviet Union, he was determined not to let his readers forget. In a 1990 *Annals* article, he says:

> It will be up to the new breed of Soviet historians, untrammelled by the blinkers of Leninism or Stalinism, to tell the true story of the unremitting attempt by the Bolsheviks to wipe out the Catholics – Byzantine and Latin – living in the Soviet Union.

He punctures the cheering at the 'end' of the Soviet era and berates those who do not remember the suffering of its millions of martyrs:

> As the West stands back in wonder at the miraculous transformation of the former Communist states in the Baltic, Central and Eastern Europe, it would do well to remember the millions of martyrs whose blood sowed

> the seeds that put down deep roots and today are budding and tomorrow will burst into flower. We can mention but a handful ... In May 1947, to go back a little more than 40 years, Catholic Lithuania had three Bishops surviving, out of eleven. In June Archbishop Mecys Reinys, of Vilnius 'disappeared' after he was interviewed by a correspondent of the Tass newsagency. In July the nonagenarian Bishop Antonas Karosas of Seinai died, and not long afterwards, the sole remaining Bishop, Kazys Paltarokas of Penevezys, 'disappeared'.

In the same article he points to the smaller countries, often sidelined in discussion of the super-powers:

> In the Baltic alone, by 1950, more than 60,910 Estonians had been deported to Russia of whom 7,129 had been sentenced to between 10 and 25 years hard labour, and 1,800 had been murdered. More than 60,000 Latvians had disappeared, including 20,000 women and 9,000 children. At least 1,700 people were known to have been put to death by 1950. By that time, more than 50,000 Lithuanians had been deported to Russia (the names of 30,000 of whom were obtained from lists left by the Russians themselves). Over 3,000 were murdered by the Russian Secret Police.[21]

He then turns to recall the brutality endured in many other places in recent Christian history, challenging the reader to draw some conclusions. As much as post-modernists wish to bury Western history, he revives it. He will not let the socialist/cultural Marxists get away with their blinkered views which ignore the victims of their tyranny:

> Who today remembers the more than 28,000 children abducted during the Greek Civil War when Communist guerrillas realised that their cause was lost, and decided to take revenge? 12,000 were sent to Jugoslavia, 3,000

Hendrikus Wong (left) and Peter Macinante (right) in the *Annals* office; James (Jim) Waldersee, a regular *Annals* writer, was a fan of George Orwell as was Fr Stenhouse; Fr Stenhouse in his old office in which he prepared *Annals* for several decades. A few years before he passed away, he moved to a new, bigger office a few doors up, in the same building (Photo: courtesy of John Madden).

Post-Soviet Ukrainian Byzantine-rite Catholics celebrating religious freedom as Archbishop, Cardinal Lubachivskyj, preceded by Archbishop Sterniuk, leaves his residence to celebrate Mass on Palm Sunday, 31 March 1991, in St George's Cathedral, Lviv (formerly Lwów). Fr Stenhouse climbed on media vans and onto balconies to get good shots for *Annals*; Fr Stenhouse praying with Pope John Paul II in Rome and meeting him in the 1990s.

Some of the 250 seminarians who have sought admission to the only Byzantine-Rite Catholic Seminary in the Soviet Union, not far from Lviv in western Ukraine (photo in the May 1991 edition of *Annals*).

Photo of Ukrainian children taken by Fr Stenhouse on Palm Sunday, 31 March 1991.

While he had no official parish, Fr Stenhouse was always attending to the needs of international students, attending graduations, advising and helping them.

in Albania, 3,000 in Bulgaria, 3,000 in Hungary, 4,000 in Romania, 2,000 in Czechoslovakia and about 500 in Poland.[22]

He especially focuses on the Ukrainian Byzantine Catholics (also known as Uniates or the Greek Catholic church) among whom Fr Stenhouse stood with his brother priests in 1991, when the Archbishop was returned to his flock after several decades' exile. He gives 'snapshots' of a long story for the *Annals* reader, almost 'driven' to do so, lest people forget their suffering and deaths of the 10 million Byzantine Rite Catholics who had perished from war, starvation, forced famines since 1914. He goes on to convey the momentousness of the return of the Archbishop to a Ukraine formerly ravaged by persecution:

> Like his humble Lord before him, when he entered Jerusalem, Myroslav Ivan Cardinal Lubachivskyj, Great Archbishop of Lviv, Metropolitan of Galicia, and Spiritual Father of all Ukrainian Catholics of the Byzantine Rite, arrived in his home city of Lviv on March 30, 1991 to be greeted by the Hosannas of a vast concourse of people ... Myroslav Ivan Lubachivskyj was coming home after 52 years. He is the first Catholic Metropolitan Archbishop of Galicia to set foot in Lviv since April 11, 1945 when Metropolitan (later Cardinal) Josef Slipj was imprisoned, along with the entire Episcopate, 1735 priests, 1090 nuns and tens of thousands of lay Catholics. All the Ukrainian Byzantine Catholic bishops died in prison except Josef Slipj who paid for his refusal to convert to Russian Orthodoxy with a further seven years in prison and exile to Siberia. He was freed only in 1963 after the intervention of Pope John XXIII. [23]

In similar vein he reminds readers of the ongoing persecution in many parts of the world – among them Zambia, Uganda, Nigeria and the Congo. For example. he includes an account of, "Heroic Nuns Murdered in the Congo" (1998) and brutal Communist regimes such as that described in "Illyria/Albania."2010).[24]

Fr Stenhouse's work with *Aid to the Church in Need* (ACN) became a unique source for articles in *Annals* and one might add, for the Vatican itself. Fr Stenhouse became Chairman of the Board for ACN in 1997 and continued in this role till 2015 and hence often travelled to places of religious persecution, frequently with director Phillip Collignon. Moreover, Fr Stenhouse also used the wider media to alert the public about what was happening as regards the persecution of *all* religions not only Catholicism (more in a later chapter).

Dialogue with other religious groups: refuting anti-Catholic myths

Many will remember the *Annals* articles which gave answers to what were considered distortions of Catholicism as they were presented in the beliefs of Seventh Day Adventists, Jehovah's Witnesses and the fake versions of Catholicism in the public square. As Stuart Rowland, accomplished member of the Melbourne Bar, stated of Fr Stenhouse:

> He was very tolerant in allowing one to express opinions but this laser accuracy would hone in on the facts and assumptions that underpinned those opinions: he would have made a devastating advocate had he chosen the law.[25]

The series of articles answering 'Bible Christians', written between 1986 and 1988, took on various misunderstandings and distortions about the Catholic faith and pointed out that none of them is novel. These articles were later put together in a publication entitled *Catholic Answers to 'Bible' Christians: A Light on Biblical Fundamentalism* (1988 in two volumes). and underwent many reprintings. In these volumes, based on *Annals* articles, Fr Stenhouse states and refutes many of the myths concerning Catholicism.[26]

One persistent myth is that there was no Bible in English before that of Wycliffe (1382), as asserted by anti-Catholic polemicist Loraine Boettner, an American Protestant Bible Teacher. Fr Stenhouse replies that while English as a written language dates from around 1150, having at least three dialects, it came of age in the time of Geoffrey Chaucer (1340-1400), a contemporary of John Wycliffe, both of whom were Catholics at the time Wycliffe made his translation.[27] Having entered the argument with this simple fact, Fr Stenhouse takes apart Boettner's case, piece by piece, replying that: the whole Bible was translated into Saxon by the Venerable Bede (672-735); King Alfred (848-899) translated parts of Exodus and the Acts of the Apostles; that King Alfred exhorted his readers to "be busily occupied in reading Sacred Scripture and in frequent prayer"; Pope Agatho, in a Council in Rome in 679 AD, strongly encouraged sacred reading by all, referring to the words of Holy Scripture; the Council of Cloveshoe (of Clyff) insisted on the reading of Sacred Scripture (by everyone), also exhorting that "the Sacraments should be in the vernacular so that the faithful may more easily draw spiritual fruit."[28] The notion that Bibles were chained to pulpits or walls is often asserted as if there were some malign Catholic desire to prevent the faithful accessing them. Given that it took at least 10 months to write out the Bible's 35,877 verses on 6,391 pages, the reason it was available in a public place was quite the opposite – to make it available to all. As with any library:

> Far from restricting access it is actually ensuring that they be accessible to as many people as possible, and not just to a privileged few.[29]

Fr Stenhouse explains that the assertions 'Bible Christians' often make are not correct. He quotes the Protestant Rev. S.R. Maitland, librarian to the Archbishop of Canterbury, who in 1844 demolished forever the myth that "No Catholic (in pre-reformation England) ever knew his Bible well."[30] None of the facts collected by Maitland support the 'Bible only' claims. Fr Stenhouse cites this Protestant ally who refers to the fact that St Aldhelm sailed into Dover Harbour in 715 AD with a Bible, and presented it to the people of Malmesbury; and refers to Offa, King of the Mercians who presented a Bible to the Church at Worcester in 780AD – with many other similar examples. Maitland adds in his account that he came across not a single instance in which the Bible was treated with disrespect in pre-Reformation times and no instance of its being kept from the people.[31] Fr Stenhouse does, however, attest to the sad fact that many of the earlier Bibles, read by King, priest and layman alike, were destroyed during the dissolution of the monasteries.

Fr Stenhouse had his unique style of presenting a fusillade of facts. He refers to Eusebius of Caesarea (265-339 AD) who speaks, in his history, of knowing the Scriptures by heart and of Origen (185-193AD) who assumed widespread knowledge of them.[32] He cites the fact that there were no fewer than nine Catholic editions of the Bible in German before 1483, the year Luther was born! Calvinist David Clement documented his seeing two copies of a Catholic version of the Bible, made in 1466 and kept in the Senatorial Library in Leipzig, pointing out that there were at least sixteen editions of this translation made before 1552, one at Strasbourg, five at Nuremberg and ten at Augsburg. Fr Stenhouse notes: "[t]hree other Catholic editions were printed at Wittenberg in 1470, 1483 and 1490 and one at Augsburg in 1518. These are referred to by Seckendorf, Luther's biographer!"[33]

Were pre-Reformation Bibles printed in the vernacular?

In reply to the charge that the Bible was not available to people in any language of the vernacular in pre-Reformation times, a mass of evidence is presented to prove that editions in the vernacular were found in Italy, Spain, the Low Countries, Poland, Sweden, Iceland, as well as the older Arabic, Syriac, Ethiopian, Armenian, not to mention the Chinese and Indian translations being produced in Rome around the time Luther was working on his translation/version of the Bible. Fr Stenhouse cites overwhelming evidence that the Bible was indeed in the vernacular of a multitude of countries prior to the Reformation.

In answer to the charge that Catholics did not read the Bible at Mass, Fr Stenhouse quotes St Irenaeus, born in Smyrna in 175 AD, saying that the saint takes it for granted that every sincere Christian "will diligently read the scriptures together with the priests in the church which is the source of Apostolic doctrine."[34] He adds that not only were they expected to listen attentively to the scriptures, but priests were to be properly trained in their interpretation: "For this reason a Synod held in Syria around 405 AD forbade the ordaining of young men who did not understand the Scriptures."[35] If people came to a church simply to read the Gospels, moreover, that was a misconstruing of the purpose of the sacrifice of the Mass. *Both* hearing the word of Scripture *and* adoring the Word of God, the author of life, were essential to the Holy Mass.

Fr Stenhouse takes on 'private interpretation'

In addition to countering the myth that Catholics supposedly were prevented from reading the Bible, Fr Stenhouse methodically takes apart the notion of private interpretation of the Scriptures. Amidst the many phone calls Fr Stenhouse constantly received, he had to answer those who announced that they were no longer Catholics but were now led by the "Spirit" and could now interpret the Bible as they saw fit. Heaven help them. Fr Stenhouse had a way of countering such claims with an irrefutable series of facts, often stunning listeners into silence. After a deep, calm breath, he would remain silent just long enough to start delivering more facts, explanations, sources and irrefutable arguments with reason, Socratic finality and a cordial smile.

Fr Stenhouse asks how one is to choose between the many thousands of Scriptural interpretations of "biblical Christian Churches in the centres of Protestantism like Britain, Germany, Switzerland and America and now spreading through the Third World?" He notes the proliferation of sects and esoteric religions from the time of the reformation, referring to the "unleashing of literally thousands of individualistic religions, all posing as Christian no matter how contradictory their doctrines, and how unbiblical their views."[36] If all are 'prophets' and all are led by the 'Spirit' then logic and reason go by the board – superstition and absurdity can breed without hindrance, each member being able to interpret the Scriptures as they wish.

Lest the reader thinks Fr Stenhouse is overstating things, he gives several examples of such private interpretation within the tens of thousands of Christian' churches: some baptise, some do not; some accept a visible church, some do not; some believe in predestination, some do not; some deny Jesus' humanity, some do not; some deny the reality of the saints, the resurrection of the body, prayers for the dead – and the list goes on. He states dramatically: "And all claim to be 'Bible' Christians!"[37] This is not to deny vociferous conflicts between Catholics on certain issues but the matter is settled by eschewing polemics and referring to what the Church had traditionally taught and Papal authority. Fr Stenhouse points out that the fierce battles between the Protestant sects had no such recourse. No sooner had Luther set up his own criterion of private interpretation of the Scriptures, than his followers set out to prove Luther himself was in error. Thus we get Carlstadt who attacked Luther in 1521; Zwingli who took his version to Switzerland (Luther called him a 'pagan'); Oecolampadius, whose disagreement with Luther ended in death, Luther describing this as his being strangled by the devil. Then there was the case of Müntzer and the Anabaptists whose followers disagreed with Müntzer and each other, each claiming to base his doctrine on the text of the Bible. Luther was dismayed at the subsequent unleashing of myriad interpretations and insisted that what *he* said was "to be taken for an inspiration of the Holy Ghost", but as Fr Stenhouse, explains:

> The effects of Luther's opening of Pandora's box are still in our midst: and flourishing in the humid soil of poverty, ignorance and credulity.[38]

Whether one agreed or disagreed, friendship remained

Annals' articles aroused much interest and whether listeners agreed or disagreed, Fr Stenhouse had the gift of drawing people into the ambience of a serious, cordial discussion and commonly perceived humanity. This applied to contentious issues within the Church as well as radically differing worldviews. He would demolish views, not people. He did not enter all controversies of the day, though he did enter some. He was not interested in fiery polemics nor gossip, nor did he respond to anger, but affirmed his readers in a more serene consideration of the facts of a situation, in which mutual respect for all was paramount. For example, in a 1986 *Annals* article, Fr Stenhouse said the distress felt at the excommunication of ex-Archbishop of Dakar, Marcel Lefebvre, was understandable, praising Lefebvrist's orthodoxy and love of the traditional Mass.[39] During one of his journeys, he went to visit Lefebvrists staying in a Greek orthodox monastery in the hills of Hardine in northern Lebanon. The meeting was beneficial, fruitful and friendly. In his *Annals* article, however, while not questioning the love of the tradition of the Catholic Church, Fr Stenhouse questioned the wisdom of the political dimension of the Lefebvrist movement and how this has influenced its fate within the church:

> It is well-known that Lefebvre's movement has the solid backing of the European Monarchists who are still disgruntled at what they see as the 'betrayal' of Europe's monarchical 'tradition' by Pope Paul VI through his support for the implementation of the decrees of Vatican II.[40]

Then he adds:

> As Pope Paul VI said many times, if all that Archbishop Lefebvre wanted was permission to say Mass in the Latin according to the Rite of Pius V, he would have granted it gladly. But sadly, the seminary of Econe is not, as Lefebvre claims, just a 'Traditional' seminary like all those that existed prior to the Council. No pre-Vatican II seminary formed its priests in a spirit of opposition to the reigning Pope, to an Ecumenical Council, or to the teaching authority of the Church. No pre-Vatican II seminaries demanded that students for the priesthood reject the official Catholic Church, in order to adhere to some allegedly 'faithful' Church for which in the words of Marcel Lefebvre, 'disobedience (to the Pope) is a serious obligation'.[41]

Fr Stenhouse was interested in generating light not heat, and sought answers to the contradictions he presented. He would admit he was wrong if presented with compelling facts, but would not withdraw from asking reasonable questions. This applied to his discussions with many others who did not share his worldview and despite divergences of viewpoints, he managed to create bridges of cordiality and friendship. Even the Marxist Bob Gould, in speaking about the death of his 'enemy', the non-conformist, dramatic editor of *Quadrant*, Paddy McGuinness, expresses some 'friendly' words about Fr Stenhouse on seeing him at Paddy's funeral. Gould places these words about Fr Stenhouse on, of all things, a Marxist website:

> One of the more human features of the event was a eulogy by the editor of the Catholic journal, *The Annals*, a rather energetic tridentine Catholic apologist, Father Paul Stenhouse. He showed genuine emotion about McGuinness's death, and broke up at the end ... In Stenhouse's eulogy there was a note of affection for a fellow editor of a slightly cranky small-circulation journal. Father Stenhouse's *Annals* found considerable room a few years ago for some interesting articles by disillusioned Stalinist Rupert Lockwood about the Australian Communist Party and Stalinism ... Father Stenhouse's emotion about McGuinness was obviously genuine.[42]

No small praise from a Marxist and anti-Catholic!

Even before he had finished his PhD, Fr Stenhouse had published an article in the University of New South Wales publication, *Tharunka*, not known for its conservative, nor its pro-Christian sympathies. He wrote his observations on Lebanon in the edition of 31 March 1976 (page 47).

More surprises came from journalist Rupert Lockwood, a Communist who was lambasted by Fr Paddy Ryan, yet who later became a Catholic and got to know Fr Stenhouse well. Lockwood was a famous European correspondent during the Cold War, spending decades in Moscow as a highly valued and trusted Communist. But in the end, he disappointed his comrades by converting to the enemy – Catholicism! He had much to say about Communism and the Petrov affair which his former comrades did not want to hear. It was quite a change to go from writing for *Pravda* to writing for *Annals* but that is exactly what happened!

Lockwood gave dire warnings about the post-Soviet euphoria, pointing to the lack of an international trial for those responsible for the merciless era of gulags, whose numbers of victims exceeded those of Hitler by many millions.

Gorbachev, no doubt conscious that so many Soviet citizens were criminally involved as murderers, perjured informers, torturers and Gulag guards, has failed to insist on due respect to victims of the Great Terror. And aware of the power of intensively cultivated Leninolatory he has shied away from including Lenin among the guilty men, despite demands for removal of his body from the Red Square mausoleum.[43]

Sending dire warnings, Lockwood writes:

> The burdens of the Russian past, never able to produce more than a sparse crop of democrats, still weigh heavily. Even in the times of Krushchev and Brezhnev, when I was in the USSR, so many Russians could forget the piles of blood-soaked linen still to be washed and proclaim: "What Russia needs is another Stalin!" It was as if they wanted this long-suffering people to march once more toward the crackle of firing squads. Hamlets anxious to find what was rotten in the State could be re-stamped with the brand of treason.[44]

Lockwood's accounts of Australian history and attitudes are incisive and counteract received wisdom. He said Australia's first foray into foreign conflict was not the Boer War or World War 1 but was actually participation in the Chinese Opium Wars. Nevertheless the Crimean War instilled a fear of Russia in Australians and Lockwood writes: "The Crimea made Russia the enduring threat. They would invade Australia – without a Pacific navy – and turn our merino sheep into borscht soup."[45] He adds to this memorably put threat that the "spectacular pinnacle rock that was such a charming feature of Sydney Harbour was razed to create Fort Denison (Pinchgut) to blast the mythical Russian invasion fleet."

Over and above the ability to reach across the divides of many worldviews and draw others into enduring friendships, as will be described further in forthcoming chapters, Fr Stenhouse managed to create a 'still point in the turning world', which could hold the centrifugal force of conflicting, even destructive views in a rational centre. When *Annals* celebrated its 115th anniversary in 2004, Fr John George MSC saw its significance in standing in what he called the 'radical centre' of the Catholic intellectual tradition, understanding very well the hostile pressures of the day. Interestingly he posted this comment on *Eureka Street* website:

> *Annals Australia* is the way to go after its 115 years of outstanding Catholic output. Re present Editor Fr Stenhouse MSC: "Fr Paul and his writing stand very much at the 'radical centre' of the Catholic intellectual tradition," Cardinal Pell said at *Annals* 115th birthday celebrations "He knows where he's come from; he knows where we are and understands the very, very real and hostile pressures that are working against the Church today. He uses his vast array of learning, his elegant writing and his intelligence to present genuinely Christian views on a whole variety of subjects and challenges that confront us."[46]

5

SOME ISLAMIC THEMES FROM *ANNALS*

All the nations shall come to adore you
And glorify your name O Lord.
for you are great and do marvellous deeds,
you who alone are God.

Ps 85: 9

... despite the problem of snipers, I took photos of West Beirut.

Fr Stenhouse

How can one discuss *Annals* without referring to its many articles on the Middle East? Fr Stenhouse's scholarship, his knowledge of Arabic and Hebrew, gave him an understanding of its complexities, in particular a deep knowledge of those pertaining to Islam. He also drew other historians and linguists to write for him on this subject, publishing some of their articles in *Annals*, among them Samir Khalil Samir SJ, John Pontifex, Walter Brandmüller, Robert Spencer, Andrew Bostom, Nina Shea, Professor Jude Dougherty, and John Newton. Those who had first-hand experience of Islamic societies, such as Fr Stenhouse's Malaysian friend Ganesh Sahathevan and Lebanese friend Joseph Assaf, were able to give firsthand accounts of how life had been in Islamic societies. As for Fr Stenhouse's own articles and books, they covered a lot of ground ranging from the history of Islam, its impact on Christianity, and its current geo-political impact on several Western countries.

For those wishing to get better acquainted with his writings, there is a collection of very informative articles on Islam to be found in the online *Annals* Archive and anyone can access them.[1] Also, the final book Fr Stenhouse wrote, *Islam: Context and Complexity* (Scholarly Press, 2019), is an edited synthesis of many of these *Annals* articles.[2] The brief biography of the author, given in this final book, indicates the wide range of his interests. It refers to the *Kitab al-Tarikh* of the Samaritan priest Abu'l-Fath (1986) and the work entitled *Futuh al-Habasha*, that is, "The Conquest of Abyssinia", which was a translation from Arabic into English of the 16th century work by a long-named author, Shihab al-Din Ahmad bin 'Abdu'l Qader bin Salem bin Uthman.[3] This latter text is a key to understanding current events in the Horn of Africa. It gives an eye-witness account of the jihads waged against Ethiopian Christians in the early part of the sixteenth century.[4]

Professor of History at the World Institute of Politics, Marek Chodakiewicz, was inspired by Fr Stenhouse's work:

> The main point of attraction for me was his omnivorous mind, and in particular his mastery of the Middle East and east Africa. Since I have been in the process of writing a monograph on "The Worlds of Islam" for a while now, I always cast about for sagacious insights and solid sources on the topic. Therefore, I was smitten by Fr. Stenhouse's original translation of arguably the best original source on jihad, by Šîhab ad-Dîn Aḥmad bin 'Abd al-Qader bin Salem bin 'Utman vel 'Arab Faqih, his 16th century study *Futûḥ al-Habaša: The Conquest of Abyssinia* (Tsehai, 2003) ...[5]

Fr Stenhouse's work on monographs on Middle Arabic grammar, Samaritan history, chronology of the Samaritan High Priests and Samaritan religion have continued to inspire many others to write further on these subjects and will continue to do so.

Travels, the Middle East, the diary

There is a particularly interesting source as regards some of Fr Stenhouse's travels among his general correspondence and papers which I was given permission to see. How amazing to walk into his old office, with many open drawers of photos, books, cameras and papers on myriad subjects. Among these papers, I came across a treasure trove, a short, hand-written diary of 25 pages, in a small lined book, lying on a desk. It recounts one of Fr Stenhouse's trips to the Middle East, in particular to Lebanon, one of many such trips in which he learned about the politics and spiritual legacy of the region. The pages of this travel diary are unnumbered. The year is not given. The diary entries are mostly for days alone, such as "Monday", but one is given as Friday 19th, another Saturday 20th, another Wednesday, 24 April. From this I deduced that the year could have been one of five different years when the dates fall on those given days. It is less likely the trip happened in 2013 as Fr Stenhouse was already quite ill then and unlikely to do such a 'risky' trip in that year. This narrowed it down and from looking at his travel documents, it is most likely that it was written in 1985 as one of his passports indicates him leaving Australia on 16 April 1985, arriving in Cyprus on 17 April, and leaving Cyprus by boat on 19 April 1985. The diary confirms that he left Cyprus by boat, his passport being stamped from Larnaca Port.[6]

Starting from the back of the book, Arabic style, Fr Stenhouse writes about leaving Australia, and the intervening stops en route to Cyprus. After first landing in Cyprus, he writes that he tries to book a seat "on a helicopter that did not materialise."[7] He mentions that Fr Franko, "a monk of the Maronite Order of St Basil came for me and we went to get some Cypriot takeaway." Given that the trip by helicopter did not eventuate, Fr Franko helped secure passage by boat from Port Larnaca to Tunisia. From here Fr Stenhouse gets flights to Lebanon, returning to Cyprus and then on to Tel Aviv. The diary is mostly about Lebanon, and records the dates of some important interviews with local Maronite religious and military figures. His eye for detail is evident throughout. Once in Lebanon, he writes:

> In the pm I went to the Maronite Patriarch's residence – was not able to see him but did manage to meet the President of the Episcopal Conference Bishop Abi Joudy ... I waited back and visited the Patriarch's chapel – built in Crusader style – simple but quite devotional. While I was waiting ... sounds of firing came from a gully near the residence of the Patriarch.[8]

Despite the sounds of firing, Fr Stenhouse aims to reach Zahle: "If I can get to Zahle [and] to Jezzine that would please me" (20 April). Travelling by car with two Maronite monks, he notes several Lebanese and Syrian checkpoints along the way:

> There were at least 15 Syrian army checkpoints through which we had to pass before arriving at Zahle. The trip was saddening as many homes along the roadside were in ruins and if their occupants had been inside when the shells struck, they would have been killed ... We passed a church that was being used as a weapons store by the Syrians ... we also noticed two or three Syrian soldiers wearing crosses, one of them was a Maronite. The rest would have been Syrian Catholic or Orthodox."[9]

No doubt many prayers were said on roads such as follows:

> Our road took us in a circuitous route, along deserted

mountain roads, set dangerously close to the mountain, with deep chasms to the side. Occasional rock falls made the trip hazardous as did the addition of the road broken to pieces either by heavy tanks and guns passing over it or by bombs.[10]

Arriving at Zahle, Fr Stenhouse attends a Maronite Mass, noting that "inside the church one could see signs of the shelling, with bits out of the ceiling." He writes that he goes with a monk, Fr Steiby Stephan, to a memorial ceremony where there were also "Ketaib or Phalangists" to commemorate "the hundreds who died in the three sieges and bombardments of the town." After the ceremony he interviews the "chief of the Ketaib, Gabriel Sayagh", along with "the Chief Minister for the region of the Bekaa" (name not listed), and has lunch with them. He then adds:

> I went and interviewed Bishop Haddad, the Melchite Bishop of Zahle. He showed me the damage caused to his residence and school ... tracer bullets left their mark.[11]

Fr Stenhouse refers to his interviews with religious and political leaders on his journey. He was squeezed into a small room, with other journalists from Arabic press and Reuters in an interview with Samir Ja'ja (also known as Samir Geagea, a Lebanese Maronite politician). He notices a painting of the Madonna and Child hanging above him. He records speaking privately to Ja'ja afterwards, who refers to "the aims of the fundamentalist sects to impose Islamic Law on all the Lebanon."[12]

On his return to Beirut, he writes:

> We picked up a Syrian soldier looking for a lift to a village on the Syrian side and it turned out that he was a Christian – Greek Orthodox. Our route back took us past the residence of Amin Gemayal and also past his brother Bashir's tomb ... one couldn't help noticing how young the

Lebanese soldiers look, by contrast with the tough looking Syrians. The country seems to be defended by children.[13]

When taken to the 'Green line', dividing East and West Beirut, he notes:

> The devastation in this area was frightening to see – with buildings literally riddled with bullets and shells and railway carriages hurriedly used as defences miles from any railway line. People were going about their business as usual – children playing in dumps, a few businesses open – the poor trying to help the poor.

Nothing, however, impedes his photographic zeal:

> Today I went into East Beirut ... The city showed all signs of having suffered terrible bombardments. I had an interview with Jean Kehedy, who is in charge of Public Relations for the Forces Libanaises. Afterwards I went back to Harissa ... despite the problem of snipers, I took photos of West Beirut.[14]

Revolvers, dangerous mountain roads, St Charbel

The diary records Fr Stenhouse's going to the Melchite monks in Harissa, visiting the statue of Our Lady of Lebanon. When leaving, he gets a lift with a wedding party and observes a revolver being placed in the glove box of the car.

Also recorded in the diary is the journey to Byblos and to the Maronite Monastery and Hermitage of Saint Charbel, comparing the latter to the monasteries of St Bernard and St Francis, set high in the mountains in beautiful surroundings. He writes:

> The road was electrifyingly twisty and narrow with deep gorges. Few towns on the way. On arrival at the monastery I found there a monk (there were 11) who had been in Australia – Antoine – who showed us the tomb of the

saint and various objects associated with him – as well as thousands of letters received from all over the world in connection with cures through his intercession. A beautiful cave-like chapel encloses his body.

Fr Stenhouse's diary also records his attempts to interview Lebanese Maronite politician Elie Karami:[15]

> We had trouble finding his headquarters as it is in the middle of no man's land and my driver was rather frightened and at times lost.

He does finally get there, and refers to a "most enlightening" interview with Karami, saying he seems "full of faith" seated under the photo of Maronite politician Pierre Gemayal.[16]

Sometime later, he interviews ex-President Franjuja (also known as Franjiyeh). In a monastery nearby he sees the "militia of Franjuja in residence." Noting the military at the house, he adds that Franjuja is "still in mourning for his son and his followers who were killed in an ambush."[17] He notes:

> Our talk lasted more than an hour and he told me more off the record than on it. He would get up and point at photos or paintings to make his point. ... he is full of Faith, a good Catholic who believes that God will take care of his people ... some of his vision for Lebanon is not different from that of Samir Ja'ja, the killer of his son. Both want a free democratic Lebanon. But they differ as to the means.

Interestingly, on 14 November 2018, Reuters reported:

> Christian rivals from the Lebanese civil war, Samir Geagea and Suleiman Franjuja [grandson of the ex-President], shook hands with each other on Wednesday, marking a formal reconciliation to end more than four decades of enmity.[18]

Doubtless, Fr Stenhouse had prayed for such a reconciliation among the Christian groups. Knowledge of the language, politics, history, his resourcefulness, diplomatic skills, and the fact he was a priest, all clearly helped Fr Stenhouse reach places not easy to access, to read between the lines, to be a peace-maker. This was a solid basis for understanding some complexities of the region and informing others about it.

Pitching it right

Yet, having seen so much, learned so much, met so many people, how was Fr Stenhouse to pitch the information and commentary about Islam at the right level for his *Annals* readers? Not everyone can say long names like 'Shihab al-Din Ahmad bin 'Abdu 'l Qader bin Salem bin Uthman' at the drop of a hat as Fr Stenhouse could. Not all can name Islamic religious minorities with consummate ease – 'Shi'a, Ismailis, Druse, Alawites, Sufis, Alevis, Aidis and Ahmadis' – as he could.[19] All things considered, he managed to explain some essential facts of Islam clearly to his readers by conveying information in easy-to-read paragraphs and articles. He knew they most likely were not familiar with Arabic terms like *jizya* (a tax paid by non-Muslims in Muslim countries) nor *dhimmi* (a non-Muslim living in Islamic countries), so he intermingled his commentary with explanations of Islamic teaching, a sensible way of writing. He was also acutely aware that there were many myths concerning Islam circulating in the media and academia and was at pains to get the facts straight. Above all, he did not wish to incite polemics, to which he was always averse. He was a genuine peace-maker wherever he went. He could appreciate the authentic search for what is genuinely holy in all human beings, as the poet Khalil Gibran expresses it:

You are my brother and I love you. I love you when you

prostrate yourself in your mosque, and kneel in your church and pray in your synagogue.[20]

Yet he distinguished between Muslims and Islam and wanted above all to generate clear and reasonable discussion about Islam with interested readers. It would not be possible to cover all issues in his articles on Islam but selecting a number of persistent themes gives an indication of his understanding.[21] Here, three major headings are selected: first, his account of some basic history and beliefs of Islam; second, his exposure of some Western myths on the subject: and, third, some insightful contemporary commentary on Islam and the West arising from this.

History and beliefs of Islam

Fr Stenhouse points out that Islam's sacred book, the Qur'an (or Koran), claims to be the first book written in Arabic known to scholars, allegedly being the direct word of Allah given to Muhammad by Allah himself, through an angel from 612 to 632 AD. In a 1989 *Annals* article, Fr Stenhouse points out that Islamic teachings in this text, held to be sacred by Muslims, are "in the form of 114 Suras or chapters made up ... of 6,200 verses (the most ancient text of the Koran dates from 776 AD)." In his explanatory style, he points out that Islamic teachings are not restricted to the Koran (Fr Stenhouse later used the term Qur'an for Koran), but include:

> The Sunna or 'conduit' containing what are variously estimated to be from 100,000 to 750,000 Hadith of 'sayings' of the prophet dating from around 855 AD ... There are four basic pillars of Islam. In addition to the Koran, and the Sunna, there is the Ijma (or consent of the Mujtahidun or learned men), and the Kiyas (legal prescriptions deduced from the Koran and the Sunna).[22]

According to Islamic belief, Allah has revealed his final message to the 'greatest' prophet Muhammad and thus, the Qur'an says, the world is forever divided into the world of those who live in *dar al-Islam* or 'land of Islam' (surrender), and who live in a *dar al-harb* or 'land of war' (meaning any country inhabited by non-Muslims), not yet subjugated to Islam. This implies a judgement of previous holy books, Fr Stenhouse says, as there were teachings in the Torah and the Gospel that Muhammad did not accept, and the Qur'an presents these as "perverted." Muslims have to interpret the Torah and the Gospel in a strictly Qur'anic fashion with severe censure, if not punishments, for not doing so.

While explaining Islamic beliefs, Fr Stenhouse points out that there are difficulties facing a Qur'anic exegete, which include many unclear words and phrases in the Qur'an, the lack of a received text such as exists for the Old and New Testaments, and the fact that Islamic commentators can't agree over the meaning of many passages whose interpretations are often contradictory.

One problem is the meaning of the word '*Jahliyya*' which, as Fr Stenhouse explains, is translated as the "Time of Ignorance", that is, the time before Muhammad came on the scene. By contrast, Fr Stenhouse explains that this was not a "Time of Ignorance" as Christianity pervaded the Middle East, and had holy books and thriving communities long *before* Muhammad and Islam appeared on the scene:

> Large numbers of Christian tribes – the Kalb, TamTmi, Taghlibi, Ayyubi and many others like the Banu Najiya – are known to have inhabited or moved around vast areas of Arabia in pre-Islamic times. Christian Arab merchants had been doing business in Arabia for centuries.[23]

In referring to the large numbers of Christian tribes in pre-Islamic Arabia, Fr Stenhouse refers to the Christian and Jewish communities of physicians, musicians and merchants to be found in Mecca for several generations, even after Muhammad. He also refers to the several copies of the Bible that were known at that time, for the Christian theologian Origen Adamantius, writing sometime before 240, referred to the Hexapla, that is the Bible in six translations, saying that he (Origen) had seen a Bible in Arabic translation.[24] There were, moreover, associations between various tribes and the Christian tribe of the Banu Ghassan had a stall close to the Ka'ba in Mecca because "they were associates of the Christian Quraish clan of Banu Assad."[25] Aramaic and Arabic (among other languages) were spoken by hundreds of tribes which had lived in that area for centuries.

Another common misunderstanding dealt with in *Annals* concerns the word 'Allah' which Christians in Malaysia have recently been banned from using as it is purportedly only an Islamic term. Fr Stenhouse explains it was used long *before* Muhammad came on the scene as Muhammad's own father had the name 'Abdullah' meaning 'Servant of Allah' and died before Muhammad was born. Muhammad's father certainly was not a Muslim. Fr Stenhouse does not stop there. He cites the writing of Ibn Isḥāq (c. 704-767), Arab biographer of the Prophet Muḥammad, whose book is one of the most important sources on the Muhammad's life, stating that a leading Christian murdered in battle in pre-Islamic times *circa* 523, whose name is Abdullah bin al-Thamir, is claimed by Ibn Isḥāq to have worn a ring that said "Allah is my Lord."[26] In addition, a pre-Islamic fragment of Psalm 78 [77] discovered in Damascus has the Greek text on one side and the Arabic text in Greek characters on the other. In this fragment, the Greek word for 'God', Theos, is translated into Arabic as 'Allah'. The earliest dated inscription in Arabic, moreover, is on a Martyrion, a church or shrine containing the relics of a Christian martyr, built in 512 AD. Texts are in Greek, Syriac and Arabic. 'God' is referred to as 'Allah'.[27] Christian sources indicate that the word 'Allah' was used for God, well *before* the time of Muhammad. To my knowledge no-one ever challenged Fr Stenhouse on this point.

Islam grows – why and how?

Fr Stenhouse gives an engaging synthesis of the history and beliefs of Islam and how they arose near the Roman and Byzantine empires and Persia. He interpolates his account with lively comments and questions. For example, he asks this question of the year Mohammad was born:

> If someone around 628 had dared to prophesy that within a decade some unheralded, unforeseen power from the hitherto barbarous and little known land of Arabia was to make an appearance, hurl itself against the only two world empires of the age, seize by force of arms the one – the Persian/Sassanid – and strip the other – the Byzantine Eastern Roman – of its fairest provinces, he would undoubtedly have been declared a lunatic. Yet that was exactly what happened.[28]

His account of the significant facts behind the expansion of Islam emphasise that both the Byzantine and Persian empires had been weakened because of their internecine conflicts for centuries:

> The rise of an Islamic State under Muhammad from 622 onwards was only possible because the Byzantine and Persian empires exhausted themselves fighting each other on and off for 126 years.[29]

The Arab forces were not unaware of the disastrous wars between the empires which had lasted so long and ended in 628 AD. In addition to taking advantage of this weakness was the fact that "[c]oercion and violence run like a *leitmotif* through the Qur'an and through the early biographies of Muhammad and his successors."[30] There was not so much a discussion of ideas but concrete plans about how to take over Medina and to attack other countries. Muhammad preached not only worship of Allah and the precepts of the Qur'an but he overwhelmingly preached *jihad* – war sanctioned by Allah as a sacred duty – and commanded his followers. not only to kill pagans but also members of their own families and tribes. Fr Stenhouse outlined much of this early period of Islam in his 2011 *Annals* article which synthesised some of the timeline and terminology of Islam:

> To understand the situation in which non-Muslim minorities in Islamic countries find themselves one must remember incidents that occurred in 627 and 628 AD during the latter period of Muhammad's fight with the people of Mecca. A Jewish tribe of the Qurayza which had remained neutral in the conflict was attacked. When the tribes people refused to convert to Muhammad's new religion they were seized and, according to Muslim sources, taken to the market place of Medina. There trenches were dug and between six and nine hundred of the men were beheaded. One only converted to Islam. The prophet then divided the women and children among the Muslims of Medina as slaves.[31]

After this, as Fr Stenhouse explains, Muhammad went north to the oasis of Khaybar, about 140km north west of Medina. Attacking the Jewish tribesmen at night, he burned their palm groves and, after a siege lasting a month, the inhabitants surrendered under the terms of a treaty called the *dhimma*, that is the law governing non-Muslims living in Muslim lands. As "[t]he land belongs to Allah and His Apostle (Muhammad)", declared the prophet, Jews and Christians could either convert, die, or pay a high tax called the *jizya* which was to be given to Muhammad and his followers. As well

Top: Fr Stenhouse (third from left) with a group in Jerusalem during the 1960s and while journeying in Lebanon, he had to avoid trouble spots. Here he sits with military personnel, discussing the lie of the land.

As it turned out we reached Rome at 10 to 11 and my flight to Athens had left when I collected my baggage. So after making a booking for that afternoon at 3.10 (with a connecting flight to Larnaca in Cyprus at 7.35 I rang John Bosman in Rome to say I'd call + leave one of tea bags. I got to Via Asmara via bus + taxi for the stay, Termini at 1.05 to discover that John who said he'd drive me to the airport was not home! So at 1.20 Jack Bolton + I went by bus to the Stazione Termini to find John waiting there + so we three went to the airport together. W[enny]

LEBANON — APRIL 16 →
We left Sydney AZ at 12.45 and after landing at Melbourne did not leave till 4.29 "due to technical problems" with brakes. Singapore at 12.00 midnight Australian time + we stayed (overstayed!) until 1.30 am. The scheduled 2 hour flight to Bangkok got us there at 3.30 but unlike Singapore we were not permitted to disembark. Our next stop is Bombay. We left Bangkok after an hour, and got to Bombay at 8.00 am. We are due in Rome at 9 am. So we will have to leave Bombay on time. Unfortunately our departure time from Bombay was 10.30 so we will be late into Rome.

Some of the 25 page handwritten text of a diary written by Fr Stenhouse on one of his many trips to Lebanon. Found among his papers in his old office; and Joseph Assaf, Lebanese-Australian friend of Fr Stenhouse. They met at Sydney University and became longtime friends. Fr Stenhouse visited Joseph's family in Lebanon (detailed account in Chapter 8).

Fr Stenhouse met Michel Aoun, president of Lebanon (1988-1990; re-elected president in 2016). An *Annals* article (1993) gave the text of his 1992 interview with Michel Aoun in exile in France.

Bringing Lebanon to *Annals* readers. A Maronite church in Hardine in Lebanon, which Fr Stenhouse visited, along with other religious sites, many dating back to the early years of Christianity; Marek Chodakiewicz, Professor of History at the World Institute of Politics, who has been inspired in his own work by Fr Stenhouse's writings on Islam; Father Stenhouse's papers included his 1975 Laissez-Passer from the Apostolic Delegation in Jerusalem, allowing him to travel in Jordan and Cyprus.

as paying exorbitant taxes, often over half of what they earned, they had to submit to Muslims in every other way:

> After some time, all the Christian and Jewish tribes of Arabia submitted to Muhammad's demands under the terms of a dhimma similar to that entered into at Khaybar. Non-Muslims were expected to provide assistance to Muslim armies ... they were to make space available in Churches and Synagogues if Muslims wanted to pray there. The dhimma which fixed the relationship of non-Muslims to Muhammad and his successors served as a model for all later treaties.[32]

Some thought that when Muhammad died they would escape the brutality. This violence, however, continued under Muhammad's successor Abu Bakr (father of Muhammad's favourite wife Aisha, hence Muhammad's father-in-law) in the so-called 'Wars of the Apostates', when some, previously forced to convert, thought they would be freed from paying the alms and wealth taxes. But there was no escape:

> Abu Bakr made it clear that he didn't care whether the 'apostates' submitted – that is gave their Islam (submission) willingly or unwillingly ... but submit they would or face the consequences.[33]

Abu Bakr and his successor 'Umar unleashed such ferocity on those wishing to withdraw from Islam, and on the Byzantine and Persian Empires, that he had no trouble luring their armies to him through abject fear and the promise of booty. When invading others' territories, the invitation to convert to Islam would be made – the *Da'wa'* card – and if this invitation to were rejected any killing and booty-taking would be totally justified. Thus, if Christians and Jews accepted Islam, they were exempted from the *jizya*, the poll tax paid by *dhimmis* to the treasury.[34] If they failed to convert they had to pay the punitive *jizya* all their lives. *Dhimmis* who paid exorbitant taxes were not second-class citizens, they were non-citizens in an Islamic state. There was a problem at one stage, Fr Stenhouse relates, when between 699 to 701, large numbers converted to Islam. This was not a good thing from a financial point of view as there were fewer non-Muslims to pay tax. So the "tyrannical Governor of Kufa in Iraq simply changed the rules. The new Muslim converts in Iraq lost their exemption from the *jizya* tax. The importance of the tax which raised money for *jihad* was paramount."[35]

Confronted with Islamic violence, the Persian and Byzantine forces were weakened by internal dissension which seriously prejudiced their chances of survival. As Fr Stenhouse explains, "[t]he vacuum was beginning to be filled."[36] The Byzantines lost the trust of many of their formerly Catholic Arab tribes who in turn elicited grievances from their harsh treatment of groups they controlled, the Nestorians and Monophysites. Fr Stenhouse speculates on what might have been:

> Had Heraclius, the Byzantine emperor, followed Belisarius's example and treated these Arab tribes more justly, one can only speculate how successful his forces would have been in repulsing the Muslim invaders....[37]

Myths about Islam throughout the Ages

The myths Fr Stenhouse was keen to expose were not just the results of differences in interpretation of texts but were, according to him, outright falsifications of history that were and still are perpetrated to this day by the mainstream media and some historians. For example, one of the greatest myths is the notion that when Muhammad died, there was peaceful coexistence for centuries till the Crusaders came. Fr Stenhouse points out that this is inaccurate, and that even Muslims say so. This view has spread its tentacles into school text books, media and popular imagination, "[n]or is scholarly work immune to post-Reformation spin against the Catholic Church and the Crusades." The myth of a peaceful co-existence owes as much to post-Reformation anti-Catholic polemic as it does to Islamic writings, while Muslims themselves acknowledge the reality of their wars and jihads. The Western myth derives from a persistent desire to depict other civilisations in a utopian way and regard Catholicism as negative. In a 2007 *Annals* article entitled "The Crusades and the Spin Doctors", Fr Stenhouse comments on such views:

> They are relics of anti-Catholic polemic from the sixteenth century onwards embedded uncritically in people's memories or lying on library shelves like landmines buried by an invading army. That they remain unacknowledged and unchallenged even now reflects poorly on modern, largely secularized, Western Societies, whose survival continues to be threatened by their refusal to confront reality. All mediaeval Crusaders were Catholic – good, bad and in between. It isn't easy for someone brought up on the historical fare provided for generations in predominantly Protestant countries, to conceive of a time when all Christians were Catholic.[38]

Fr Stenhouse points out that the overwhelming extant evidence indicates something very different from what is widely believed. Following the death of Muhammad in 632, many places fell to invading Muslim armies, including: Mesopotamia (633), Damascus (635), Alexandria (643), the latter sounding the death knell of Hellenic civilization that once enriched the whole of the Near East, Cyprus (648-9), Carthage (698), Tangiers (708), indeed virtually the whole of North Africa. Less than eighty years after Muhammad's death, Muslim armies poured across the Strait of Gibraltar into Spain, the intention being neither co-existence, nor dialogue over scones and tea, but violent takeover. By 721 the Arab Berbers had overthrown the ruling Catholic Visigoths in Spain and after the fall of Saragossa, the Muslim armies set their sights on France:

> By 720 Narbonne had fallen. Bordeaux was stormed and its churches burnt ... in early spring 732 . A basilica outside the walls of Poitiers was razed. 'Abd al-Rahman headed for Tours which held the body of St Martin who died in 397.[39]

In 732, Charles Martel and his Frankish army were able to halt the Islamic advance, 100 years after the death of Muhammad. But that was not the end of it as attacks on France continued and Arab forces took Avignon (734) and Marseille (838). The list of invasions is long and makes for grim reading. Subsequently came the fall of Crete (826), Sicily (827), Palermo (831) and Messina (842). Then followed Islamic raids along the Adriatic involving the destruction of Anco, Naples and places along the Po river, not to mention Bari where were held the relics of St Nicholas of Myra ('Father Christmas') which were taken by Khalfun, a Berber chieftain in 840. Then came the invasions of Italy in 846 of which Fr Stenhouse states:

> The two most revered Christian shrines outside the Holy Land, the tombs of Saints Peter and Paul, were desecrated, and their respective Basilicas were sacked, as was the Lateran Basilica along with numerous other churches and public buildings. The very altar over the body of St Peter was smashed to pieces and the great door of St Peter's Basilica was stripped ... Romans were desolated and Christendom was shocked at the barbarism of the Muslim forces.[40]

Having given this overview of Islamic invasions of Europe, Fr Stenhouse explains that it was not till Pope Leo IV (847-855) united Naples, Amalfi and Gaeta, that the Papal fleet was able to repel the Muslim forces, survivors of the battle being brought to Rome to help build the Leonine Wall around the Vatican. But this did not prevent the Arab forces continuing their wars for they invaded and took Malta (870), Taranto (880), Syracuse (878), Cosenza (1010) and Sardinia (1015); and the list goes on. This is not to mention the Muslim incursions of the Alps and the robbing and murdering of pilgrims trying to reach Rome and the Holy Land.

The new millennium saw the situation go from bad to worse when, in 1009, the Fatimid Caliph of Egypt ordered the destruction of the Holy Sepulchre in Jerusalem. Thus the invading Arabs destroyed the tomb of Jesus, the Dome, and other parts of the Church. For eleven years Christians were forbidden even to visit the rubble or to pray in the ruins. Pope Sergius IV appealed for help to go to the Holy Land and rebuild the destroyed site but his appeal fell on deaf ears. Fr Stenhouse also recounts the sad toll of destruction within North Africa:

> At the beginning of the fifth century, two hundred years before Muhammad appeared, there were seven-hundred Catholic bishops in North Africa ... Two hundred of them attended the Council of Carthage in 535. By the middle of the 900s there were forty left. By 1050, as a result of 'peaceful coexistence,' there were only five left ... in 1076, before the calling of the Council of Clermont, there were only two bishops left ...[41]

Fr Stenhouse asks several times if there is any reader who still believes that the period from the death of Muhammad (632) till the calling of the first Crusade (1095) was a period of peace? He describes how the two bishops left in North Africa had to import a newly consecrated assistant bishop from Rome in order to consecrate other bishops for North African Catholics. Also he writes how Pope Gregory VII had dreamt of forming a Christian League to defend the Holy Places. Yet it was not until the Seljuk Turkish capture of Jerusalem that it happened. It had taken 463 years for Europe's Catholics to combine forces and rise up in defence of themselves.[42]

Fr Stenhouse says it is misleading to claim that the Crusades represented a war of aggression against Islam. One can do no better than quote his clearly outlined reasons:

1. The Crusaders were not primarily interested in fighting Islam. The Crusaders fought [when necessary] to open up a safe pilgrimage route, and to repossess the Holy Places, swept away in the first heady days of Islamic jihadism after the death of Muhammad in 632. I say 'when necessary,' because cities controlled by Muslims – most of which had majority Christian populations were not attacked or occupied when they did not offer resistance. The Turkish Emir of Aleppo made no attempt to stop the crusading armies when they passed by Aleppo ...

2. Had the Crusaders really sought to destroy Islam they would have occupied Aleppo and cut Antioch off from Damascus and, thereby, from trade and military routes to Arabia and to Egypt. Everything between the desert and the Mediterranean would have been closed to Muslim forces. They did not.

3. Had the Crusaders sought to destroy Islam they would have occupied and garrisoned the whole of Cilicia – not just Antioch – and cut the Turks off from the principal land routes to Egypt and Arabia. They did not.

4. Had the Crusaders sought to destroy Islam they would have captured Damascus and controlled the whole of Syria, the route to Jerusalem, and all the land routes that connected Arabia to Egypt and the West. They did not.

5. Had the Crusaders sought to destroy Islam they would not have set up individual fiefdoms along the way, draining much-needed military resources to garrison them and leaving the liberation of Jerusalem to around 4% of the initial force of 300,000 men – an estimated 12,000 armed men of whom only 1,200 were mounted knights.

6. Had the Crusaders sought to destroy Islam the majority would not have withdrawn after Jerusalem fell to them on July 15, 1099, and returned to their estates in France, Italy and Sicily. One year after the liberation of Jerusalem, there were only 300 western knights and the same number of foot soldiers in those parts of southern Palestine controlled by the Crusaders.
7. Had the Crusaders sought to destroy Islam they would have ensured that the knights who remained in Jerusalem, Acre, Tripoli, Antioch, Edessa, Karak [Syriac for 'fortress'] ... and the numerous other Crusader citadels that stretched as far as Aqaba on the Red Sea, were adequately reinforced and supplied ... They did not.
8. Had the Crusaders sought to destroy Islam after Jerusalem fell to them in 1099 they would have adopted a less defensive and security-conscious posture, and conquered the neighbouring countries, cities and towns dominated by Muslim rulers, instead of entering into treaties with them as they did, e.g. with the Fatimid Caliphs, and later the Mamluk Sultans, of Egypt, the Emir of Hazart ... and even with the Emirs of Damascus. In 1104 and 1151 the Emirs of Basra allied themselves with the Crusaders against Damascus. In 1147 the Muslim commander of Hauran ... asked the Crusaders for help against Damascus.[43]

Fr Stenhouse had an informative, tenacious and reasonable way of making his points.

Other myths

Another myth Fr Stenhouse tackles is that of the meaning of Islam. Various groups assert that the word 'Islam' means 'peace' implying that it is a peaceful religion. He says two meanings are usually given for the word in Arabic – 'submission' and 'the religion of Islam' – explaining that Islam does not mean 'peace' and that no Arabic dictionary confirms this claim:

> ... while one sympathises with peace-loving Muslims for

wishing that it did, pretending that it does helps no one, and perpetuates a myth that obfuscates what is really at issue: the profound influence exerted by sections of the Qur'an and the Sunnah – Islam's religious patrimony – on the bloodletting and cruelty and chaos that fills the world's TV and social media.[44]

Fr Stenhouse's intention here and elsewhere is to draw a distinction between those Muslims who are genuinely peaceful and essential Islamic teachings which are not necessarily so. Islam, being submission to God, is not just a religion for it embraces the whole spectrum of life, political, social and religious, and implies submission to those who wield authority in the name of God in all these areas. There cannot be submission to the authority of non-Muslims. This is taught in madrassas, that is, in Islamic schools and has implications for the rights of women, of non-Muslims, and on the very notion of a pluralist society. When one adds the beliefs allowing under-age marriage and the killing of apostates, this conflicts with Western beliefs which prohibit such practices. It underlines the fact that the notion of 'culture' cannot be used as a justification for what is illegal in the host society to which many have fled after wars in their own countries. Here, it is apposite to recall that most victims of Islamic violence are Muslims.

Another myth, arising this time from morally relativist Western society, is that one idea is as good as another. But that surely cannot condone tolerating the violence of some beliefs.[45] As Fr Stenhouse observed:

> The conspiracy of silence in the mass-media when fundamentalist Islamic violations of the rights of Muslims and non-Muslim minorities are concerned – the ongoing slaughter of Christians and other non-Muslims by the Laskar Jihad in the Moluccas and the island of Sulawesi in Indonesia, is an example – has done much to convince the

likes of Usama bin Laden that their cause is just and that many in the West approve of it.[46]

While Fr Stenhouse always encouraged dialogue wherever possible, he insisted that this could not occur at the cost of authentic understanding of the beliefs on all sides and never at the cost of injustice.

Commentary on Islam and the West

While unflinchingly direct, Fr Stenhouse's analyses are always threaded with future hope of understanding between Islam and the West. As the West has forgotten many of its core beliefs, he saw it as easily overwhelmed, not understanding how to assert its own historical legacy with reason. When the Archbishop of Canterbury expressed the view that Shari'a law might find a place in Western society, Fr Stenhouse points out that, while the West may have its various political problems, in dealing with Muslims, "[t]he West is dealing with contradictory, opposed and apparently irreconcilable *political systems*. Islam is not some routinely familiar religion – or even an exotic religion – with a political face. *Islam is an intricate political system with a religious face.*"[47] He goes on to explain that the Archbishop appears to assume that the Shari'a of Islam is only *religious* law; and that fatwas emanating from Shari'a courts would affect only questions of a religious nature – garb, dietary laws, prayers, religious obligations, pilgrimages, training of imams, defining sins. Fr Stenhouse indicates that "the reality is otherwise", pointing out that there is a political dimension to Shari'a law, adding, "[w]hat we are witnessing, in essence, is a flexing of legal muscles brought about by competing jurisdictional claims made by two systems of *civil* laws: those governing Western democratic societies [in this instance, British law] and those civil/religious/social laws that govern Islamic societies." He states:

> Islamists are seeking, quite literally, to live [and have other Muslims live] under Shari'a rather than under British Law. Only one of these competing systems can be supreme. The Archbishop recognizes that there is a problem but seems unaware of the danger of ceding jurisdiction to a group of Islamic Shari`a scholars who deny that compliance with Shari`a is optional ... Laws of a political, juridical and religious nature are `absolutely similar from the Muslim point of view'.[48]

He emphasises such points as he sees Western legislators dabbling with the notion of Shari'a law, imbibing their limited knowledge from the newspapers and regarding it as compatible with a secular political society. They, he cautions, "are digging a grave for Democracy", as laws of a political, juridical and religious nature are absolutely similar from the Muslim point of view.[49] While the West separates Caesar and God, Islam does not.

Indifference or the failure to understand some facts about Islam is impacting many societies and Fr Stenhouse berates those who do not try to understand Islam:

> TV and the media generally, especially the internet, have given new meaning to the words 'bystander.' and 'onlooker'. Not always unwittingly, the media have become Terrorism's fifth column as they carry its grisly message, and extend its scope world-wide until no corner of the planet is immune to it.[50]

Not being a bystander, Fr Stenhouse questioned aspects of the insertion of Islamic Studies in Australian Catholic tertiary institutions.[51] For example, in a 2007 *Quadrant* article he expressed concern at the establishment of the Fethullah Gülen Chair for Islamic Studies and Interfaith Dialogue, within a Centre of Inter-Religious Dialogue at the Fitzroy campus of the Australian Catholic University, Melbourne.[52] While all for genuine inter-faith dialogue, Fr Stenhouse put forward the notion of 'taqiyya' as a possible motive for the appearance of dialogue while advancing Islam's cause. Taqiyya, while having various emphases in the schools of Islam, refers to the Islamic principle of permissible dissimulation and deception in difficult situations. He wondered how many knew whom they were promoting: Muhammed Fethullah Gülen is a Turkish Islamic scholar, leader of the Gülen movement, an international, faith-based civil organisation once aligned with Turkey's government, but since then outlawed as 'terrorist'. Gülen has promoted dialogue with other cultures and since 1999 has lived in exile in the United States.

In his 2007 *Quadrant* article, Fr Stenhouse simply queried the establishment of this Chair in the context of Islamic expansionism using the principle of taqiyya. His concerns were dismissed by Greg Barton, who did not answer the questions Fr Stenhouse asked: how much funding was there from Gülen himself and other groups? Is it prudent for Catholic institutions to accept funding from groups supporting Gülen?[53] Fr Stenhouse asked for clear answers in an age where transparency is paramount. His concerns were also dismissed in the 2016 doctoral thesis of Sureyya Nur Cicek, without addressing any point he had made. Such dismissal is something Fr Stenhouse would never do, as he always listened to varying viewpoints and would give an answer. Here he genuinely sought reasons for discounting taqiyya in this situation. None was given.[54]

Fr Stenhouse considers it a serious obstacle in Islam that no one person has authority to speak on behalf of all Muslims and their many schools: There are several groups: five major Sunni 'theological' schools, the Maliki, Hanafi, Shafi'i, Hanbali and Zahiri; and two Shi'a Schools, the Ja'afari and Zaidi. Despite the many schools, the suras or chapters of the Qur'an are believed to contain 'the very words' of God, so they are beyond discussion. So the only outcome possible, were religious dialogue to take place, would be submission to the teachings of the Qur'an and the authority of the Sunna or Hadith. Fr Stenhouse, however, does not stop there but looks at some figures within Islam who *have* reflected on it throughout history. He turns to Mahmoud Mohamed Taha, an Imam from Omdurman in Sudan, who sought to bring justice to his fellow Muslims, acknowledging that Shari'a does not treat women and non-Muslims equally with male Muslims. Fr Stenhouse notes that Mahmoud Taha understood that the 'peaceful' verses of the Qur'an derive from the earlier Meccan period of Muhammad's preaching, and those inciting violent jihad from the later Medina period.[55] Taha looks at the fact that the violent verses were not abrogated and asks about the nature of abrogation itself. Basing what he says on the Qur'an itself, he proposed that the Medina texts had fulfilled their purpose and that the earlier Meccan teachings "had been postponed, not abrogated permanently."[56] Thus it was time to return to the original Meccan peaceful verses. Though his desire was to invite discussion, Mahmoud Taha's teachings were met with fierce hostility from the Sudanese Islamic establishment and Taha was arrested, tried and hanged on 18 January 1985. Fr Stenhouse praises him for his "courageous and far-seeing spirit" and hopes it may inspire others to spread his message.[57]

Fr Stenhouse praises the Shiite Imam Mohammed Tawhidi for promoting peaceful discussion about Islam on mainstream Australian TV.[58] He also notes an attempt by more than 120 Muslims in positions of authority from around the world, who wrote an Open Letter (on 19 September 2014) to Abu Bakr al-Baghdadi (now deceased). The letter drew extensively from the Qur'an, the Hadith and classic Islamic texts, in rebutting the ideology of ISIS. Later that year Egypt's Abdul Fatah al-Sisi himself addressed the leaders of Egypt's al-Azhar Mosque on 28 December 2014, in an attempt to dissuade impressionable young Muslims from extremism:

> You imams are responsible before Allah. The entire world is waiting on you. The entire world is waiting for your work ... because the Islamic world in being torn, it is being destroyed, it is being lost. And it is being lost by our own hands.[59]

These were words of a Muslim leader to fellow Muslims. Fr Stenhouse also took great interest in the post-Regensburg meetings between Catholic and Islamic leaders in 2005. He was a long-time friend and admirer of professor of Islamic studies Fr Samir Khalil Samir who, in September 2005, participated in a study meeting with Benedict XVI on the concept of God in Islam at Castel Gandolfo. Fr Stenhouse published Fr Samir's article about the then Pope's address to Muslims in *Annals*, in which he addressed people of good will, speaking of 'our' concern for terrorism. Fr Samir states:

> On August 20 in Cologne, Pope Benedict XVI has his first big encounter with Islam, speaking with the representatives of Muslim communities. In a relatively long speech, he says, "I am certain that I echo your own thoughts when I bring up one of our concerns as we notice the spread of terrorism .... I know that many of you have firmly rejected, also publicly, in particular any connection between your faith and terrorism and have condemned it."[60]

Fr Samir lays emphasis on the universal 'dignity of the human person' quoting what he saw as a "crucial sentence" in the Pope's speech:

> "Only through recognition of the centrality of the person," the Pope goes on to say, "can a common basis for understanding be found, one which enables us to move beyond cultural conflicts and which neutralizes the disruptive power of ideologies."[61]

He adds the surprising statement that the "dialogue with Islam and other religions cannot be essentially a theological or religious dialogue" but one approached in "broad moral terms" as a "dialogue of cultures and civilizations."[62] And this led to the following reflection by Fr Samir:

> Thus, even before religion, there is the voice of conscience and we must all fight for moral values, for the dignity of the person, the defence of rights ... Therefore, for Benedict XVI, dialogue must be based on the centrality of the person, which overrides both cultural and ideological contrasts.[63]

Here we witness, one might say, the notion of bringing Aristotle and Aquinas to Muhammad. If the notion of the dignity of each person, so central to Aristotle and Aquinas, were agreed upon by Islamic leaders, this would have profound consequences. Fr Stenhouse notes that some commentators might doubt the sincerity of such attempts at intercultural dialogue, but he, like Fr Samir, places great value on them, if they are well-informed. Even if they appear to fail, they may prompt bystanders to a more reasonable viewpoint. He certainly berates the West's much vaunted tolerance, saying it is often a "product of thinly disguised indifference, born of incomprehension regarding the present, and ignorance of the past and served with an unhealthy admixture of confusion and an underling fear ..."[64] He exhorts his readers to become more knowledgeable about Islam, to have confidence in their own beliefs, to reinstate the sacred in the daily life of the postmodern West, and above all, to build bridges of understanding with those who are genuine seekers of what is good and true.

6

Reaching out to the World, Universities, and Cardinal Pell

*For he has not despised or abhorred
the affliction of the afflicted,
and he has not hidden his face from him,
but has heard, when he cried to him.*

Psalm 22: 24

Fr Stenhouse had an extraordinary network of friends with whom he co-operated in all kinds of ways for the Church. A deep thread in his life was his long association with the organisation Aid to the Church in Need (ACN) and its director Phillip Collignon. The work of this organisation echoed that of the Missionaries of the Sacred Heart. Like the MSC order, appearing in the darkness of post-Enlightenment France in the nineteenth century, ACN will be forever engraved in twentieth century history for its sudden appearance like a burst of light amid the darkness of post-World War II destruction. It will be forever remembered for its ongoing assistance to the poor, refugees and the spiritually persecuted around the world.

Many have heard of the organisation but not many know how it came into existence. It is an extraordinary story. ACN is an international Catholic organisation which was established after

World War II by the 34-year-old Dutch Norbertine priest Father Werenfried van Straaten. In 1947 he saw the needs of millions of refugees in Germany and sought to provide help for them in some way.[1] He had no money, few connections, owned nothing. Nevertheless, like many followers of Christ when he saw suffering, he sought some way to alleviate it. And this took the form of 'an idea', of begging for food from Flemish farmers nearby who responded by giving slabs of bacon to him. Like a postwar busker, he kept begging for food from farmers. This became known as the "revolutionary Battle of the Bacon" for the hungry and the poor. May it be forever recorded in history that those farmers gave generously. As former Australian director Phillip Collignon says:

> One of the first things that Fr Werenfried requested from his fellow Flemish country folk was bacon, to help feed the destitute refugees. He knew that the country folk had more food than money, and were willing to share what they had. The response was amazing and so much pork was collected that Father Werenfried became known as the "bacon priest."[2]

Aid to the Church in Need (ACN) was first named 'Iron Curtain Church Relief' because it specialised in helping the new millions of refugees fleeing Communism. In time it came to focus not only on refugees from Eastern Europe but on all parts of the world where the Church was persecuted.[3] Fr Werenfried launched his program of providing wheels for the many "rucksack priests", that is, Catholic clergy from among the displaced refugee population who sought to minister to their scattered flocks in war-torn Germany. By 1950 Fr Werenfried was financing the first "chapel trucks" which were converted buses, with swing-out altars, used as mobile churches to bring the Mass and sacraments to the scattered Catholic refugees. So from handfuls of bacon and chapel trucks grew the mighty organisation we know today. The headquarters of ACN are based in

Königstein in Germany. During his pontificate, in December 2011, Pope Benedict XVI elevated the importance of ACN's charitable work to a Pontifical Foundation of the Catholic Church. Today, ACN offers annual financial support to more than 5,000 projects in 140 countries with 23 offices around the world.

In the midst of its growth, ACN set up an office in Sydney in 1963, under another Norbertine priest, Father Coenen. But it was not until the Berlin Wall fell in 1989 that Phillip Collignon was to meet Fr Stenhouse. By that time various members of the Collignon family had served as directors, and now Phillip, after a chance meeting in Sydney with Fr Werenfried's niece (Ton Willemsen), was invited to become ACN's new director, starting in 1990. Phillip recalls that he had, "no Curriculum Vitae, no preparation" for the job.[4] Of this he says:

> I now look back on the timing of my appointment as quite providential. I remember walking into that interview with a newspaper headlining the collapse of the Berlin Wall, which then saw atheistic Communism collapse like a 'pack of cards'. Fr Werenfried, Ton and ACN worldwide had been working towards this momentous occasion for decades and here I was being appointed at this historic time in world and Church history.[5]

It was also providential that the fall of the Berlin Wall led to Phillip meeting Fr Stenhouse. What a time! What a meeting! Just as ACN was trying to resurrect the forgotten churches of the old Soviet Union, Fr Stenhouse could apply his zeal and knowledge to this effort. Not long after, he accompanied Phillip to many places on behalf of ACN and in 1997 became the Australian Chairman of the ACN Board, which position he held till 2014. Thus arose a fortuitous working relationship between an MSC priest, Phillip and ACN, which aided the survival of Christianity in a century of war, displacement and disintegration. With his language proficiency, Fr

Stenhouse could travel to places of persecution, write about them, and attend the annual meetings of the organisation at the General Secretariat and Project Headquarters in Königstein. *Annals* readers became used to his accounts and its writers regularly heard words, "I'm off to Germany for a few weeks!" It was not only that he could speak German (he once translated a page in German for me at short notice) but he could communicate with ACN members from around the world with ease in their languages and hear reports of persecuted Catholics and at first hand.

Aeroflot, Chernobyl and jumping on vans

The journeys with Fr Stenhouse that remain vivid in Phillip's memory were those to the Ukraine, Korea, China and East Timor. Some aspects of the journey to the Ukraine were described in a previous chapter, but there was more to it which Phillip related to me.[6] It was actually Phillip who was asked to go to the Ukraine in 1991 for ACN but it was suggested that he take a journalist with him. Who to ask? It was his first year as director of ACN and he did not know the world of Catholic journalists well. He asked around for someone and the name 'Fr Stenhouse' came up. He recognised the name, knew of *Annals*, and one thing led to another and he finally met him. Thus began the long association. It was especially on this initial journey to the Ukraine on 30 March 1991 that Phillip realised Fr Stenhouse was a highly competent journalist, a very keen observer and, as Phillip learned, "was his own man" and would do extraordinary things to obtain his story. For example, during a Ukrainian Palm Sunday procession in 1991, Phillip saw Fr Stenhouse jump on top of a media van. It only took a few seconds and soon he was taking good quality shots amidst the crowds and media brigade.

This was the time of the end of the Soviet Union, and to reach here Phillip and Fr Stenhouse experienced their first ever flight on Aeroflot, in fact the first Aeroflot flight from Rome to Lviv. On reading this last sentence, if a shiver does not go up your spine, you have probably never flown Aeroflot. I have. When once flying between Moscow and Riga I experienced such bureaucratic bungles, technical confusion and dubious food that I prayed fervently in preparation for eternity. On disembarking, I was so relieved that I wanted to kiss the ground like Pope John Paul II used to do. In telling me of Aeroflot, Phillip's voice was shaking from time to time. No doubt the flights have now improved.

When in Lviv (also known as Lwów) Fr Stenhouse and Phillip blended into the huge Palm Sunday crowds welcoming Myroslav Ivan Cardinal Lubachivskyj, Great Archbishop of Lviv, Metropolitan of Galicia, and Spiritual Father of all Ukrainian Catholics of the Byzantine Rite. Phillip thought he had lost Fr Stenhouse in the throng a few times, but the latter would always crop up in unusual places, talking to Ukrainians, on top of various vans, in alcoves and on high balconies. Phillip was looking for him at one point and then suddenly saw him on a high balcony with the Archbishop himself within a small entourage. In those heady post-Soviet days, Fr Stenhouse managed to speak with priests, journalists and even dined with Communists, all of which he relayed in his *Annals* articles about this journey. This was superb reportage.

This trip coincided with the fifth anniversary of the Chernobyl disaster. Before he left for the Ukraine, Phillip recalls his family saying something along the lines, "Whatever you do in the Ukraine, don't go to Chernobyl!" They thought that such a visit might permanently irradiate him. One day, however, Phillip was standing in the lobby of their hotel and says he heard Fr Stenhouse announcing that the press corps were going to Chernobyl! Phillip ended up going with him:

I was in the process of sneaking back to my room to avoid

getting on the bus, when Fr Paul came bounding down the hotel stairs, full of zeal, with the knowledge that he was off to Chernobyl. I tried to politely say that I thought it best that I stay in the hotel but, in his inimitable style, he managed to get me onto the bus and off to the disaster site of Chernobyl.[7]

It turned out that journalists had been suddenly given permission to go to Chernobyl by the new Ukrainian authorities – sometimes such permission was given, sometimes not; this time it was. Within seconds, with some apprehension, Phillip found himself in a press van heading to the airport to board a twin engine Aeroflot flight from Lviv to Kiev. Having survived the flight they were placed in one of several press vans moving through one radioactive exclusion zone after another. Imagine hearing the Geiger counter on the back seat of the van emitting 'rat a tat tat' drum beats, indicating increasing levels of radiation. Fr Stenhouse was not perturbed in the slightest and in this way the two arrived in Chernobyl. Emerging from the press van, they felt an eerie stillness, saw the empty apartment blocks, the abandoned playgrounds, the apocalyptic desolation. What a symbol of the destruction wreaked on human beings by an uncaring political system, where the layers of unaccountability were like those of Dante's Hell. Phillip said that he heard of elderly people returning later to their apartments in Chernobyl crying, "what does it matter?" Their dire need for accommodation evidently outweighed any estimation of their own lifespans.

To Ekaterinburg, prison camps and South Korea

Meantime Fr Stenhouse's travel documents (in his old office) reveal very detailed itineraries to various parts of the world. If anyone wonders if he visited Russia – yes he did. There is one most interesting itinerary regarding such a journey. It is unclear whether this was for ACN work, but without doubt he would have seen and heard a great deal there and communicated his observations. For example, in 2001, an itinerary for a journey to the Ural region for 11-20 June 2001 has Fr Stenhouse arriving in Moscow, meeting with a Fr Michael Ryan, then having dinner with a religious sociologist from the Keston Institute, Sergej Borisovic Filatov. The next day, Tuesday, 12 June 2001, Fr Stenhouse leaves by train to Ekaterinburg and arrives there on Wednesday. Over the next few days, he visits the Novo-Tichinski Convent with 100 nuns, meets with Archpriest Foma Abel, in charge of a prison chaplaincy, followed by a visit to prison Camp 349/12 and a meeting with Jurij Michailovic Korjagin and other staff members. During this time he visits monasteries in the Ural mountains, travels to more prison camps, then to Celjabinsk, next to Niznij Tagil, and lastly Simferopol. He visits a Catholic parish in Celjabinsk run by Fr Wilhelm Palesch and other priests of the Focolarini group and later Orthodox Metropolitan Iov in this town. This is the bare outline of his itinerary, dramatic enough to read but doubtless much more occurred on the journey.[8]

Another journey Phillip recalls with Fr Stenhouse was the one to South Korea in the early 1990s. No, they did not gain access to North Korea, but knowing Fr Stenhouse's outreach to Catholics and his assiduous collection of information on the state of the Church, they would have learned much of the situation. Both he and Phillip would have heard from South Koreans about how Catholics and Christians generally were surviving under persecution in the North and this, doubtless, would have reached Königstein and Rome.

China, rats and fires in East Timor

In 1997 Phillip and Fr Stenhouse took an ACN trip to China. The ACN team were accompanied by Professor Audrey Donnithorne, daughter of former British missionaries in China, who knew a lot about the country, and who witnessed some of its major historical shifts (she died on 9 June 2020 at the age of 97). A review of Donnithorne's remarkable book *China in Life's Foreground* (2019) states that the "period of Audrey's memoir is tumultuous in China's history, ranging from the end of the Qing dynasty to the vicissitudes of the Communist revolution and its aftermath" and notes that Audrey was particularly well-informed about the various Christian communities there. Fr Stenhouse and Phillip could not have had a better source of information.

Finding accommodation was another matter entirely. One could not rely on getting Catholic groups to accommodate them as that would put them at risk. They stayed where they could and at one stage Phillip and Fr Stenhouse found themselves sharing a hotel room in Sichuan. During the night Phillip says that he heard Fr Stenhouse suddenly wake up on the other side of the room with a torch in hand to see a rat crawling up his arm which he then shooed off in a matter of fact way. The rat joined its rat mates and perhaps all fled at Fr Stenhouse's stern command. Another time, when sitting in a modest dining room ready to order lunch, Phillip wondered why they were the only ones there. Fr Stenhouse, ever observant, looked around and pointed out the rat droppings on various tables and suggested they leave – which they did. These encounters did not stop Fr Stenhouse enduring all kinds of physical obstacles to reaching wherever he wanted to go. Phillip said he was fearless and at one point saw his priest friend half way up a cliff, wondering how to get to the top to reach a group of Catholics at the summit in order to make contact with them.

Fr Stenhouse's never-ending sense of observation must be a general 'Stenhousian' family trait as I saw it in his brother Richard's eyes and in his cousins and nephews. The eyes move silently here and there, taking in all kinds of information. Fr Stenhouse's observation and reflexes actually saved people's lives! Phillip remembers that they went to East Timor in 1999 with Fr Stenhouse to see how ACN could help the majority Catholic country in the aftermath of its war with Indonesia. They were staying at a monastery dormitory at one stage, where the 'hired help' usually slept, and at some point during the night a lit candle fell to the floor, starting a fire. Fr Stenhouse woke up in an instant, shouting "Fire! Fire! Leave the building!" before the conflagration really took hold. He saved several lives on that occasion.

Following up on violations of human rights

Phillip spoke of ACN being very grateful for Fr Stenhouse's support for the organisation in so many different ways, in helping to boost its finances, using his investigative, scholarly and linguistic skills to good use. Miranda Devine, writing in the *Daily Telegraph*, refers to his journey to Syria and his views of the 'Arab Spring' about which he had written in *Annals* and *The Australian* and spoken about in radio interviews:

> Australian priest and scholar Paul Stenhouse, recently returned from a visit there, [Syria] warns of the consequences of destabilising the Assad regime, imperfect though it is. The charity he chairs in Australia has put together figures that show the catastrophe for Christians and other minorities in the Middle East amid what is being called the "Arab Winter". In Egypt Coptic Christians, who comprise more than 10 per cent of the population, are being slaughtered, and their churches burned.[9]

Fr Stenhouse's information-gathering also contributed significantly to reports on increasing persecution of Catholicism and other religions.[10] In this he was a very up to date investigative journalist, very much a thinker of his time. In a 2014 radio interview he spoke about the state of persecution of religion in the world, pointing out that Article 18 of the United Nations Declaration of Human Rights states:

> Everyone has the right to freedom of thought, conscience and religion; this right includes freedom to change his religion or belief, and freedom, either alone or in community with others and in public or private, to manifest his religion or belief in teaching, practice, worship and observance.[11]

Quoting from an annually produced report to which he had contributed, Fr Stenhouse points out that of 196 countries in the world, religion is under attack in 81, among them North Korea, China and Burma, as well as others in the Middle East and Asia. He observes that political solutions rarely succeed and merely exacerbate conflicts, adding that Sunnis, Shiites, Christians, Druze and Alawites more recently lived in some kind of peace in the Middle East until political extremists entered the scene. He comments on the persecution of the Rohingyas in Burma, noting that when one minority group is persecuted, this usually leads on to the persecution of other minority groups. He speaks favourably of the United Arab Emirates building Christian churches and even a temple and synagogue as a "candle in the darkness." The interpolation of relevant information from various organisations made *Annals* an effective, up-to-date source of information on persecution of the Church. Its pages carried fund-raising advertisements for ACN which gave readers a practical way to help and be part of the 'solution'.

Under Fr Stenhouse's chairmanship, ACN also had a 'triple A rating' with the finance department in Germany with its Secretary General at the time, Philipp Ozores, mentioning that the Australian office was "the most efficient in the world."[12] Fr Stenhouse's assistance with intrepid ACN information-gathering led to

Top: Fr Stenhouse at Westminster Cathedral Hall, London on 20 February 2004, speaking on behalf of Aid to the Church in Need and with an ACN Delegation (circa 2014) including the Cardinal-Archbishop of Seoul, Andrew Yeom Soo-Jung (third from left) and Father Matthias Hur Young-yup (second from right). Below: Phillip Collignon (president of ACN for 27 years) and his wife who often went overseas with Fr Stenhouse to areas of persecution in the Church and people coming to greet Archbishop Myroslav Ivan Cardinal Lubachivskyj in Lviv in 1991. Fr Stenhouse wrote several *Annals* articles about the Ukraine.

Clockwise from top left: Ukrainian official testing for radiation on the way to Chernobyl (Ukraine) and wreckage in Chernobyl (photos by Fr Stenhouse, circa 1991); Fr Stenhouse in in East Timor, 2011, with Bishop Belo (centre) and Phillip Collignon (left); Karl Schmude, long-time friend who worked with Fr Stenhouse to establish Campion College; Fr Stenhouse during his visit to China with Phillip Collignon in 1996. Of this photo Phillip says: "We were high in the mountains in search of a remote Catholic village. The locals thought the best way to get us there was in the back of a truck via a very dodgy mountain pass. It was dangerous but I had 'Indiana Jones' Stenhouse beside me as my personal guardian angel!"

Fr Paul Stenhouse's 1982 *Annals* article on the Chinese Catholic communities in Australia, with Chinese translation below. He was long interested in the history of Christian communities in China; Fr Stenhouse at Campion College at the 2019 Australian Chesterton Society conference. This took place on 19 October, exactly one month before Fr Stenhouse died on 19 November. It was his last public address; Dean of Campion College, Paul Morris, standing with Karl Schmude at the funeral of Fr Stenhouse on 25 November 2019.

The new president of Aid to the Church in Need, Bernard Totounji, with his family; Cardinal Pell at ease, talking about his friendship with Fr Stenhouse and good friends sharing some reflections together on 10 January 2012 in Canberra at the National Gallery of Australia exhibition: "Renaissance: 15th & 16th Century Italian Paintings from the Accademia Carrara, Beramo" (reprinted with permission: photo taken by Stuart Walmsley, for the *Canberra Times*).

widespread transmission of the results not only in *Annals*, but in many mainstream and radio interviews. Without doubt much of such gathered information would reach the Vatican. Who knows what discussions transpired behind the scenes, and what discreet meetings led to various levels of negotiation with religious and political leaders of other nations in discussion of the material and spiritual needs of their people.

Fr Stenhouse and Karl Schmude – the idea of a university

At the same time as he was working with ACN, editing, writing and investigating religious persecution around the world, Fr Stenhouse helped start a university. While many know of Campion College in Sydney, and the distinctive mark it has made on the tertiary education scene, few know of Fr Stenhouse's encouragement during its inception, establishment and growth. Karl Schmude, librarian, scholar, conference organiser and editor of Chestertonian journals, was a prime mover behind the establishment of that university. He recalls that he had many conversations with Fr Stenhouse, during its years of preparation. As you may imagine it is not easy to start up a university. The first meetings of the Campion Board actually took place at the MSC Monastery in Kensington, Sydney, at the suggestion of Fr Stenhouse himself whom Karl says he "cajoled" to join the Board – yet another venture to which Fr Stenhouse willingly lent his hand. Knowing the situation of the post-modern, morally relativist West and its growing anti-Christian ambience, Fr Stenhouse perceived the urgent need for a liberal arts college which could preserve the literary, historical and spiritual heritage of the West in a context where sectors of tertiary education had lost the plot. He encouraged Campion with all his might.

Karl Schmude laid the groundwork for the new university. Born and raised in Sydney, he then moved to Armidale in October 1970, shortly after his marriage to Virginia, joining the University of New England Library where he worked for 30 years. He had trained as a librarian following a BA at Sydney University and a Diploma of Librarianship in 1967 at the University of NSW, not far from the MSC Monastery, close to where Fr Stenhouse was, though at the time Karl was not aware of this.[13]

At university Karl studied English, Latin, Psychology and Government (as Politics was called at Sydney University in those days) for his BA, during the years 1964-66. University campuses over that period were turbulent, and Karl says he became politically active in 1965, at the height of the Vietnam War and during the huge controversy over conscription. He was actually in favour of Australia's participation in the War, believing that the cause was justified, as it gave the people of South Vietnam a chance of determining their own future without domination by North Vietnam and China. In this, Karl voiced the views of many East Europeans, who wished to spare Vietnam the fate they had suffered under Communist tyrants. While many might not have been in favour of conscription, a number of Australians became increasingly aware of Communist brutality and wished this on no-one.[14]

Karl had his first contact with Fr Stenhouse in the early 1970s, his earliest correspondence with him being in 1973. He reflects:

> I can't recall meeting him in person at that time, but probably by correspondence when he published an article I had sent him for *Annals*. My parents were long-time subscribers to *Annals*, and I would have begun reading the journal after I left university in the mid-1960s, and began writing occasional articles and book reviews for journals like *News Weekly* (Melbourne) and the *Catholic Weekly* (Sydney) – and then for *Annals*.[15]

By the mid-1970s Karl had begun travelling to Sydney for library meetings, some of which would have been at UNSW. As he knew of Fr Stenhouse, this would have provided a convenient opportunity to meet him in person and discuss matters of mutual interest, which included the whole world. From then on, Karl always tried to drop in to see him in the Kensington monastery when he was in Sydney, assuming Fr Stenhouse was not in Kazakhstan, or Timbuktu. He got to know him well and spoke via phone, and via occasional correspondence on a myriad number of topics. With Fr Stenhouse, as his friends came to know, there were always never-ending conversations.

Karl's working life covered areas which were to be of great benefit in the future establishment of a university. In the first phase of his life, his work in librarianship (1968-2000), mainly in a university setting, gave him ample experience of organisation on a grand level, as anyone working in a library will know. Of this Karl says humbly:

> I enacted the Peter Principle at the University of New England, rising to my highest level of incompetence – and then staying there! I became Deputy Librarian in 1973, and University Librarian in 1984.[16]

The second phase of Karl's work ensued when he resigned in 2000 to undertake bringing a dream to reality, in conjunction with his long-time, generous friend, James Power (senior). The establishment of a Catholic liberal arts college had been the hope of many but with these courageous pioneers it became reality when Campion College opened in 2006 in Toongabbie. This followed years of international research carried out by Karl during the New England years. Beginning in 1977, he was fortunate to receive a Fulbright scholarship to the USA. This was not only of direct professional benefit, but it providentially put him in touch, as he recalls, "with various leaders of the Catholic liberal arts colleges springing up in America in the 1970s – such as Fr Joseph Fessio

SJ (founder of the St Ignatius Institute at the University of San Francisco, and later founder of Ignatius Press) and Warren Carroll (founder of Christendom College in Virginia)."[17] This phase of planning for a liberal arts college in Australia ensued from seeing how well they were functioning in the United States, and in learning how they did it. It was during this phase of planning that many conversations with Fr Stenhouse took place, gave encouragement and provided a venue for the first meetings of the Board.

Karl recalls some coincidences between his life and that of his friend. He says:

> I later completed (1979-81) a postgraduate degree in History at the University of New England. It was a Master of Letters (M.Litt., the same degree that UNE awarded Fr Stenhouse in 2014, when he produced a biography of his great-grandfather, John Farrell). A further coincidence is that I asked Fr Stenhouse to speak on John Farrell at our October 2019 Australian Chesterton conference at Campion College. Given his rapidly declining health, it was a little miracle that he managed to come and speak.[18]

Fr Stenhouse could barely walk by late October but he made his way to the Campion College podium and informed and entertained his listeners in witty Chestertonian style, albeit with a quieter touch, with his account of John Farrell and the literary and political milieu surrounding him in the nineteenth century.[19] The audience showed evident appreciation and the atmosphere was electric. Karl reflected about the fact that Fr Stenhouse had given it when he had advanced cancer, and observed that it was "a triumph of will over capacity – with the aid of divine grace!"

Cardinal Pell's memories of Fr Stenhouse

Fr Stenhouse's reputation as a priest and scholar was known to Cardinal Pell, long before they met. Both were openly loyal to the papacy in times of Western cultural decay and worked to bring the teachings of the Church into ever clearer perspective. Cardinal Pell was only too happy to reflect on his friendship with Fr Stenhouse when we met in a gracious, relaxed interview in Sydney in July 2020, which touched on many themes besides.[20] He recalled that he met Fr Stenhouse "in about 1997" when the latter came to Melbourne with Frank Devine for the blessing of the MSC Chapel in Croydon. Cardinal Pell had invited Cardinal Francis George of Chicago to come in order to bless the Chapel. In the aftermath he found himself at dinner with Fr Stenhouse and Frank Devine among others, all launching into discussion of matters of mutual interest. It appears there was a deep trust on a personal and ecclesial level from the outset. Not long afterwards they met to discuss issues local and global, how to help oppressed Christians around the world and much else. The friendship was significant to the thoughts and actions of both men and not long after they met, Cardinal Pell began writing for *Annals*.

Cardinal Pell recalled Fr Stenhouse's intellectual qualities, describing him as "an absolutely outstanding intellectual" and "the very fine writing" which issued from this. He added that he was "a wonderful Catholic and a wonderful human being" saying "he was a charming, courteous and learned fellow" and "had a great gift for friendship." In particular, he referred to Fr Stenhouse's reaching out to others from many religious and cultural backgrounds. He recalled in particular his friendship with the Jewish Professor of Semitic Studies (Alan Crown) and considered the panegyric about him one of the finest things he wrote.

He reflected, "I used to chuckle that he would insist on driving ... even in his 80s!" Clearly this did not faze the Cardinal and they went to restaurants, to other friends' houses, to Camden and Cobbitty, areas where Fr Stenhouse had grown up and where his mother was buried. Cardinal Pell recalls him speaking of the poverty of his childhood and how, after the death of his father, the two boys and their mother had to live with relations on whom they were dependent, which was difficult at times. He said Fr Stenhouse spoke of this without animosity but memories of the poverty of his childhood seemed to have affected him deeply and never left him. This is doubtless why many of the students he helped sensed his particular compassion for those who were poor, lonely and in need.

When I asked the Cardinal what topics he and Fr Stenhouse spoke about, he mentioned that they both greatly respected the then Pontiff, Pope John Paul II – "he was a great enthusiast of John Paul II" – and they talked about the general situation in the Church. Lebanese Maronite friend Joseph Assaf also recalls Cardinal Pell coming to his house and having discussions over dinner about political instability, war, oppression in various countries, particularly in the Middle East. It was at dinners such as these that geopolitical situations were analysed, along with the work of Aid to the Church in Need. Future plans were hatched.

When questioned on how Fr Stenhouse kept his calm in eras of social and political unrest, he believed Fr Stenhouse's spiritual stability followed from his "immense knowledge of Church history". On a more personal note he said he himself was very grateful that he had studied Patristics at Oxford and so was able to acquire a thorough knowledge of Church history. He said in his case, and in the situation of Fr Stenhouse, "it gives you an immense understanding of the froth and bubble ... I remember encouraging people into Patristics", underlining the need to study the past, so as to have an anchor in the present era. He pointed out that Cardinal Newman (now a saint) entered the Catholic Church after reading deeply about early Christian history as indeed many have done. When I noted that there was an almost anti-historical vein in current times, Cardinal Pell said there was an ever greater need to study our history as Catholics. This emphasis on 'roots' or, as others might say, going to the sources, has been a glaring need in my own field of psychology, for there is a quasi-amnesia about the history of psychology itself.

In our conversation, Cardinal Pell also reflected on "the great challenge and tragedy" of the current era in Australia, the "defection of the Anglos – by them I include the Irish", and the pervasive task of "bringing them back". When I spoke of the priests who had come from overseas he said that he was extremely grateful for their work, noting that there had been some opposition due to their "conservatism" in some quarters. He recalled the great number of Australian missionaries sent overseas at one point, numbering 300 one stage, while now there was only one diocesan missionary from Sydney working overseas. While speaking of the good work of the Indian, Polish, African and other priests here I questioned him on his attempts to get some priests from overseas, to "kidnap" them to come to Australia, especially from Poland. He answered quickly that he was not very successful in kidnapping but expressed his gratitude for the Polish priests who had come here, naming the Michaelites, to which I added the Pauline priests and those of the older missionary group in Australia, the order of Christ the Priest. He warmly agreed and restated his gratitude to all the priests from overseas.

Taking into account the current cultural instability, Cardinal Pell was emphatic in praising Fr Stenhouse for his loyalty to his vocation in shifting times where views of a "different orientation" and "hostile views" surrounded him in the prevailing cultural turbulence, adding, "I admire him so much for this."

When touching on issues relating to his time in Rome, Cardinal Pell recalled that he spoke to the North American College about five years earlier about China and how things had seemed much better then. He even mentioned that they had thought of the possibility of a Chinese Constantine. He lamented how different things were now and how the intentions and actions of the Communist Chinese were quite clear with regard to the Catholic Church, Christians in general and in terms of global politics.

Showing an ever lively interest in books and scholarship Cardinal Pell also recalled books he had read, on the subject of what had made the West so significant, mentioning the work of Philip Jenkins and that of Rodney Stark. He also recalled being given a book by the retiring head of the Vatican Bank on the Japanese expedition to Europe in the nineteenth century, to find out how the West was so successful. He thought this kind of expedition into different cultures to learn what works best is of benefit to all groups, observing that the person who gave him the gift was perhaps suggesting such an expedition on the part of the Vatican, an investigative foray involving 10-20 people to find out what works best in various cultures. Giving a book as a gift could be a way of making a subtle point. Cardinal Pell clarified that he was not talking about missions or evangelisation, which the Church has done well for millennia, but about matters of organisation and governance where the Church might benefit.

Cardinal Pell mentioned one area in which Fr Stenhouse influenced him was in his understanding of the Middle East, it being one of his "greatest intellectual debts to Paul ... I owe him a great debt for that." Particularly after 9/11, Fr Stenhouse had been able to put events in some perspective, but Cardinal Pell being a historian, wanted to go to the sources and see for himself. He recalled that with the help of Fr Stenhouse he "read the Qur'an, not absolutely every part, but most of it." He added, "See after September 11, I had some people coming to me saying the Muslims were like the Uniting Church." Simultaneously there were people, among them, Pakistani Christians, come to me saying something different namely that "as soon as they come to power they are radically different." He recalled that this was what an African bishop had told him too. He sought peaceful outreach to all groups.

Another thing Cardinal Pell noted was that Fr Stenhouse "participated in high level official dialogue in Iran ... I know that for an absolute fact", adding, "I don't know how long he lasted as his views were perhaps not to the liking of the Iranian leadership." His attempts to communicate with Shiite Muslims did not endear Fr Stenhouse to the Americans either. Both the Cardinal and Fr Stenhouse yearned for peace in the Middle East, the Cardinal noting that the "Sunnis and Shiites killed more of each other than they killed of us." He had no doubt that Fr Stenhouse's involvement was nothing other than that – trying to help attain peace. In the Cardinal's view, "he was not a hater at all. He wanted to be very clear about what they were really at ... and in many cases he was right."

The desire for peace on the part of Fr Stenhouse drew him into many situations that were decidedly not peaceful. Once, the Cardinal recalled Fr Stenhouse telling him that his friend was in the hull of a warship near the Middle East, and the shelling was so loud that Fr Stenhouse had tinnitus for the rest of his life.

Despite the unrest of the current age, the Cardinal stressed the importance of interfaith dialogue, arguing that it was "better to be talking together than squabbling more seriously." In this regard, some of our best interlocutors for Islam, among others, were Turkish Muslims: "I gather most of the leadership who spoke to us were followers of Fethullah Gülen who seemed more open to deal with" though many had been victims in Turkey's recent troubles. (Muhammed Fethullah Gülen, mentioned in the previous chapter, is a Turkish Islamic scholar, regarded by some as a terrorist, by others as a peace-maker).

It was with some surprise, however, that Cardinal Pell heard of the chair of Islamic Studies being opened at the Australian Catholic University in Melbourne, none other than the Fethullah Gülen Chair in the study of Islam and Muslim-Catholic Relations. Cardinal Pell insists he had nothing to do with this decision, but after some time, one of the Fethullah Gülen members approached him saying that few had enrolled in their courses and related that they were rather upset with this and would even have to consider shifting. This being the case, Cardinal Pell noted that the complainant also stated that a priest called Fr Stenhouse was questioning their movement and could he, Cardinal Pell, stop this meddlesome priest from writing his analyses and critiques of Islam, upon which the Cardinal replied, "no-one can control Fr Stenhouse."

Cardinal Pell reflected that Fr Stenhouse was "very charitable in his judgments" although, "he [Fr Stenhouse] said to me that I was more charitable in my judgments than he was himself." He added that their mutual friend Tony Abbott, who had gone to see him not long before he died, remembered Fr Stenhouse saying to him (Abbott) that "he was looking forward to seeing the face of Christ."

7

THE PEOPLE HE KNEW

Faithful friends are beyond price
No amount could balance their worth
Faithful friends are life-saving medicine
And those who fear the Lord will find them

Ecclesiasticus 6:15-16

For many decades the life of Fr Stenhouse moved in harmony on several simultaneous levels, all emanating from his priesthood: his editorship of *Annals*, his work with Aid to the Church in Need, his scholarly work, and his friends, some of whom have been already mentioned in previous pages. There were many friends in his life. No-one would ever be able to understand Fr Stenhouse without noting his wonderful capacity for friendship and the following pages will give testimony to this. Some tributes have already been written, such as that of Fr Peter Malone entitled *Fr Stenhouse: A Distinctive and Distinguished Missionary of the Sacred Heart* (2020) – and may many such tributes continue to be written. Given that it is impossible to include all his friends in any one volume, at the very least I can try to refer to some, though I include 'all' in spirit. Friends, you know who you are, whether named here or not. All who knew Fr Stenhouse have unique memories of meetings, kindnesses, conversations and have memories that will long outlive his death.

Of course, to begin with, Fr Stenhouse held his family in special affection, especially his mother, as is clear in an account she wrote about Cobbitty, the house, the land, the surrounding community, addressing her memoir to "Dear Paul", revealing within it her own distinct literary gift.[1] In this typed account in Fr Stenhouse's office, she writes of family events and a place "that was filled with history for me" and has a detailed memory of uncles, aunts and grandparents, all of which would have delighted Fr Stenhouse who revelled in these genealogical explorations.[2] May Stenhouse also contributed historical photos and other materials to the Camden Historical Society. Among Fr Stenhouse's books lay a copy of *The Journal of the Society of Australian Genealogists*, along with many genealogical trees drawn up by himself.

Fr Stenhouse's brother Richard recalled, "I was close to my grandmother" and that Paul was "closer to his mother" though they all greatly cared for each other.[3] Richard told me of the airmen's families who were boarders at their Camden house and of going into protective mode after fellow school students warned him that Paul might be throttled for being "too smart." And while Paul went into journalism and the priesthood, Richard went on to become a mechanic, relating some escapades in this area of work – having to deal with unions, mechanics, and bosses of all kinds. Then he moved into sales/general management and had a career with 3M (a US industrial products company) spanning more than 30 years. Though the brothers pursued differing paths, there is a great similarity in their sense of delight, their humour and keen sense of observation. Though there are but a few photographs from their childhood, Richard said that as adults both he and Paul became interested in photography. Fr Stenhouse's old office was filled with organised drawers of travel photos.

Richard, his wife Gloria and two sons, Jamie and Gerard (Ged), were in regular contact with Fr Stenhouse. Jamie is a chartered accountant as is his brother Ged who lives in Canberra. It was at Jamie's house where we met after the funeral and conversed around a table in the backyard. Based in Sydney, Jamie was able to meet his uncle Paul for lunch during Jamie's lunch hour in the city, often at the Queen Victoria Building. Jamie told me he heard all about his uncle's travels and was amazed at his exploits and several passports. He heard of his uncle's travels to Lebanon during the war and was touched at seeing so many friends at his memorial evening and funeral, himself giving heartfelt tributes there.

A gift for friendship

Then there was his spiritual family. Fr Stenhouse was friendly to the priests and brothers at the MSC monastery. Sometimes in his office, I witnessed how Fr Stenhouse would call out joyfully to passing priests, as if he were an Italian barista inviting them in for a cappuccino.

There were common memories with several generations of MSC priests. Fr Stenhouse had known Fr (later Bishop) Eugene Cuskelly, Bishop Des Moore, Fr 'Doc' Rumble and Fr Paddy Ryan. He knew Fr Jim Littleton, Fr John Kelliher, Fr Michael Fallon, Fr Pat Austin, Brother Jack Boelen, Fr Peter Malone, Fr Peter Guy, Fr Arthur Stidwill, Brother Kevin Guthrie, Fr Chris McPhee, Fr John Conroy – to mention some.

MSC priest Fr Jim Littleton, former MSC Provincial, school principal and lecturer, recalled in his obituary that Fr Stenhouse had a very busy life of ministry to people who sought assistance: "... there was rarely a day when he was not out of the monastery involved in some sort of ministry while at the same time finding time to prepare another issue of the *Annals*."[4] Fr Littleton, who taught Fr Stenhouse history at the Apostolic School during the 1950s, wrote articles for *Annals*, one being an interesting series entitled "The 'Bully' and the War on 'Humbug'" about the hostility towards the Catholic Church in Australian journalism and history.[5] He ended up travelling with Fr Stenhouse to many places, flying, driving and walking. In fact, as Fr Littleton told me, both of them went to Broome, to Darwin and covered much inland Australia. They travelled overseas (mostly during the 1990s and 2000s), to Malaysia, Burma, Vietnam (through Hanoi, before it became a popular tourist trail). They also travelled to South America in the 2000s to Buenos Aires, and visited Rosario (where Fr Stenhouse's great-grandfather, John Farrell was born). Fr Stenhouse was ever at work while travelling, observing and collecting information. Nevertheless, Fr Littleton recalled "plenty of light-hearted moments" and in fact he considered his friend an "extrovert" and "a great conversationalist."[6]

This point about being an 'extrovert' is interesting. Strange to say, others did not see Fr Stenhouse as such an extrovert. Fr John Conroy and Brother Kevin Guthrie, while noting his friendly conversations, thought he was rather reserved at times, keeping his thoughts to himself.[7] MSC Superior Fr Kelliher, also thought him an introvert. OLSH Sister Mary Ruth thought him more reserved and "not so outgoing" while being "an incredible influence" on overseas students in his compassion and outreach.[8] It happens sometimes that people can seem to be both introvert and extrovert. They shine in particular situations and seem extrovert, yet still have a more introvert nature. Fr Stenhouse could discuss, debate, laugh and be verbally provocative, but there was that 'silent interior council' to which he withdrew when he was thinking about an issue, or was being diplomatic.

Some other priest friends

Fr Arthur Stidwill, a missionary in Papua New Guinea for over 30 years (in Milne Bay and Port Moresby with Bishop Des Moore), met Fr Stenhouse in 1968 when he came to the St Paul's Seminary for Late Vocations, located within the Sacred Heart Monastery.

The people he knew

He remembers Fr Stenhouse seeming "uninterested", almost aloof at first, and Fr Stidwill was less than enthusiastic when chosen to share a car journey with him to Douglas Park on the death of an MSC member. Whatever happened during that journey, however, changed Fr Stidwill's mind forever: "I became of a disciple of Fr Stenhouse", explaining that he came to understand his "goodness" and his "warm, loving" personality. He considers him a "man of great charity", a "very devout priest", "faithful to his daily Mass", and though a "great intellect" he "did not show off."[9] In later years, Fr Stidwill used to walk past his office a few times a week and have lively conversations with him. He considered Fr Stenhouse to be a "fantastic car driver" who knew all the back streets, often going with friends for coffee in Zetland near the monastery, for companionship and the exchange of dramatic stories.

Another long-time priest friend, Fr Pat Austin, remembers Fr Stenhouse being a voracious reader at the seminary, asking for many articles to be printed by Fr Austin when he was the "copier on duty." Fr Austin himself had spent many years in missionary work on Bathurst Island (1969-79) and at Milne Bay in Papua New Guinea (1988-1996), having many stories to share with his priest friends. He also called Fr Stenhouse an "introvert", happy with his books, very focused on *Annals* and his pastoral work with overseas students. Fr Pat Austin recalls Fr Stenhouse knocking on many doors to get things done for students, calling on State MP Deirdre Grusovin (sister of Laurie Brereton) to help with various matters: "If there were any problems, she would do things."[10] Fr Stenhouse's network went beyond party lines and backgrounds in seeking assistance. Fr Austin remembers what he called his "intentional generosity", adding that he had a "remarkable capacity for [empathising with the]sufferings of people."

Another MSC priest, Fr Michael Fallon, author and chaplain, knew Fr Stenhouse from the time of his entry into the Apostolic

School in 1953. He gave the following moving tribute to his brother priest: "I could go on forever speaking of his amazing mind. but he did have an even greater gift: his heart." He said what many felt about Fr Stenhouse's kindness, adding that he did not "know a hundredth of it ... I don't know of anyone who experienced need and turned to Paul who did not experience his loving, practical and committed care."[11] Some people help others in a general 'one off' way but Fr Stenhouse went well beyond the call of duty in contacting families, befriending them, reassuring them their children were well. He was a trustworthy mentor and guide to many, and even argued with university authorities if there were anomalies in the students' enrolment or training programs.

In his tribute, Fr Fallon recalled:

> Paul would meet people at the airport, deliver them to appointments, find them accommodation, accompany them to immigration tribunals, badger university administrations – and any academic who he thought could help on their behalf. He also took on the role of reassuring anxious parents, worried about their children overseas. And finally of course he could marry them and baptize their children. Paul was, indeed, a missionary of the Sacred Heart of Jesus. It was from his faith in God as revealed in the heart of Jesus that Paul derived his inspiration.[12]

Fr Fallon notes in the same tribute that he could "hear Paul" in something John Henry Newman wrote in *A Grammar of Assent*: "I do not care to overcome people's reason without touching their hearts."

Another MSC priest, Father Peter Malone, who lectured at Yarra Theological College was a long time friend of Fr Stenhouse. Fr Malone has also had long experience of the media. He headed the Catholic Film Offices of the Pacific from 1989-1998; was president of OCIC, the International Catholic Organisation for Cinema, from 1998-2001; and world president of SIGNIS, the World Catholic Association for Communications, 2001-2005. He is the Pacific representative to the SIGNIS Cinema Desk. He recalls meeting Fr Stenhouse in London, during his several visits there.

> If he wanted to go out he preferred McDonalds. I think he must have dined in the highest of places so to speak. But he was very ordinary and he enjoyed that kind of ordinariness. And in going to the films I had to make sure that there was an action show, probably compensation for all the intellectual activity, but we had to find an action show which he would enjoy. So I did want to stress that kind of ordinariness about him.[13]

Fr Malone emphasises that while Fr Stenhouse was "outstanding, distinguished and distinctive", he was also "very ordinary" and the "friend of many" and a true confrere of the Missionaries of the Sacred Heart. He recalls conversations with him on various topics including Middle Eastern politics and Jungian psychology. Fr Stenhouse could converse on virtually any topic and if anyone ever brought up the subject of Antarctica, no doubt he would have been able to discuss its flora, fauna, and the history of Catholic chaplains there.

Another friend who went back a long way was Fr Peter Guy who met Fr Stenhouse in 1966. He thought Fr Stenhouse "an exceptionally intelligent fellow" and in many ways "a private person" with "an open, loving and compassionate heart." Fr Guy thought his friend more reserved in the past, becoming more open as time went on. One day, he recalls running into Br Paul Whelan at the Kensington monastery, the latter saying, "I have just had the most wonderful conversation with Paul Stenhouse!" This is the kind of thing many said about him. Fr Guy also remembers the great help given to ACN, especially to the Ukrainians, on the return of Archbishop Lubashevski in 1991. This was of particular significance also because Fr Guy grew up with Ukrainian friends, learned to speak Ukrainian and was chaplain to the Ukrainian Uniate community. He was a skilled linguist himself and could share much about pre- and post-Soviet Ukraine with Fr Stenhouse in lively and engrossing conversations. Of his help to university students, Fr Guy said that Fr Stenhouse "became their father" and noted his contact with their parents. Fr Guy said that he got to know Fr Stenhouse even better, when he, Father Guy, was superior of the MSC Monastery in Kensington. He described Fr Stenhouse as a traditional priest, in his life and in his preaching.[14]

Fr Paul Glynn, Marist priest, missionary and author, was also an enduring friend of Fr Stenhouse. When the latter was ill, Fr Glynn sent him a book on prayer entitled *Hearers of Silent Music*, with an encouraging inscription saying, "you have been in my prayers." Fr Stenhouse also knew Father Matthew Attia from St George's Coptic Orthodox Church who came to his funeral.[15] Later when talking about his dear friend, Fr Attia said with deep feeling, "He loved the Christians of the Middle East. He rallied for us and our systematic persecution." He added, "Fr Stenhouse was a man of prayer, a man of conviction and principles." Fr Matthew said that Fr Stenhouse attended several ecumenical services which were conducted to express "solidarity for the suffering and hardships of ME (Middle Eastern) Christians." In a poignant tribute from one priest to another, he said, "He was a humble priest. He was a wonderful icon of the shepherd."

Some years ago when visiting St George's Coptic Orthodox Church, I remarked on the pile of *Annals* at the back of the church and was told that they had stocked them "for years" and that Fr Stenhouse "had just been to visit them."

Trish Kavanagh

Fr Stenhouse had several cousins, one of whom was Trish Kavanagh, barrister and judge, the wife of Laurie Brereton. Introducing herself as 'Trish', we met at Fr Stenhouse's funeral and it was a pleasure to meet her again to hear many reminiscences about her priest-cousin. She related to me that she did not meet her cousin in childhood but only later, when he was a priest. She said she thought the connection was that her father was a second cousin of Fr Stenhouse's mother, May Stenhouse, who was a "self-educated, wonderful woman" and that "his faith came from her."[16] She remembered her cousin Paul with affection, recalling his rich, varied life, and that while he travelled the world, he was always weaving in and out of the lives of his family, marrying, baptising, officiating at funerals, doing a baptism in the year before he died. When his mother died, Fr Stenhouse said a Latin Mass for her at the church in Cobbitty, where her childhood home had been.

Trish had left school in 1968, having benefited from a Dominican education in Sydney and after Teachers' College, taught in Sydney and Cootamundra. She related that, after some time overseas, she went to study law at UTS (The University of Technology, Sydney) and was the first woman graduate to undertake a PhD there, graduating in 1980. She went to the Bar in 1981 for eighteen years, and then was an industrial judge for fourteen years. Prior to this, she recalls interesting times helping Fr Stenhouse with *Annals* in the 1960s and 70s, describing them as "the boom times."[17] She remembered going to many Catholic schools and talking to students about *Annals*. She also wrote theatre and film reviews, enjoying "the best seats in the house" as a good *Annals* review would boost ticket sales. Once, she was with Fr Stenhouse and Fr Peter Malone at the performance of *Fiddler on the Roof* during the 1970s and her cousin rose and disappeared backstage. She and Fr Malone suddenly saw

Fr Stenhouse coming onto the stage arm in arm laughing with the leading star, Topol, both speaking Hebrew!

For about a year, Trish helped her cousin go through Samaritan manuscripts. Many were in very bad condition, with smudged sections on some pages. Trish regularly came to the monastery to help organise archival material which he needed to carry out his scholarly research, driving into the monastery grounds in her canary yellow beach buggy, which Fr Stenhouse borrowed on occasion to visit others, or to go for a swim. Trish recalls that he had a "thirst for knowledge" and "grew into his intellectual life", noting that his gift for languages was a discovery to him, a gradual process, an unfurling of his talents through time, adding she had never encountered anyone with such a gift. She said "no one has the gift of tongues like Paul" for he perceived the need for the study of languages in order to understand Scripture and history.

As we sat together at a cafe, Trish described her cousin as "a most modest, accomplished, humble person", who wore old sweaters and "always travelled economy." This depiction brings to mind the simplicity of Pier Giorgio Frassati (1901-1925), the Italian saint, who when he was asked why he travelled third class by train, responded "because there is no fourth class." Trish said Fr Stenhouse was "a simple, direct person." While he spoke with men of high position, in politics, and within the Church, he never sought advancement for himself, such as the position of bishop, though apparently it was put to him several times.

Trish spoke of his unceasing work with Aid to the Church in Need, recalling the story, of him hiring a boat from Cyprus to Lebanon to deliver medicines not available there at the time.[18] When in Syria, he apparently tried to access a place that was being bombed in order to reach some war victims, but was unable to do so and thus remained in Damascus. She thought he "was the eyes and ears of the Vatican in many countries he travelled to." She was adamant that "his judgement was always sound – he did daring things but did not take ill-considered risks. And very significantly, he was not fooled by bureaucrats." This is no mean praise, coming from a judge.

Fr Stenhouse was a regular visitor at her family home, sometimes ringing after he had said 4.30am morning Mass at the monastery. Having completed several hours of prayer, he would come over for breakfast, enjoying French pastries from a shop nearby. There were many discussions on various issues, noting that "he and Laurie had a lot of debates." She thought he became "more conservative" as he grew older and on occasion she took him to task for some of his views. Trish observed that "there were many dimensions to Paul", and seemed lost in thought saying, "he had a deep spirituality" adding "of that there was never a doubt."

Peter Macinante and "sources close to the *Annals* Office"

If there was anyone who saw the daily goings on in the *Annals* office, it was Peter Macinante, who came to work there in 1982. His industrious colleagues at that time were Jennie Hiatt, Andrew Mobbs and other volunteers. Peter was to stay there (apart from a few periods overseas) for nearly forty years and, after the death of Fr Stenhouse, has stayed on performing invaluable organisational work. Interestingly, he is related to Fr Stenhouse in that their grandmothers were sisters, both being daughters of John Farrell, their great-grandfather. There is something moving about Peter remaining in the office in that this connection still remains, with memories of the *Annals* years still abounding. In fact Peter is always engrossed in administrative matters, as he sits daily in the wood-panelled *Annals* office, surrounded by ceiling to floor bookshelves, several computers, and alcoves. There is still much to do for Peter is to become archivist for the MSCs. Peter's wife Gloria has also performed invaluable administrative work for the MSC order in their Coogee house.

As I came each week to look up old editions of *Annals* and delve into papers for this book, Peter recounted some anecdotes. He remembered there was no such thing as 'desk top' publishing when Fr Stenhouse joined *Annals*. Cut and paste meant scissors and glue which is exactly how Fr Stenhouse designed the layout for those early editions. During the 1980s there were regular trips to David Graphics, run by Alan David, who was a donor and helped *Annals* in various ways, such as working on four colour plates each month for the cover page. Then there were various Sydney printers along the way, among them O'Loughlin Brothers who did the initial work. As Peter recalls, the printing went to Canberra Publishing and Printing in 1981 where a Catholic colleague John Smith handled the typesetting. Fr Stenhouse was always adept in finding printing contacts. How many know that Mr Hoe, of Joy Publishing in Hong Kong, printed all the books by Chevalier Press written by Fr Stenhouse and Fr Fallon, and some other material besides?

Fr Stenhouse had to work at breakneck speed to get the journal printed month after month. When the typesetting was completed in Canberra, Peter and Fr Stenhouse had to call there to check that the new edition was in order, and only then was it printed. After this, there was a journey back to Sydney to prepare the next month's issue, when out came the glue and the scissors!

Nearly wiped out by a tanker, Mother Machree and covert operations

It was on a trip to Canberra that, as Peter recalls, "we were almost wiped out by a petrol tanker" which looked as if it was going to "run the red lights." The problem was that Peter and Fr Stenhouse had to avoid crashing into it and there was "much terrifying skidding, jack-knifing, and screeching of brakes." Peter says, without batting an eyelid, "we escaped death by millimetres." The angels were surely working overtime.

Looking back, Peter recalls that Fr Stenhouse used a "secret weapon" in promoting *Annals*, which aroused the curiosity of readers, a centrefold which would reveal the "Saints for the Month" to appreciative acclaim. Also the "beautiful artwork of Hal English" (the "Hal-cyon" days) and the work of Kevin Drumm added a certain panache. Peter said, during the 1980s, *Annals* "sold like hotcakes" and also published the early work of artist Matthew Hatton (who created the Olli Syd and Millie mascots for the 2000 Olympics) and the reviews of Bill Collins, the famous 'Mr Movies', before the renowned James Murray came on board as a film reviewer.

Peter came to call Fr Stenhouse, "Fr Perpetual Motion", as he was always racing off to important commitments here and overseas, his constant "war cry" being "Andiamo!" (in English "let's go!"), often adding "mamma mia, this isn't getting the baby bathed!" Fr Stenhouse would come from his upstairs office, asking Peter to check on a detail, calling out that he needed everything "immediately, if not sooner." Anyone who knew Fr Stenhouse knew how scrupulous he was about the accuracy of original sources, no matter how long it took. Many friends would also recall his cry of astonishment, "Mother Machree!", though no-one quite knew who Mother Machree was. It turns out that there was a popular radio song shortly before Fr Stenhouse was born and he likely heard it as he was growing up. Other frequent expressions were "Hell's bells and buckets of blood!" and "Let's skedaddle!"

Peter knew of Fr Stenhouse's overseas journeys to report on the plight of Christians in the Middle East, the Balkans and Central Asian Republics, though he never saw the detailed itineraries. He remarks, tongue-in-cheek, "covert operations were assumed – for his own safety of course."[19] Fr Stenhouse did say of his trip to Timbuktu that there were "not many Catholics there." Given that it was 100% Muslim, one can imagine him saying a quiet Mass there, at some risk to himself.

At some point, Peter Macinante and Jennie Hiatt decided to carry out some covert operations of their own. It turns out that someone had given Fr Stenhouse a 'wave ski', a kind of surfboard with a contoured space to sit in, which Fr Stenhouse purported to use. It would be strapped to the roof of the car and the editor of *Annals* would disappear for hours on end. He alleged that he would paddle on his wave ski from Watsons Bay to the Opera House and back. This was hard to believe, as Fr Stenhouse was not known to be sporty. Peter and Jennie followed one of these disappearing drives one afternoon from the monastery and ended up in Darling Point hidden behind a tree watching the waters of Sydney Harbour. Peter recalls the surprise of seeing Fr Stenhouse on the wave ski: "lo and behold, he came paddling energetically past us heading in the direction of the Opera House." He returned to the *Annals* office, never doubting Fr Stenhouse again. "This was the end of our covert operations!"

Peter says of Fr Stenhouse, "unlike the mother of the Maccabees, he just could not say 'No' and helped so many people here and overseas."[20] He also recalls him using his final energies to produce the last edition of *Annals*, which might never have been completed without the constant nursing care of Therese Compton who came to the monastery months before he died to help him out. One can add that this last and previous editions would not have come about without supporters including Peter Beswick, Jim Giltinan, Joseph Assaf and many others. When finances were squeezed, and they often were, as the expenses incurred in running a hard copy journal were enormous, Peter Macinante often heard Fr Stenhouse exclaim, "Hang the expense, give the canary another seed!" Speaking at the final *Annals* lunch Peter asked his priest friend to forgive him "for any split infinitives" over the years, adding with tears in his eyes that "Father Paul lives on in our treasured memories of him."

Nephew of Fr Stenhouse, Jamie Stenhouse, with his wife Jennifer and children front left to right Alexandra and Emma.

Another nephew of Fr Stenhouse, Gerard (Ged) Stenhouse with other family members, mother Gloria Stenhouse, daughter Rachel (left) and Alexa (right) at the Baptism of niece Alexandra Stenhouse; Fr Arthur Stidwill MSC, who worked as a missionary in Papua New Guinea and shared many conversations with his longtime friend Fr Stenhouse.

Annals Office Manager Peter Macinante with Greg Tait, MSC librarian who helped Fr Stenhouse with some computer difficulties; Fr Pat Austin MSC, who was a missionary in PNG, did seminary studies with Fr Stenhouse and recalled his "voracious reading"; Jennie Hiatt who worked in the *Annals* office for over 20 years; Greg Quinn, who helped Fr Stenhouse with numerous computer matters over the years.

In Fr Stenhouse's old office, Peter Macinante holds one of the many cameras used by Fr Stenhouse while travelling; Trish Kavanagh, cousin of Fr Stenhouse who helped him with *Annals* and some scholarly tasks in earlier years. Fr Stenhouse came regularly to have coffee, pastries and discussions with Trish and her husband Laurie Brereton; Hendrikus Wong with Fr Stenhouse on his graduation day; Vony Sugiarto with Fr Stenhouse on her graduation day at the UNSW on 15 April 1994.

A great triumvirate of thinkers, writers and journalists. From left to right: Fr Stenhouse, Giles Auty and Peter Coleman, sharing a jovial moment; below left, James Murray, renowned film reviewer for *Annals* standing with Christopher Dawson; Fr Stenhouse had friends in many places. In 1987 he took some students and staff from Daramalan College in Canberra on a pilgrimage to the Holy Land. With him were Fr Bob Irwin and Fr John Mulroney and the story was written up in the MSC school magazine.

Memories of city driving and hamburgers at Hungry Jacks

Another essential link in *Annals*' story is Jennie Hiatt who worked in the *Annals* office for over twenty years. She initially came to help part-time at the MSC Chevalier Book Shop in the 1970s, assisting Margaret and Bernard Carrick who worked there. Not long afterwards she transferred up the corridor to the *Annals* office, when Fr Stenhouse returned from Dubrovnik in 1981 and worked there till 1999. Jenny performed a multitude of tasks, mainly managing the subscriptions at first, becoming good friends with Peter Macinante, who managed other aspects of the journal. When the House of Mary Masses were looming each month (which, as previously mentioned, Father Stenhouse had instituted) Jennie and Peter would go and set up the church of Our Lady of the Sacred Heart in Randwick for Fr Stenhouse or another priest to say Mass there.

Fr Stenhouse visited Jennie, her husband and four children in nearby Kingsford. Over dinner he would answer any questions the Hiatt family had about the future of their children's studies, the faith, and anything else that cropped up. Jennie recalled, as was the experience of many other friends of Fr Stenhouse, that it was "like we were friends forever." He would call by at around 10.30pm and have an omelette on toast, as if he were a member of the family.

Living close to the monastery did make it easier in dealing with publishing matters for Jennie. Sometimes Fr Stenhouse would enter the *Annals* office with the announcement, "We're going to Drummoyne" or wherever it was that *Annals* took them. Jennie often found herself not only handling '*Annals* drops' at many destinations but also driving Fr Stenhouse to places where parking was not possible, often around Alexandria and inner city destinations in Fr Stenhouse's Ford Falcon (a step upwards from the old blue van). This was where Jennie would wait for him to emerge and then drop him back at the monastery. After driving around Sydney, sometimes they would try to grab lunch at Vito's in Kingsford or at Hungry Jacks in Alexandria. Jennie, along with many other people, can testify to Fr Stenhouse's liking for hamburgers. I would not be surprised if, someday, *Annals* afficionados organise a memorial *Annals* hamburger lunch in Alexandria's Hungry Jacks!

The words that came to Jennie's mind about Fr Stenhouse were "kind", "good friend", "always helping out the Asian students", and "wonderful conversationalist." In particular Jennie recalls conversations about Rome, the city he particularly loved, and she and her husband were among that those privileged to experience one of his uniquely superb guided tours there.

Annals and the unforgettable digital angels...

Those who have worked with *Annals*, remember the impressive assistance of Greg Quinn easing its transition to the digital age. Not only did *Annals* transition from France to Australia, from the nineteenth century to the twentieth, but also lived on the cusp of the digital revolution.

Greg came to Australia from New Zealand, having attended Catholic schools in Auckland and Wellington, which he says hold "wonderful memories for him."[21] In Australia, Greg worked as a programmer for Deloitte and Deloitte Haskins and Sells. One fateful day, he heard that a Fr Stenhouse from a monastery in Kensington needed a programmer. Unaware of who Fr Stenhouse was, Greg recalled: "Peter Pettorino organised a meeting sometime in 1981-2."[22] On first meeting Fr Stenhouse, Greg remembers he was very impressed with this priest, for while he was not a computer person as such, he "knew what he wanted."[23] Greg, being an adept programmer, found a way to write databases copying individual cards to a disc with relevant categories and labels. He said Fr Stenhouse would ask him "to pop over" and come to do maintenance and Greg

The people he knew

said he "was happy to do it."[24] Thus the digital world gradually entered the life and operation of *Annals* and Greg's system kept it going to the end. Greg says they had discussed having a website for *Annals* but Fr Stenhouse's illness prevented this from getting off the ground. It was a great boon that, at some stage, an *Annals* Archive was established, with a wide selection of articles.

Greg remembers that Fr Stenhouse would speak to him in his office which was "well organised' and "all was in its place." Sometimes he would suggest a bite to eat – and yes, they would head to Hungry Jacks in Alexandria for a hamburger. Other times, Greg would also be invited to have dinner at the monastery, about once a month, with the conversation ranging across many subjects. He remembers how busy Fr Stenhouse was, working on *Annals*, his books and especially the one on John Farrell. He saw his priest friend "quite a bit" in the last few weeks. Greg saw that he was deteriorating rapidly, as he sat next to him in the office, with Fr Stenhouse telling him how "bad the pain was", but that he was at peace with what faced him. Not long before he died, Fr Stenhouse went out with Greg for one final hamburger together at Hungry Jacks, but by then he could only walk with difficulty, so he stayed in the car. Greg remembers that he enjoyed the hamburger very much. On the way back Fr Stenhouse asked Greg to drive to La Perouse which Greg did. After the car was parked, they chatted while gazing at the lights of Botany Bay. Greg was delighted to be part of *Annals*, and said he missed his dear friend whom "he cherished dearly."

There were several other people who, from time to time, were involved in computer matters related to *Annals*, among them academic Paul Compton, Greg Tait, Hendrikus Wong, Tony Bonanno and Vonny Sugiarto, all of whom helped greatly at various times when needed. Greg Tait, the MSC IT consultant, particularly helped with occasional emergencies and kept Fr Stenhouse's personal computer maintained, upgraded and operational for many years. Fr Stenhouse was a quick learner, though he had definite ideas of layout and what programs to use. He was a good friend of all his digital angels.

"I had never met a priest like that" – Hendrikus Wong

Originally from Indonesia, Hendrikus Wong remembers meeting Fr Stenhouse through friends in early 1992 and that he had "never met a priest like that."[25] He could not get over how this priest had so many Asian friends – from Hong Kong, Indonesia, China and Malaysia – and remembered that at times he wore a kind of bomber jacket whose memory brought back laughter, as it had for many other of Fr Stenhouse's friends.

Before coming to Australia, Hendrikus had attended a school run by the Sisters of Our Lady of the Sacred Heart in Jakarta. He converted to Catholicism after his brothers, mother and father had converted. Then the family looked to Australia for further education. Hendrikus first came in the late 1980s following his sisters who were studying at high school and TAFE. His whole family applied for permanent residency (PR), and this was granted in 1987. However, when his father died in 1989, Hendrikus had to return to Indonesia to look after family matters till 1992 – which affected his PR status. He approached the Australian Consulate in Jakarta, asking to return to Australia and they granted him what he called a "last chance visa" to return to Australia where he had to stay for three years – which he did. After this, he travelled to Indonesia again in 1995 to work for a while in Jakarta. He had already met Fr Stenhouse in Sydney, remarking, "I was surprised when Fr Stenhouse visited Indonesia in early 1998 – he had been invited by an Indonesian friend".[26] By that stage Hendrikus was married to Paula and they had twin babies, four months old. When they met, the subject of Baptism came up. Fr Stenhouse nearly hit the roof asking, "Why didn't you have the babies baptised as quickly as possible?" Hendrikus admitted, "I was a convert and did not have a lot of knowledge on the subject and was jolted by his comment." Fr Stenhouse explained that the sooner the baby got baptised the better and so, "my wife and I went immediately to have the babies baptised by the local priest in Indonesia."[27]

On his return to Australia later in 1998, Hendrikus found it difficult to get a job in Sydney. As Peter Macinante was relocating to Singapore for a while with his wife, Hendrikus was asked if he wished to work in the *Annals* office – which is how he came to work there. He has good memories of Jennie Hiatt and Stephen Smith and came to handle many jobs within the office, especially dealing with *Annals* subscriptions, cutting out articles, researching, acting as a courier, organising bank transfers and encoding. He was happy to have had this time working at the MSC monastery, for his early education was with the Order in Indonesia and it gave him a sense of connection, remembering with gratitude that his elder son was tutored by the OLSH sisters nearby.

When Peter returned from Singapore, Hendrikus told me he had moved on to work at Notre Dame University and handled *Annals* work at night. He remembers Fr Stenhouse "as a person with a purpose, with perfection – not 100 percent but 110 percent perfection", working from morning to night. Then he would head out at night visiting friends – he was always very pleasant to everyone. Peter remembers that "Fr Stenhouse helped me with my Catholic faith through his writings, through Dr Rumble's books." He speaks with deep affection: "I owe him, for me and for my family,"[28] adding, "I like him because he never treated us differently as Asians. So many of his friends came from different backgrounds. He was a good priest, always giving us good example ... He always did his best to help us in every way."

"Paul and I developed a perhaps unlikely but almost instant rapport" – Giles Auty

Anyone meeting the renowned *Annals* writer Giles Auty would have been struck by the extraordinary knowledge and breadth of his life experiences. His conversations with Fr Stenhouse would doubtless have resembled some witty, Chestertonian, literary fireworks. It was always sheer delight for anyone to converse with Giles, so sparkling the discourse on all kinds of topics, ranging across the KGB, Sussex villages, music, Slovenian tennis tournaments, the landscape of Georgia and the glories of Western art. Giles told me he had attended an Anglican boarding school in England, receiving a classical education, "learning Latin at eight, French at nine and Ancient Greek at eleven."[29] He also had a very erudite family but recalls that "[n]either of my parents were churchgoers and my father's surname identifies our background for those who understand such matters as being of Huguenot stock." He further recalls his conversion to Catholicism at age 28:

> Auty is in fact the name of an ancient village and chateau near Montauban in South West France. My boarding school was of a moralistic, strict and Anglican persuasion and I did not become a Catholic until in my late twenties after much travel and a spell of front-line military service.[30]

Having a keen sense of the beauty of nature from childhood, Giles wanted to be a painter. In the course of his art journey, however, he became a journalist, focusing on art and culture, spending time in Russia, Slovenia and Georgia, working at one stage for the Moscow Branch of the Russian Union of Artists, rubbing shoulders with colonels of the KGB, before the Soviet Union ended. At his funeral on 7 October 2020, artist Tom Storrier told the story of Giles finding a copy of the *Spectator* on a railway seat in London, with an ad for an art critic in it. Giles applied for the job and got it. His deep understanding of art, his love of the visual world and his astonishing ease with words on many other subjects besides had found a home.

Giles was an ardent anti-Communist, and tried to help people of Soviet run countries by participating in 'events' to raise money for them, including an international tennis tournament organised by the Slovenian Journalists' Association. When he came to Australia to take up work as a journalist he recalls:

> My first meetings with the late Father Paul Stenhouse took place usually in the company of senior journalists such as Frank Devine and Paddy McGuinness who are ... now no longer with us. All four of us enjoyed an easy but very genuine friendship. As a newcomer from the other side of the world I was initially very much the outsider when I arrived in Australia in 1995 to take up work for The Australian as their national art correspondent covering the whole continent. Before that I had worked for 11 years for the English weekly The Spectator and other national and international magazines such as Apollo which covered major national and international artistic events.[31]

Giles found it easy to bond with people of many different backgrounds. One can imagine the profusion of knowledge and anecdotes transmitted between himself and Fr Stenhouse, and many of these were recorded in *Annals* for over 17 years.

> For people from entirely different backgrounds with only our Catholic faith obviously in common Paul and I developed a perhaps unlikely but almost instant rapport. I began writing for Annals back in about 2002 and fairly soon 'graduated' to the magazine's editorial board in the distinguished company of such major Australian writers as Pierre Ryckmans and Christopher Koch.

Speaking of his youth Giles observed the similarities and differences of his life with that of his priest friend: "Paul and I hailed basically from small-town rural environments at different ends of our world ... and were also much the same age." He adds, while "Paul hailed from Cobbitty in NSW, I was born in the ancient Kentish brewing town of Faversham which boasts not only Britain's oldest brewery but one of England's best and longest Elizabethan streets off which my maternal grandfather ran a timber business beside the town's estuarine creek."[32] There were other notable differences:

> While his father died not long after his birth, mine tended to remain a very remote scholarly figure whom I came to see as 'the man at the bottom of the garden' from his habit of retreating regularly there with a portable table and either a selection of enormous books or vast piles of the examination papers he was regularly commissioned to mark. The huge books in question were copies of the 1933, 13 volume *Complete Oxford English Dictionary* for which my father latterly become a senior reader contributing some 26,000 original entries to the 1970 supplement. To say my father was impractical is a major understatement: neither he, nor my sole sibling – an older sister – could ever drive a car or perform even elementary practical tasks. Perhaps for these simple reasons I was never tempted to be a 'pure' scholar myself.

Speaking of the erudition of Fr Stenhouse he reflects:

> I doubt I could ever remotely have emulated anything like Father Paul's mastery of Arabic languages or his extraordinary erudition regarding the history of Islam itself. But who else on our planet possibly could?

Of his own love of the physical world, he says:

> Outside my principal interests in painting and writing

which I subsidised for a long time by playing and teaching sport, my cerebral interests tended to embrace philosophy and politics rather than any more esoteric subjects ... Passionate love of the physical world basically underlies my love of painting which I first learned at the hands of a professional painter whose home lay in one of the most beautiful rural hamlets of England near Canterbury. It even has a wonderful name: Old Wives' Lees.

Giles says that it was at "Father Paul's behest" that he wrote about *Brexit* and the so-called 'Long March through the Institutions' for *Annals*. This has led him to reflect on what was happening to Western civilisation and on his political leanings:

I am probably far more of a political – if not religious – conservative than the late Father Paul yet he trusted me to present my case and argue it honestly and humanely. "What on earth do you want to cover next?" Father Paul would ask nervously on his regular visits to houses we owned in Australia and – for a period – in England.

When in Britain, Giles and his wife Annouchka would show Fr Stenhouse some of the wonders of rural England "such as my favourite village of all time Lodsworth in Sussex. The wonderful illustrator E. H. Shepard spent the last 20 years of his life there – living happily I hope on the royalties earned from immortal children's books such as *Winnie the Pooh* and *Wind in the Willows*." Giles recalls:

On an idyllic summer day my wife, Paul and I drove from our house near Hampton Court to the wonderful pub at Lodsworth where the three of us had lunch. Thereafter we adjourned to sitting on the wall of the churchyard of an early church which would, of course, have been Catholic in its infancy at least. No happier memory of Father Paul could possibly stay with us than memories of that most English of days. The two Airedale terriers we owned during our days of knowing each other – Humphrey and Harry – adored Father Paul and mere mention of his name was enough to send both into frenzies of anticipation.

On the sadder, post-Fr Stenhousian world Giles said he would sorely miss his friend but as things turned out Auty himself passed away on 24 September 2020. One of his last comments on his dear priest friend was:

> I am glad, if it is true, that Father Paul missed knowledge of the current Chinese virus. Humankind inhabits the sole viable planet in God's boundless universe. The folly of humankind in the past 50 years of Postmodernism seems limitless. Let's pray that rather a sharp rap on the knuckles may return us to our senses and that it has not come too late for us all.

For now, Fr Stenhouse and Giles Auty will be watching the folly of humankind and our planet from another world and seeing its perturbations in quite another perspective.

"He liked westerns" – film reviewer James Murray

Many *Annals* readers will recall the interesting, if not scintillating film reviews of James Murray who had a long friendship with Fr Stenhouse. James, who had an entertaining flair for bringing the essence of the film world to the written page, wrote reviews in *Annals* for 25 years. Many people consulted them while wondering whether to see a film or not. James recalls that, at one stage, before he came on the scene, Fr Stenhouse had handled some film reviews himself, as had Fr Peter Malone and Bill Collins. With an eye for piquant detail, James recalls that, Bill Collins had taught Latin at Sydney University and was "pre-Vatican II".[33]

James was born in Glasgow, came to Australia in 1960 and worked on *The Advertiser* in Adelaide, "a proper broadsheet then." He met his wife Jenny when they were both working on the children's publication, *The Young Australian*, in 1961 – they were married in Adelaide in 1963. They returned to the U.K. not long afterwards and lived in London for ten years. James worked for Granada Television, interviewing many celebrities. Then at some point, the Murrays decided to exchange the excitements of Granada for the Antipodes. They had eight children and now have many grandchildren, recently sending birthday greetings to one of them via Zoom, during the Coronavirus crisis.

Counting David Stratton as a friend, James insists that though he loved movies, he was not a 'scenist' and "a lover of movies as such", but was very selective and withheld praise from those that did not deserve it. James liked the medium, and given that movie going was an increasingly expensive activity, he did not want people to waste their money on commercialised nonsense. He spoke well of the 'quality movies' sometimes shown on SBS World Movies. He wrote with riveting, superlative analysis of Mel Gibson's *The Passion of the Christ*:

> In the role of a lifetime, Jim Caviezel plays Christ with a conviction a heartbeat from the heroic. Yes, the movie is blood-boltered in the ferocity of the scourgings and the crucifixion. Mediaeval some have called these tortures, reaching for the all-purpose pejorative of hacks whose vocabulary is inadequate to their deadline task. Gibson then is not being gratuitously violent, he is making a creative link between the pain we inflict on each other with the redemptive pain endured by Christ. Gibson's violence is metaphoric of the 20th century, the cruellest of human history, in which millions suffered so much pain and death under regimes that were national or supernational, and ideological rather than religious, in their inspiration.[34]

Conversation with James is permeated with drama and candour.

When I asked James what his favourite film genre was he had no hesitation in saying "the western" and recalled many discussions about these with his priest friend. Both shared a great liking for these heroic, bang-bang stories that have been so much a part of American mythology. Among Fr Stenhouse's books on the Church Fathers, saints, and histories of Lebanon, there was a pile of old paperback westerns, among them *The Leaden Cache* by Noel Loomis, *Squatters Rights* by Frank C Robertson and *Gallows Ghost and the Long Wire* by Barry Cord.

James mentioned the famous 1968 paperback western called *True Grit* by Charles Portis, first published as a 1968 serial in *The Saturday Evening Post*. The novel is told from the perspective of a devout, church-going woman named Mattie Ross, who seeks retribution for the murder of her father by scoundrel Tom Chaney. There are many adventures, barroom brawls and confrontations in the story. Mattie joins up with an ageing, trigger-happy Reuben J. "Rooster" Cogburn, played by John Wayne in the movie version of the book for which Wayne got an Academy Award for best actor.

Recalling an interview at the Dorchester in London with a renowned American western writer, Louis L'Amour, James, knowing heroes in westerns have 'survival packs' they take everywhere, asked jocularly if the author had a survival pack in real life. To his amazement, L'Amour took out one survival tool which he had brought to this interview. It was a steel mirror with a hole in the middle of it, which L'Amour explained was highly useful if one was lost in the desert and had to focus on getting a signal to a plane.

James then asked me out of the blue, "What was Stalin's favourite movie?" I had no idea and was surprised to learn that it was the American western, "The Lost Patrol" by the famous director John Ford. Apparently, Stalin loved the movie so much that he ordered a Russian remake of it, called "The Thirteen" (1937) by Mikhail

Romm, as the first Soviet 'eastern' – a pun on the word 'western'. But it was the Western 'westerns' that appealed to Fr Stenhouse more, particularly with their heroic defenders of the good and the true. One is left imagining the delightful conversations that Fr Stenhouse, James and Jenny enjoyed over Shepherd's Pie, not to mention Moussaka in the visits to a favourite Greek restaurant nearby and at Christmases spent together. Fr Stenhouse was involved in the spiritual life of the Murray family. They not only shared discussions of bang-bang westerns but of the spiritual heart of the Western world and where its culture was headed.

"I shamelessly drew on his knowledge" – Greg Sheridan

The sense of immense respect and affection felt by many journalists for Fr Stenhouse is echoed by Greg Sheridan, the long-serving Foreign Affairs editor of *The Australian*. Sheridan described Fr Stenhouse as much more than a friend, adding that he had presided at his (Greg's) wedding and had given much wise counsel. He reflected:

> Paul Stenhouse was a gifted polymath, a cosmopolite of astonishing diversity and virtuosity, a prodigious reader, a knower of infinite facts and theories, and a deeply wise, friendly, good, pastoral priest ....[35]

Greg admits that he "shamelessly drew on his knowledge about Islam, Indonesia, the Balkans, Lebanon, the Middle East more widely, medieval Christianity, contemporary Christianity and any other subject which from time to time I needed input on" That is quite a comment from one as well-versed in history and politics as Greg is. He had been introduced to Fr Stenhouse through someone he considered another polymath, John Wheeldon, associate editor of *The Australian* when Sheridan joined that paper in 1984. He remembered John had an immense admiration for Paul and the two would converse on several topics, in several languages from time to time, to get a point across, oblivious to other listeners in the room.

One day Fr Stenhouse was present at a talk which Greg gave to a small group about Islam in Indonesia. Of this Greg says, "Paul rose to ask a question. He lavished my feeble remarks with unjustified praise and then, politely and kindly, took them apart piece by piece." He reflected: "And here is his true genius. I liked him just as much afterwards as before and while I was perhaps none the wiser for the encounter, I was certainly better informed." There was no point scoring, no put down, simply an invitation to clarity. In an age of ideology and buzz words, there are not many who can engage in debate with a person expressing a conflicting view and enjoy the conversation. Fr Stenhouse could disagree with a point of view in a consummately agreeable way. Greg points to Fr Stenhouse's friendship with many journalists of varying views, his cheerful demeanour and loads of common sense in all kinds of situations. He particularly remembers the "deep, priestly, pastoral personality" which was at the base of his being able to talk to anybody. No doubt this was helped by Fr Stenhouse's boyhood conversations with the visitors and inhabitants of Camden, and his innate inclination, indeed continually burning zeal for wisdom and understanding.

8

FRIENDS WITH THE WHOLE WORLD

There is nothing on this earth more to be prized than true friendship

St Thomas Aquinas.
De Regno ad Regem Cypri, Book 1.

Fr Stenhouse was friends with people from many differing backgrounds – Malaysians, Indonesians, Armenians, Lebanese, Syrians, Ukrainians, Poles, Italians, Tobagans, Chinese and Vietnamese among other groups.[1] If you went to see him at his office, he might take a call from Canberra, Damascus or Kuala Lumpur while you were there. He befriended people easily and deeply. These were not just friends in passing, they were friends with whom Fr Stenhouse struck a deep chord, eliciting gratitude and loyalty. For example, one student wrote a card to "Dearest Father Paul", thanking him for everything especially his "friendliness and tender care," adding that Fr Stenhouse brought "so much warmth and comfort to my heart in this 'hostile' foreign country." He signs off, "With the love of Jesus."[2] There were many cards and mementos in Fr Stenhouse's office, deeply felt testimonies from those he met and helped.

This reaching out extended especially to Jewish and Muslim groups. Recall the story of his going to see *Fiddler on the Roof*, and going backstage afterwards, emerging out arm in arm with the main star, Chaim Topol, exchanging jokes and stories in Hebrew, to the amazement of onlookers. He befriended Jewish fellow students and scholars and spoke Hebrew so fluently that, as previously noted, he marked University and HSC Hebrew exam papers for many years. Moreover, Fr Stenhouse held such a high regard for the Jewish professor of Semitic Studies at Sydney University, Professor Alan Crown, his mentor and advisor on many matters, that he wrote a moving tribute to him on his death:

> He may have inherited the name Crown from his parents, but he earned the title 'CROWN' – the Crown of Torah, through his own merit, his sharp intellect and his deep respect for scholarship. He will be remembered by his family, his colleagues and his students – may his memory be for a blessing.[3]

Stuart Rowland recalls "visits to Professor Alan and Mrs Sadie Crown" in the round of people Fr Stenhouse regularly called in on.[4] As well as his interest in Judaism and his Jewish friends, Fr Stenhouse could reach out to Muslims in a unique way. Many will never forget his journey to Syria in 2011, as war flared up there. He went to Damascus to meet with none other than the grand mufti of Syria, Muhammad Badr Din Hassoun, and spoke in Arabic with him for several hours asking him questions of the Sunni Muslim view of the war. His conversation with this Muslim leader was a confirmation for Fr Stenhouse that the war was not something from within the country but from outside influences. Fr Stenhouse told me that he had comforted the Mufti who had lost his son in the recent war. Here was a Catholic priest comforting a Muslim leader. It came naturally. Fr Stenhouse had no trouble seeing our common humanity across many divides. In fact, this meeting was valuable first hand evidence, the account being published in *The Australian* and other mainstream sources.[5]

"I love Lebanon" – many journeys with Joseph Assaf

There were friends outside writing and publishing with whom Fr Stenhouse became a virtual family member. While he had many friends in the Australian Lebanese community in Australia – priests, scholars, businessmen and politicians alike – one person who had a deep connection with him was Joseph Assaf. Joseph was only too happy to talk to me about his "dear friend" in a long conversation in his office on 16 December 2019 and much of what follows is taken from this interview.[6]

Joseph migrated to Australia from Lebanon in 1967 and met Father Stenhouse at Sydney University in the Department of Semitic Studies when they were in the same class studying Arabic as a language, Joseph recalling that this was "about 1969 or 1970."[7] This meeting in class turned into a lifelong friendship which influenced Fr Stenhouse deeply, opening up much of the Middle East to him, historically and spiritually, not only through books, but the lived experience of a close friend. It drew him to the Assaf family whom he visited many times.

Joseph was born in Hardine, in Lebanon, to a Maronite Christian family and was one of six children. As a young man, he decided to migrate to Australia, the land of dreams for a budding businessman. He describes his journey from Beirut to Sydney in his fascinating book, *In Someone Else's Shoes* (2008). Yet, he nearly did not make it. On the day Joseph was booked to leave Lebanon he checked in to his flight with an "as requested" brand new pair of shoes, this rule being enforced to protect Australia from soil, seed or plant material detrimental to the country. Joseph's flight was cancelled and passengers were sent home and advised to come back on another day. When Joseph returned to the airport and began the check-in process he was asked to remove his old shoes and put on the new shoes. But, alas, he had worn the new shoes already. He was therefore prohibited from boarding the flight. That is until some kind stranger working for the airline was touched by Joseph's enormous disappointment. This stranger began searching through the luggage of other passengers and eventually found a brand new pair of shoes that he gave to Joseph to wear on the flight. They were much too big for him but they did the job. He boarded the flight and began his journey "In Someone Else's Shoes".

Joseph came to love his new country where he worked in factories, saved his money and enrolled at Sydney University. It was there he met Fr Stenhouse who, as noted above, was himself a young student studying Arabic (among other subjects). Their friendship began and was to develop into one of great influence for both men throughout their lives. For Fr Stenhouse, Joseph, through his lived experience, opened up much of the Middle East to him, both historically and spiritually. Then when Joseph married his wife, Angela, Fr Stenhouse was welcomed into their family and he visited them often.

Joseph remarked that Father Stenhouse's ability with languages was so good that he not only ended up speaking fluent Arabic, but knowing several of its dialects. He said Fr Stenhouse also studied Aramaic and other ancient languages in order to understand better the contexts in which Christianity and Islam had grown, explaining, "Fr Stenhouse always wanted to go to the sources, the beginnings."[8] Joseph also remembers visiting Italy during those early years, and being given a guided tour by Fr Stenhouse whom he commended as "an excellent tour guide." His priest friend told him to "forget the tour operators" and then gave a rich account of the cultural history of Rome, its catacombs, churches and other sites of religious significance. Joseph realised his priest guide knew the city better than anyone.

At some point Joseph became involved in some of the activities of Fr Stenhouse. On some of these trips, Joseph invited Fr Stenhouse to his own family home in Hardine up in the Lebanese mountains with its surviving groups of Maronites. For the young priest it must have opened up a new world. He recalls that Fr Stenhouse was enthralled with the early Christian history of the country, walking around, taking everything in, saying at one point to Joseph, "I love Lebanon."

Joseph estimated there were dozens of trips to Lebanon over the years during which Fr Stenhouse met Lebanese religious leaders, monks and politicians, both Christian and Muslim. But it was this contact with Joseph's own Maronite village up in the mountains that really ignited him. For in Hardine, the young priest saw where Saint Nimatullah, one of the greatest Lebanese Maronite saints, had lived. It is not hard to understand why Fr Stenhouse came to love this Christian area, which had survived so many invasions. Hardine, with its 30 monasteries and hermitages, has been called the 'Lourdes of Lebanon' and pilgrims, Christians and non-Christians, have long found it a peaceful retreat. Father Youssef Saleh has said that Hardine is the place where one can hear "voice of silence, meditate, pray and feel close to the Creator."[9] Its very distance from major cities afforded it some protection throughout history and, as those who knew Fr Stenhouse understood, he was always drawn to Christian groups that had survived against the odds. As Joseph told me, Fr Stenhouse would walk around the mountains alone, visiting monasteries, talking to people he met, praying and absorbing the spiritual atmosphere of this remarkable place – and not only here, but in Israel, Syria and Jordan.

Taking *Annals* readers on the journey to St Nimatullah

Writing about St Nimatullah (sometimes rendered Nimatallah by Fr Stenhouse, though Nimatullah is used here for consistency) in a 1998 *Annals* article, Fr Stenhouse took his readers on a journey of discovery few Australians had heard of:

> Nimatullah, whose name means 'God's blessing' was born in 1808 in Hardine in North Lebanon. His baptismal

name was Yussef or Joseph and his Maronite Catholic family raised him in the Aramaic traditions and the archpatriarchate of Antioch, and especially in the monastic traditions of their ancient Catholic Rite ... He was one of the six children of Girgis Kassab of Hardine and Marian Raad, from Tannurin. Four boys in his family became priests or monks. Nimatullah was 20 when he entered the Lebanese Maronite Order of Monks that had been founded in 1695, spending the two years of his novitiate in the Monastery of St Anthony of Quozhaya, close to the Qadisha or the Holy Valley of the Maronites'.[10]

The typical Stenhousian focus on detail is fired by a holy zeal to have others know about the saint: how Nimatullah founded schools for poor children at Kfifan and Bhershaf, how he lived through the terrible massacres of Maronite Catholics, how he witnessed the desecration of many churches by the Ottomans in 1840 and 1845. Nimatullah dedicated himself, Lebanon, and his Order, to the care of the Virgin Mary, having a devotion to the Immaculate Conception, and being thrilled with the defining of the Dogma in 1854, not long before his death. He had refused any elevation to be Assistant General to the Maronite Order saying, "I would rather die than be Abbot General", convinced of his inability to meet the demands of high office. But in the end he did take it on, and as Fr Stenhouse relates, continued to teach theology while insisting his students speak Syriac (the Aramaic of Lebanon and Edessa, now Urfa in Turkey), rather than Arabic or French, in order that they understand the ancient liturgical language of Maronite Catholics. All this would have been music to the ears of Fr Stenhouse, as would have been the fact that St Nimatullah taught the future Saint Charbel Makhlouf (1828-1898, his body being incorrupt) who was canonised by Pope Paul VI in 1977, as well as Saint Rafqa-Ar-Rayès (1832-1914) the nun who was canonised by Pope John Paul II on June 10, 2001.

Fr Stenhouse compares the saintly life of Nimatullah to that of St Thérèse of Lisieux, in that the focus of his life was on ordinary, daily activities dedicated "to the glory of God and the building up of the Church ... Nimatullah was genuinely self-effacing, and preferred the life hidden in God."[11] Fr Stenhouse writes that after his death in 1858 Catholics, Orthodox, Druze and Muslims came to venerate him. There were Muslims in St Peter's Square on 10 May 1998, for his beatification and later for his canonisation on 16 May 2004. After his death, many miracles were granted through his intercession, among these, making a blind man see, healing a paralysed man, bringing back a dead child to life, healing another from cancer, as well as healing those afflicted with psychological ailments.[12] He was widely known as a wonder-worker as was his student, St Charbel.

The canonisation of Nimatullah in St Peter's Square in Rome included the reading of a Biblical text in Arabic. The Lebanese President Emile Lahoud expressed his gratitude to Pope John Paul II, on behalf of his 50,000 countrymen gathered in Rome for the ceremonies, as well as those back at home, noting that the Pope had called his country "a nation that is a message" during his visit to Lebanon in 1997. The president movingly said to the Pope: "You have given Lebanon a lot and I am most grateful for your tremendous love." He might well have said it to the priest-journalist too who was endeavouring to make Lebanese saints known and loved. In fact, Pope John Paul II sent a letter from the Vatican in 1996, imparting an Apostolic Blessing and to officially thank Fr Stenhouse for his 'publication.'

Dinners and a Committee for Lebanon

Fr Stenhouse was a regular visitor at the home of Joseph and Angela Assaf, sharing many meals with a great collection of friends including politicians from both sides of the house.

Joseph had established the Ethnic Business Award, which

celebrated the many contributions of migrants in Australia. At one of these award dinners, Julia Gillard was seated next to Tony Abbott, to her surprise. When she showed some hesitation to sit where she was placed, Joseph said, with exquisite charm, that his group had planned the event and organised the seating. Thus Tony Abbott and Julia Gillard came to sit together! Joseph always managed to bring people together in a positive and harmonious way.

In 1986, when Joseph's American cousin Monsignor John Esseff, who was head of the Pontifical Mission Society, visited Australia, he met Fr Stenhouse. Being of Lebanese background, Monsignor Esseff was greatly concerned about the war in Lebanon (1975-1990). On hearing eyewitness accounts of suffering, Joseph recalls Fr Stenhouse's deep concern for the fate of the Christians and all victims of war in Lebanon. At one of the dinners at Joseph's house, the idea arose of forming a committee to help Lebanon and holy plots were hatched. Joseph invited politicians to become involved, from all sides of politics, among others, Peter Baume (Liberal), Laurie Brereton (Labor), Senator Wheeldon (Labor, later to become editor of *The Australian*). There was much exchange of information and Fr Stenhouse was able to disseminate accurate reports to them about the situation in Lebanon, and to the mainstream media: *The Sydney Morning Herald*, *The Financial Review*, *The Australian* and other outlets, as well as in the *Annals*. This bipartisan Committee for Lebanon was a remarkable achievement being not only a conduit for factual information but also a way to get aid to those who needed it.

In 2013, Tony Burke, then minister for Immigration, Multicultural Affairs and Citizenship, and Scott Morrison, then shadow minister for Immigration, were in Lebanon as part of a delegation to witness the ordination of a new Maronite bishop, Bishop Tarabay. At this time, they also visited Joseph in his home village of Hardine, 80 kilometres north-east of Beirut.

Joseph recalls Morrison being deeply moved, seeing how people in Hardine had lived there since Phoenician times, fighting for their faith, noting how this mountainous location had always been a refuge for the persecuted. Joseph related to me that he thought the trip had influenced Morrison's politics, for during a parliamentary speech, Morrison mentioned not only Israel, but the Maronites as an example of people of faith surviving against great odds.

Joseph said that Fr Stenhouse was always up to something, always an agent for Christ, constantly trying to find usual and unusual ways to help persecuted Christians. His fearless journeys to aid war victims and gather information led seamlessly into his future work with Aid to the Church in Need.

One story, referred to in a previous chapter, was that concerning Fr Stenhouse's attempts to get medication to the Christian victims of war, Lebanese and Syrian refugees. This was extremely difficult as the normal means of sending anything by post or courier were unlikely to succeed, being lost through corruption or resulting in the death of the courier. In 1987, during the Lebanese war, Fr Stenhouse asked (begged) for medications from pharmaceutical companies in Australia and himself took his large consignment of donated medicines to Cyprus. From there he hired a boat and crew, headed for Lebanon, and sailed into a coastal Lebanese port, and was thus able to get the medications to where they were needed.

Fr Stenhouse met several politicians, among them Maronite Christian Michel Aoun, who served as Prime Minister of Lebanon from 1988 to 1990, being appointed to that role by the departing Lebanese President Amine Gemayel. When Aoun was appointed, there was political unrest and Syrian army forces invaded several Aoun strongholds, whereupon Aoun fled to the French Embassy in Beirut. Having been granted asylum, Aoun then went to France, living there between 1990 and 2005, where Fr Stenhouse visited him in exile, having a lengthy interview published in 1993, a coup for *Annals*, indeed for any media outlet. Here are some questions asked:

> *Annals* [Fr Stenhouse to Aoun]: You're well known as a person who speaks his mind, who speaks directly and clearly and sincerely. And I think in the past this fact has cost you dearly because you were criticised not for not being a good general but for not being a good politician. When you are returned to power would you follow the same course. Would you be as direct, do you think?
>
> Michel Aoun: When things are really threatening our existence we should speak the truth whatever it is; we have to say it frankly and loudly. And we cannot hide. Sometimes it may be wise to remain silent but never should we deny the truth.[13]

Fr Stenhouse then questioned Aoun about the recent elections in Lebanon:

> *Annals* [Fr Stenhouse to Aoun]: Well, do you think that ... the more recent elections in Lebanon, give any hope for a brighter future for the country in regard to its relationship to Syria?
>
> Michel Aoun: No. Anything that's done in Lebanon right now [1992] cannot be legitimate, because the Lebanese people didn't participate in it. It was something imposed by the occupying forces: not agreed to by the people, or approved by the people. The recent elections in Lebanon, were boycotted by the Lebanese people. More than eighty per cent didn't participate in these elections because they considered that the result was known before the vote ... Free elections cannot be made in an occupied country. Free elections can only be made under a true National Government or in a period of transition under United Nations control.[14]

Friends with the whole world

Things were to change dramatically. Aoun had founded the Free Patriotic Movement in 1994 which has significantly influenced events in Lebanon.¹⁵ He was to find himself catapulted onto the political stage once more. Aoun returned to Lebanon following the withdrawal of the Syrian Army in 2015 which, along with the assassination of Rafic Hariri on 14 February 2005, became a catalyst for dramatic political change. The massive protests of the so-called Cedar Revolution helped achieve the withdrawal of Syrian troops which led to a change in government. After fifteen years of exile in France, Aoun again became a leading force in Lebanese politics, making strategic alliances with an array of political groups. Fr Stenhouse was immersed in Lebanon's complex history and the fate of its Christians, never ceasing to explain it all in *Annals*:

> LEBANON was given independence from French mandate rule in 1943. But it wasn't until December 31. 1945, when French troops withdrew, that Lebanon really stood alone, as a free, independent, sovereign state. The transition to Democracy from a League of Nations mandated territory and former feudal, tribal-based dependency of the Ottoman Turks [to cover only a tiny fraction of the political history of this most ancient of lands] had only two years to run – an impossible task – when Israel gained independence in 1948, and Lebanon found itself plunged deep in the whirlpool of intrigue and treachery that has characterised Middle Eastern politics before and since. The West cannot continue to be complacent about the fate of Lebanon's Christians – Maronites, Melkites, Armenian and Orthodox. Like Egypt's Copts and Iraq's Assyrian and Chaldaean Christians, they have had to co-exist with Islam almost from the time of Muhammad's death. Our survival as free people is contingent on theirs.¹⁶

While Fr Stenhouse's enlightening accounts might take a few

readings to grasp, especially when he threw around names like Abd-al-Aziz ibn Abd-Allah ibn Baaz, he wrote with extraordinary clarity and understanding. He sensed a man of integrity in Aoun and felt impelled to defend him against Western media distortions.[17] When Aoun was elected to the National Assembly in 2005, his Free Patriotic Movement won only 21 seats. However, greater participation was to come during the following decade. And on 31 October 2016, Aoun was elected President of the Lebanese Republic. Fr Stenhouse followed the intricacies of this situation in a way few journalists did, always inserting a spiritual focus into his dealings with politicians. Who is to say? Perhaps he influenced the course of Lebanese politics through his moral support for Aoun and his dissemination of this Maronite Christian's views in the West?

From his first days in Lebanon, travelling with Joseph Assaf, Fr Stenhouse grew to love its saints, its courageous people and its rich culture which he helped transmit to a wide readership. Joseph stated joyfully that devotion to Saint Charbel is growing fast, that in many Australian churches his image adorns their walls, pointing out that in New York's St Patrick's Cathedral there is a side altar dedicated to him. There are reports of miracles through his intercession and one can be sure he was bombarded with prayer during the COVID19 pandemic.

When Fr Stenhouse was sick, Joseph was praying for him but changed at some point saying, "I started to ask HIM for things." He declared that with Fr Stenhouse's death, he knows that "there is a committee in Heaven praying for Lebanon." And on that intercessory committee is Fr Paul Stenhouse!

John Madden and "Andiamo Giovanni!"

A lifelong Australian friend who remembers Fr Stenhouse from schooldays is John Madden. John, a solicitor, recalls a 1968 class retreat just before Easter at St Joseph's College, Hunters Hill, in Sydney, given by three MSC priests, one of whom was Fr Stenhouse. In a very evocative, written memoir he recalls:

> I well remember the first time that I met Fr Paul Stenhouse. It was at Saint Joseph's College, Hunters Hill where I had been boarding since 1963. The year was 1968, just before Easter. Three MSC priests were at the college for a few days preaching a retreat to various class groups. The three MSC priests were Frank Fletcher, Tony O'Brien (I think) and Paul Stenhouse. At that time I was 17 years of age and one morning at about 8:45 I was about to walk out of the Sixth Form accommodation block through a full-length glass door on the ground floor. Approaching the door from the other side was a young priest wearing his habit, of course. I stood back and held the door open for him; he came through; we smiled at each other and bade each other a good morning. I was later to learn that the young priest was Father Paul Stenhouse.[18]

John remembered that in those days Fr Stenhouse travelled from Kensington to North Sydney early each morning to celebrate Mass for the "Brown Sisters of Saint Joseph". Then, after Mass Paul would drive over to St Joseph's at Hunters Hill in the famous blue *Annals* van which John adds has "long since been consigned to the scrap heap."

Later in 1968 John met Fr Stenhouse when he and Fr Frank Fletcher stayed at his parents' home in Lithgow in the August school holidays. John had decided to join the MSCs and Fr Fletcher, who was the vocations director, came to meet John's parents, bringing Fr Stenhouse with him. John and Fr Stenhouse became good friends and John used to come up from Croydon seminary and from Canberra, at various stages of his formation, to meet Fr Stenhouse and his cousin Trish Kavanagh, and to help in the *Annals* office. John recalls:

At Kensington (or "Kenso" as Paul habitually referred to it) I spent my days helping him in the *Annals* Office – running errands, driving proofs to the courier at Mascot late at night to catch the last truck so that they could be at the printers the following morning, proof-reading articles, and even being trusted at times with reviewing a couple of books.

Those times at Kensington enabled me to meet other MSCs I might not have otherwise met until much later, people such as, the late Fr John McMahon (Provincial Superior at the time), Fr Morty Kerrins (Superior of the house) and Fr Ted Lambert (Provincial Bursar), Dr Leslie Rumble, Br Barney Delaney, Br Ross Mulvihill, Br John Collins, Fr Peter Dignam, Br Tom Comerford, Br McNamara, Fr Laurie Bayliss, Fr Gabriel (Mick) Saap, Fr Aub Collins ... I was also pressed into service to wait on the bishops' dining tables at meal times; in those days the Australian Bishops' Conference used to meet twice a year at St Paul's National (late vocations) Seminary which had been constructed by the bishops on the MSC Kensington property. When table waiting was over I would then return to the Annals Office to help Paul.[19]

Fr Stenhouse called John 'Giovanni' and, as well as editing *Annals* and lecturing at the late vocations seminary, would say, "Andiamo, Giovanni, come with me and we'll go and visit some friends." Then would begin a series of visits, as John relates:

We would tear around Sydney fairly late at night dropping in to say hello to people. We were always made very welcome. Sometimes we would pay brief visits to 3 or 4 people in a night. I thought that Paul drove like a maniac, tearing up to traffic lights which were already red from a distance and then slamming on the brakes. But he knew Sydney and all its back roads and short cuts like the back of his hand. I met all sorts of people on those occasions, people from all sorts of backgrounds, professions, social and economic circumstances from the high to the low ...

On one of these night time drives to visit people Fr Stenhouse taught John how to count from 1 to 100 in Italian and soon he could quickly count from 1 to infinity, adding, "I still can, not that I often have occasion so to do." After the visits, Fr Stenhouse would prepare to work for another two hours, until 2 am, and would be up again about three hours later to start a new day. On one occasion they visited Bill Collins:

> Amongst all those people was Bill Collins (Mr Movies) who at that time before he was married lived with his mother in Jannali. Bill had a studio film theatre in the back garden and after dinner he would ask, "Well, what would you like to see?" The little theatre was packed from floor to ceiling with cans of 16mm film, LP soundtracks, books about the movies, movie and studio souvenirs of all kinds and movie theatre posters.

On another occasion they were driving in North Sydney around 10.00 pm:

> Paul saw a café with the lights on. He said, "Hey, Giovanni, would you like a cup of tea?" So in we went. The Greek proprietor was tidying things behind the counter. Paul asked for a couple of cups of tea. The proprietor said, "Sorry, Mate, tea's off." Paul's so characteristic response in such a circumstance was, "But can't you boil some water or something?" to which the proprietor responded, "Oh, alright then." And as we began to turn from the counter to a table, Paul said to me (so that the proprietor would hear), "Who's ever heard of tea being off?!"[20]

John recalls Fr Stenhouse's long hours of work: "That very late to bed, very early to rise, went on year after year and I just do not know how he did it." In 1974 John was sent to Downlands College to teach for 12 months but adds: "I left Downlands and the MSCs at the end of the first school term." He had not told Fr Stenhouse of his decision to leave and study Arts/Law. Meantime he worked in the School of Physics at the University of NSW. One day, John was walking along High Street on the left hand side footpath towards Randwick and heard a car horn give a toot:

> I stopped and turned around and it was Paul who had no idea what I was doing at that time; he had probably been giving me space to sort myself out after leaving the MSCs and leaving it to me to get back in touch with him. It was so good to see him and we took up regular contact.

John recalls Fr Stenhouse going to Rome in 1976 as secretary to Fr (later Bishop) Eugene Cuskelly, the Superior-General at the time. Then followed his stay in Croatia and the Balkans and the work on his thesis "in the roof cavity above a church close to the sea wall and run by the Jesuits in Dubrovnik."

After his priest friend returned to Australia, John mentions the "Slovenian hunting boots" which also came back with him, memorable to many of Fr Stenhouse's friends, among them Giles Auty who was told by Fr Stenhouse that he had almost died in the Slovenian snow and hence the need for them.

John attended Fr Stenhouse's doctoral graduation ceremony, along with provincial Fr John McMahon MSC, in the Great Hall at Sydney University in 1982, where he met Paul's brother Richard, his wife, Gloria, their two small boys, Ged and Jamie, and Professor Alan Crown and his wife, Sadie. Though Father Stenhouse's life was henceforth divided between his priestly duties, scholarly work, journalism and outreach to students, John met him when time permitted. He notes that "Paul loved languages; those close to his

Professor Alan Crown, Professor in Semitic Studies at the University of Sydney, world renowned scholar and author, was a good friend of Fr Stenhouse; Joseph and Angela Assaf attending the 2013 Ethnic Business Award ceremony; Joseph Assaf (on the right) brought people together from all sides of politics and all backgrounds, with Scott Morrison in the centre. Joseph was able to show Maronite sites to Morrison in Lebanon. Morrison was deeply moved by this and publicly testified to the courage of Maronite Christians in the Australian Parliament.

The cover of *Annals* showing St Nimatullah, about whom Fr Stenhouse wrote at length; Fr Stenhouse saying Mass for the Trinidad-Tobago community at Kensington Monastery of the Sacred Heart with Fr Gerard Wooling; The snow-covered heights of Hardine in northern Lebanon where Fr Stenhouse often stayed.

While en route to or returning from Lebanon, Fr Stenhouse often passed through Rome. Here he is with Fr Petro Zulian MSC, at the MSC General House at Via Asmara in Rome where I visited shortly before the canonisation of St John Paul II. I heard the two priests conversing in fluent Italian; Fr Stenhouse standing with his friends from Trinidad and Tobago after one of their annual Masses at the Sacred Heart Monastery in Kensington; John Madden, long-time friend of Fr Stenhouse who met with him over several decades. Fr Stenhouse used to call out "Andiamo Giovanni" when they were going somewhere; Stuart Rowland (centre) with Fr Stenhouse and Fr Peter Guy on the wedding day of Stuart and Tracey Rowland, 28 November 1992.

Fr Stenhouse stands with pilgrims at the opening of Domus Australia in Rome. Peter Fisher, who contributed to *Annals*, is to the right of Fr Stenhouse; Margaret Fisher (second from right) sitting with Fr Stenhouse and guests at Domus Australia at its opening: from the right: Fr Stenhouse, Margaret Fisher, Danny Casey (former Diocesan Business Manager) and Annie Casey.

heart were of course: his own native tongue ... He would quite often read a passage out to me, usually in Latin, Hebrew or Arabic, and say, 'Isn't that beautiful!'" John noted Fr Stenhouse's sensitivity to sounds, saying, "He appreciated euphony."

Of the busy life of his priest friend, John reflects:

> After Paul returned to Australia after all those years he was still constantly on the move, travelling abroad to meetings, convocations, to deliver learned papers and such like. One year he walked the Silk Road with Martin Walsh. He was always so busy he would forget what he had or had not told me. I would sometimes ring him to suggest, for example, a luncheon meeting in Berrima, and he would say, "Oh, Giovanni, sorry but I can't, I'll be in France." Me: "You didn't tell me that you were going to France!" Paul: "Oh, Giovanni, I'm sure I did." Me: "When are you leaving?" Paul: "In about 2 hours from now."

On another occasion they shared their Catholic heritage at the L'Abbaye Sainte-Anne de Kergonan in Brittany:

> In 2001 I was in Europe for 3 months. Paul was coming to Rome and so we had the opportunity to spend some time together in the Eternal City which we both loved. A couple of months later and I had moved over to France where I was staying at L'Abbaye Sainte-Anne de Kergonan in Brittany. Paul had had to come back to Rome again for some purpose and so made a side trip to see me at Kergonan on his way home. They were wonderful days that we passed in that beautiful abbey with all its Masses and Offices sung in choir in Gregorian Chant.

"Paul intrigued many people."

John recalls his loyalty, particularly to his own parents (John and Edna Madden) whom Fr Stenhouse visited in Lithgow, showing them places they would not otherwise have seen. John reflected on the wide network of people Fr Stenhouse knew from all walks of life, among them, the television news reader of many years, James Dibble; the "redoubtable, inimitable and irreplaceable" NSW Supreme Court judge, Roddie Meagher QC; Paddy McGuinness; Rupert Lockwood, erstwhile Communist; Roland Liang and his wife Belinda, longtime residents in Hong Kong; Australian composer, the late John Antill and his wife; Giles Auty and his wife, Annouchka; the renowned sinologist, novelist, translator, thinker, author, and deliverer of a wonderful series of the ABC's Boyer Lectures in 1996, Pierre Ryckmans (aka Simon Leys), and his wife Han Fang; the cartoonist Hal English; and Kevin Drumm – of whom John says, "not only was Kevin's work such an adornment to the *Annals*, it was also Paul's way of helping Kevin to keep the wolf from the door"; and remarkable as it may seem, John remembers one surprising regular subscriber to *Annals*, Patrick White:

> Patrick White was a subscriber to the *Annals* over many years. Very shortly before Patrick died, Paul returned to Kensington after being away for some time, possibly overseas. A couple of days after Paul had returned someone at Kensington gave him a message. The message was that Patrick White wanted Paul to visit him. Unbeknown to Paul, Patrick had sent the message from his death bed. Paul rang the number immediately but was told by Patrick's nurse or housekeeper that Patrick had died the day before. So much for people being slack about passing on messages! I hope that Patrick did not feel that he had been rejected. Who knows it might have been a death bed conversion like Lord Marchmain's?[21]

Interestingly John asked Fr Stenhouse how he came to have so many friends:

> I once asked Paul how he came to number all those

fascinating people amongst his friends. Paul replied to the effect that most of them would have no interest in him save for the fact that he was a Catholic priest, and that was the case even though most of them were lapsed Catholics, Protestants or non-believers. I think that there is some truth in that but also much exaggeration on Paul's part. But I do think that Paul intrigued many people.

This intriguing quality has been noted by some others who met Fr Stenhouse. Perhaps it derives from the sheer range of activities he engaged in, eliciting astonishment, wonder and curiosity. Perhaps it was that he had time for others, despite his many journalistic deadlines. Perhaps it was the unusual nature of his life, travelling to many parts of the world at a moment's notice, gathering much information in overt and covert ways. Or perhaps it was the amazing contrast of seeing deep compassion beneath a scholarly demeanour, a kindness coming not from 'on high' but emanating from a humble soul who saw himself as an ordinary pilgrim in a world of suffering. John has lasting memories of Fr Stenhouse's kindness, of willingness to help whether it was car trouble or a need for deeper advice. He saw many instances where Fr Stenhouse helped others, as on the day it poured with rain in the city and they saw a lady without an umbrella, without street awnings above her, trying to hail a taxi. Without hesitation, Fr Stenhouse went to her with his umbrella, courteously helping her hail the taxi. John also remembers Fr Stenhouse giving character references to some desperate people:

> ... he seemed always to be turning up in court to give pre-sentence character references for all manner of ne'er do well. On one occasion he was rung up by a Sydney detective criticizing Paul for giving a convicted criminal a reference. The detective said to Paul, "You're on his side!" Paul replied, "For Heaven's sake! I'm a priest! If someone asks me for help I can't just turn them away!"

John recalls Fr Stenhouse's assiduousness with *Annals*, his refusal to raise the subscription rate, and his generosity in sending it to people who could not pay. He notes that his priest friend was "well aware of his shortcomings", and could discuss, and disagree, yet always reach out for understanding, listening attentively. In reflecting on this long friendship, John tries to capture the essence of a remarkable person:

> Paul was so gentle, so kind, so understanding of the human condition. He never turned anyone away. He loved the Church and her ways. He said to me once "the Church has never judged anyone for not living up to what it teaches; it has only judged people for denying what it teaches."[22]

"Stuart, Stuart, that is just superstitious bibliotry"

You could not ask for a better tour guide of historical and biblical lands than Fr Stenhouse. Such was the exceeding good fortune of young Stuart Rowland in meeting Fr Stenhouse on such a tour of the Holy Land, Turkey, Greece and Rome in 1985. He recalls, "I was 18 years old from provincial Toowoomba ... Meeting Paul had the quality of the shock of the new."[23] As well as noting his many languages, Stuart remembers his "prodigious knowledge of the ancient world" and an ability to discuss contemporary international and domestic issues, and in particular his "laser accuracy" which would "hone in on the facts and assumptions that underpinned those opinions", adding "he would have made a devastating advocate had he chosen the law." While on pilgrimage, Stuart made what he thought was some innocent remark about a Scriptural passage and Fr Stenhouse replied, "Start, Stuart, that is just superstitious bibliotry!" Stuart had not long ago converted from Anglicanism to Catholicism and was on a journey of philological, philosophical and theological discovery – and who better to do this than with Fr Stenhouse?

Stuart's memories are very vivid, recalling:

> ... regular visits to Paul's elderly but razor-witted mother; visits to the elderly mother of Fr Frank Fletcher MSC; visits to Professor Alan and Mrs Sadie Crown ...; visits to Lady Fairfax; a flying visit to Cardinal Clancy at Swifts to drop off some papers (I stayed in the car); and very many visits to elderly, sick and dying friends and clergy at the Little Sisters of the Poor at Drummoyne, as well as visits to random families all over Sydney. In all of these instances Paul showed his kindness, urbanity and a sense of humour. His care for, and engagement with, all of these people in equal measure shone through.

Stuart also remembers an astonishing capacity for work: "Paul left no talent buried or mouldering. He treasured time as a gift and filled his life accordingly." He worked long into the night:

> ... after one late evening visit to dear old Jim Waldersee (the *Annals*' contributor and proof reader of many years), Paul took me for an ice-cream on the way home. As he dropped me home I said you'd better get some sleep now. Again, came the gentle reply: "Stuart, Stuart I have 800 words (in French) due for La Croix by 2am." These qualities of service, I came to understand, all grew out of the integration of his commitment to Christ and a desire to serve Him – to make the Heart of Jesus known and everywhere loved, to paraphrase the motto of his order.
>
> To a young fellow in his early twenties Paul seemed to have Indiana Jones, Sherlock Holmes and Father Brown like qualities. Perhaps he did, but as one of his brethren (now deceased) said to me: Paul is "sui generis!" The elderly priest went on to tell me that the late Fr George Cody MSC could not decide whether "Stenhouse" was a spy for ASIO, a spy for Israel or a Communist. Of these outlandish attributions the last was perhaps somehow encouraged by

Paul's longstanding and abiding friendship with the late Cyril Pearl and his wife Patty.

Stuart became a barrister but of all his accomplishments, he says his marriage to Tracey Rowland was "the best day of his life":

> ... On 28 November 1992 Father Stenhouse witnessed my marriage to Tracey Harrison. The best day of my life – or perhaps the day that truly symbolized my very best decision. Paul nurtured us through it all wonderfully in an affectionate way with funny little quips. I was unable to attend Paul's funeral. Tracey is in Rome, so she could not go either. A posthumous edition of Annals arrived. It was like the anniversary card or call that would have come on Thursday, and it was real!
>
> The words of my wife Tracey (in her book "Portraits of Spiritual Nobility" – applied there to James V Schall SJ – Tracey's other father-figure), express much better some of the things I am trying to say here about Paul: "For those of us who knew him...there is a sense that we haven't just lost a friend, we have lost one of the old-style renaissance-men...We have lost one of the giants!" Fr Paul Stenhouse MSC priest, scholar, journalist, father to many, and dear friend: Ave Atque Vale![24]

An enduring friendship with Margaret and Peter Fisher

Another friend, Margaret Fisher, recalls meeting Fr Stenhouse in a circuitous way in the 1990s, through various friends. From there grew a long-lasting friendship with Margaret, husband Peter and the two children. Margaret says that "he baptised all our grandchildren."[25]

In her youth, Margaret had done a short course on Public Relations and not long after, in 1986, was catapulted into being a Liaison Officer in Parliament for Labor's Janice Crosio, the first woman minister. This experience stood Margaret in good stead for her future work in consultancy which involved getting major projects approved and helping with development applications. While Margaret worked in consultancy and ran her own business, Margaret Fisher Associates, Peter worked in Forestry and wrote several articles for *Annals* related to this for over 10 years, especially about Murray Redgum forests.

    She said Fr Stenhouse came regularly to visit at their home in Sydney – there were not only many interesting serious conversations but also relaxing moments. Fr Stenhouse visited the Fishers' holiday home in Lennox Head, enjoying walking, swimming and conversation, though he was less keen on watching sport on television. Perhaps we must thank the Fishers for Fr Stenhouse's knowledge of cricket, such as it was, as he could converse about it capably in other situations as we shall see later.

    Fr Stenhouse was also a tour guide for the Fishers in Italy. However, what others considered suitable hotel accommodation differed from his view, which was usually at the cheaper end of the scale. Margaret tells of a trip down the Amalfi coast with a small group of friends for which Fr Stenhouse had booked the accommodation in advance – which proved to be very spartan. Spartan was 'normal' for Fr Stenhouse so, if food was included with the hotel fee, as it was in Sorrento, there was no going out to restaurants as Fr Stenhouse insisted that they all eat the hotel food as it was wasteful not to. She said it was pasta almost every night. But the guided tour was excellent. When walking around Rome, Fr Stenhouse would take his camera and sometimes, asking his friends to wait a while, would slip into churches, buildings and side streets. On one occasion there was a riot Italian style, with overturned cars and broken shop windows in the Piazza del Populo and naturally the journalist-priest went to find out more, to film it, emerging not long after.

Margaret came to realise just how simple and unmaterialistic Fr Stenhouse was, especially his habit of hanging on to his clothes until they were worn out. She decided to take him to Sydney's David Jones one day to buy him some new clothes as a gift, prompting his comment that he had never been to this store in his life. In fact, sometimes Fr Stenhouse asked the Fishers for advice on some worldly issues. Once, when there were some students living in a house in Randwick, worried about a tree that was threatening to fall on their abode, they asked Fr Stenhouse for help, who in turn asked Margaret and Peter for help. This was already the era where you could not chop down trees. After some intervention with the local Council, the matter was solved, with the tree chopped down. Fr Stenhouse also came to know friends and neighbours of the Fishers when they moved to Cabarita (in Sydney) assisting them with spiritual advice. Once, he was given a leather case for carrying a chalice when travelling, which he much appreciated. Margaret said his simplicity was evident in his fascination with supermarkets and in enjoying friendly conversations with friends in coffee shops at the local shopping mall.

Margaret and Peter were very knowledgeable about how to get things done. When (then) Archbishop Pell came to Sydney Fr Stenhouse suggested to her that "[t]he Archbishop needs some of your expertise." In fact Margaret's experience would prove invaluable when she was invited to join the Project Controls Committee for the building of the Domus Australia in Rome. She told me the Catholic Church had bought an old monastery and turned it into an Australian guest house. As you can imagine, this involved much negotiation with Roman authorities. If you think it difficult to deal with Australian organisations it is another thing entirely to deal with Italian ones! She said she visited Rome 12 times in three years to sit on a Committee including Cardinal Pell, Daniel Casey and Steven Newton. All ended in success. In addition, Margaret has been a member of the Professional Committee for the Archdiocese of Sydney and the board of Governors at Notre Dame University in Sydney.

A particularly moving journey came when Fr Stenhouse asked the Fishers to take him to Casino, where he was born and where his father had worked and died. It seems he felt he could ask the Fishers who willingly obliged. When they arrived at Casino, he saw the very house in Barker Street where the young Stenhouse family had lived. The Fishers took him to the Catholic church, thinking that Mass for his father had been said there on his death. However, Fr Stenhouse then asked to be taken to the Anglican church and they learned that the funeral service for his father had taken place there, as he was Anglican. One can only imagine the deep emotions passing through him.

Like other friends, Margaret and Peter found Fr Stenhouse "generous to a fault." Whether he brought Archbishop Pell to their house for dinner, or disappeared into Roman riots, they were very spiritually united in doing all they could for the good of the Church.

"He walked into our shop one day" – the friends from Trinidad-Tobago

Tania McLeod spent her early years in Trinidad which she recalls being very Catholic, despite the widespread practice of voodoo. The history of Trinidad begins with the settlements of the islands by Amerindians, specifically the Island Carib and Arawak peoples and both islands were visited by Christopher Columbus on his third voyage in 1498 who claimed them in the name of Spain. Trinidad remained in Spanish hands until 1797, though it was largely settled by French colonists. Tobago changed hands many times, between the British, French, Dutch, and Courlanders, but eventually ended up in British hands following the second Treaty of Paris (1814). Leaving its sad history of slavery, in 1889 the two islands were incorporated into a single crown colony and eventually obtained independence from the Britain in 1962 and became a republic in 1976. In recent times, it has become a refugee haven for Venezuelans who nowadays often sail the six kilometres separating Venezuela from Trinidad to escape political unrest.

Trinidad's history had a permanent affect on Tania's outlook and life. In particular, she mentions being educated by the Sisters of Cluny, for whom she has nothing but praise. In childhood she lived near the coast which was frequented by smugglers plying their trade. She experienced social unrest on the island, with announcements from loudspeakers – "Anyone who can go home, go home now." This was a prelude to military activity as people scuttled home. Sometimes Tania would hide in fear, hearing soldiers marching past. There would be lockdowns, no television, uncertainty – these were the years before independence.

Tania's mother was from Trinidad and her father was Australian who had lived in Trinidad for 20 years. Tania says her mother "was a trailblazer" having worked as a company secretary and manager in a jewellery firm in Trinidad. With the growing civil unrest there, however, the family decided to move to Australia. Her father Bruce departed first in April 1960 preparing the way for his wife Odette and their children to move later in the year. Before leaving the island, the family had witnessed pillaging of the churches, but in a masterstroke, Bruce managed to buy many of the religious artefacts, saving them from destruction, and shipping to Australia. These rescued religious objects pointed them in the direction of their new life. They opened an antique shop in South Dowling Street, Sydney – McLeod's Antiques. Many people came to see them, including Catholic clergy, seeking to buy sacred objects for chapels and churches. Meantime, Bruce was very active in bringing members of his community together, with Masses said for their families, as most were Catholic. He had no hesitation in doing this even though, while his wife Odette was Catholic, Bruce was Anglican.

Then one day, Fr Stenhouse walked into McLeod's Antique Shop out of the blue. It was "around 2000", according to Tania. He started talking to Bruce as he looked around. And so began the first of many interesting conversations and beautiful friendships. Bruce's first impression was that Fr Stenhouse was "well-read" and "knowledgeable about everything." As time went on the McLeods realised how true this impression was and the friendship grew. In time, Fr Stenhouse came to say an annual Mass for the Trinidad-Tobagan community at the Sacred Heart Monastery in Kensington and people from Guyana and Barbados would join them too. A student priest from Trinidad, the future Father Gerard Woo Ling, came to assist at Mass and this group gave him support during his studies and following his ordination to the priesthood.

Tania particularly remembers the fact that Fr Stenhouse would always come to join the community after Mass for lunch in the grounds of the Sacred Heart Monastery. There was something of a collective shock when the Trinidadians realised their priest friend knew about cricket, especially, as she says, "Trinidadians are crazy about cricket." This is doubly amazing as Fr Stenhouse evinced so little interest in other areas of sport but, as previously stated, he acquired sufficient knowledge of cricket from the Fishers to converse with his new Trinidadian friends about it. And there was something else that attracted him to cricket. Not long ago, Fr Stenhouse learned that he was related to Victor Trumper, the famous Australian cricketer, so this no doubt added great spice to what he said about it. Moreover, among the papers in his office, there were many pages of diagrams of cricket bowling positions and other explanations of cricket moves. So the never-ending conversations on cricket, history and antiques persisted, which is how Fr Stenhouse became a beloved friend of the Trinidad-Tobago community. When he celebrated Mass for the community in September 2019, he announced that this would be his last for them, preparing his saddened friends for his death. The McLeods spoke on behalf of the community:

> Fr Paul was so much to so many – a friend, advisor, advocate, confidante, teacher, journalist, scholar, linguist, he was the editor of the *Annals* publication (Chevalier Press), spiritual advisor and counsellor, a priest – to name but a few. Fr Paul was a firm believer in the Catholic Tradition and Teaching. He was devoted to the Blessed Virgin Mary and a great encouragement to those who knew him.[26]

9

SOWING COURTESY AND KINDNESS IN COMMUNITIES EVERYWHERE

> *A tree is known by its fruit; a man by his deeds.*
> *A good deed is never lost;*
> *he who sows courtesy reaps friendship,*
> *and he who plants kindness gathers love.*
>
> Saint Basil the Great (330 AD-379 AD)

> *He taught me selflessness, to care for the less fortunate in society.*
> *He would go out of his way to help a student in need,*
> *never counting the cost or the inconvenience.*
> *Fr Paul would just respond ...*
>
> Archbishop Julian Leow, friend of Fr Stenhouse.

Listening to the stories of Malaysian accountant and businessman Chris Lim is to hear wonderful accounts of courage, studies and achievement. It is to hear of a long friendship with Fr Stenhouse, his mentor and spiritual guide, and a deep gratitude shared by many Asian students who benefited from the wisdom of their priest-friend.

Chris came to Australia from Malaysia in 1962, attended the University of New South Wales and completed a Bachelor of Commerce degree there and then became a Chartered Accountant. The 1960s was the dynamic era of the Colombo Plan when numbers of students from Malaysia, Singapore, India, and Hong Kong were sponsored to study in Australia. The Colombo Plan was a regional initiative at the time and supported around 20,000 students between 1952 and 1985. In fact it was the University of New South Wales (UNSW) which first welcomed these scholarship students from regional countries. The Catholics among them would have been attracted to the nearby church of Our Lady of the Sacred Heart in Avoca Street, Randwick.

Chris lived in the Randwick area and came into contact with MSC priests in an era when several of them were assigned to live in the presbytery adjacent to Our Lady of the Sacred Heart (OLSH) church. Along with other Asian Catholics he went to Mass there and sought advice from priests as they were far from home. The MSC priests reached out to the increasing numbers of Asian students there – from Malaysia, Indonesia, Singapore, Hong Kong – and helped them in many ways which they do to this day. It was in this setting that Chris met Fr Stenhouse as he recalls, "sometime in the 1960s."[1]

After studying, some students returned to their home countries to take on various positions in their chosen fields, some quite eminent. Some stayed in Australia and entered various professions and areas of business. After his commerce and accounting studies, Chris opened up a retail sports shop in Belmore Road, Randwick, which sold rugby, soccer and cricket material. He remembers students and priests often coming into his store. With other Catholic Malaysians, he speaks of being "closely associated" with the priests in that parish, exchanging news and forming a network that would last all their lives.

The Randwick Asian Catholic Community and its wide reach

In 1980 a group of Asian students, with the MSC priests, formed a Randwick Asian Catholic Community (RACC) about which the 2015 edition of the OLSH magazine says:

35 years ago, Fr Ted Collins, then our parish priest noticed a growing number of Asian students in the parish. He thought that it would be a good thing for these students to meet besides coming for Mass and invited those interested in forming a group to meet him. He convinced Fr Lucas Leung OFM to assist, and on 5 October 1980, Frs Collins and Leung met with seven university students Andrew Lim, Anthony Lim, Christopher Lean, John Ho, Jono Gunawan, Joyce Voon and Valerie Wong. They discerned that group needed to provide a mix of social and spiritual activities, and the Randwick Asian Catholic Community (RACC) was born.[2]

They met at Ventnor, a historic sandstone building near the OLSH church. Ventnor was a venue for many associations (and still is) and is listed by the National Trust. The commemorative article quoted above also states:

> The RACC was blessed with much support from clergy and parishioners. It would be remiss of me though, not to name Br Valens Boyle SM, John and Catherine Sumantri, Paul and Annie Lau, Frank O'Connor, and Celine and Chris Lim, all of whom have been constant supporters of the group.[3]

The students from RACC went on excursions and retreats together within Sydney and beyond. They met at each other's houses, undertaking a great deal of outreach to the Little Sisters of the Poor, St Vincent de Paul work as well as Christmas carolling at the nearby hospitals and helping each other in times of need.

When Chris met Fr Stenhouse "sometime after a Mass" it was the beginning of a long friendship.[4] While Fr Stenhouse had not been there at the beginning of the organisation, when he did arrive on the scene, he became well known and beloved by many, within and beyond the borders of the RACC. Paul Lau and his wife Anne also remember Fr Stenhouse well. Paul became a chartered accountant and distinguished himself in the financial world as did Ken and Wendy Yap who were also students and members of the RACC. Sim Wee Teng found a ready guide and mentor in Fr Stenhouse and maintained lifelong contact with him.

One of the students, Julian Leow, had studied building and architecture at UNSW. On completing his studies, he secured a job in Singapore with a Japanese construction company and eventually returned to Malaysia to work in the 1990s. He entered the seminary and became a priest, more recently rising to be Archbishop Julian Leow, holding the most senior position in the Catholic Church in Malaysia. It was a pleasure to correspond with him. In a written account sent to me on 17 August 2020 (the following quotations are from this), he recalled:

> It must have been in 1985 in Randwick when I first joined RACC (Randwick Asian Catholic Community). Fr Paul was the Chaplain of RACC (or was it still Fr Pat Sharpe at that time … my memory fails me) and it must have been during our weekend Bible Study at Ventnor, OLSH that we must have met.

He describes Fr Stenhouse as a "father figure" to many as "we were overseas students in a foreign land":

> As chaplain for Overseas Students, he made it his personal commitment to assist in any way he could, any overseas student who encountered problems dealing with issues of education, immigration, financial, social and even personal … In my years of knowing Fr Paul, he had became a priest, a mentor, a friend and an inspiration towards my priesthood.

Archbishop Leow acknowledges Fr Stenhouse's influence:

> He taught me selflessness, to care for the less fortunate in

society. He would go out of his way to help a student in need, never counting the cost or the inconvenience. Fr Paul would just respond ... He really cared for those under his charge. He used to visit us students in our flats, usually late at night. He showed his care and concern in concrete ways, going out of his way to resolve all kinds of issues. He made time for others, even when he had very little of it for himself. Fr Paul was truly a Good Shepherd to many of us.

He is adamant Fr Stenhouse helped in his decision to become a priest. In 1994, he joined the College General Major Seminary in Penang, as a seminarian. He talked about his priestly vocation with Fr Stenhouse:

> ... [Fr Stenhouse] said he could get me admitted to the seminary in Sydney and serve the flock in Chinatown. I told him I was born a Malaysian for a purpose and needed to return home to respond to the call there.

The Archbishop notes Fr Stenhouse's further impact: "... he also taught me to expand my intellectual capabilities. He could speak 13 languages and almost gave up on Mandarin, which I believe was the last language he tried to master." The Archbishop perhaps sent him the teach yourself Chinese books which were found among Fr Stenhouse's books after his death.

Of their meetings in the following years, the Archbishop mentions that Fr Stenhouse stayed in his house in 1987 (in Seremban) and that he met up with his priest friend in 2003 and 2013 (in Sydney). Especially memorable was Fr Stenhouse's 80th birthday celebration in Kuala Lumpur and his Sydney meeting in 2018 where the Archbishop describes the last time they saw each other: "He was unwell but never complained nor made it known to others how serious his condition was." In a moving tribute he said, "[h]e reported the truth and never feared to express it. He was a truly humble giant."

Another Malaysian of Indian background, who befriended Fr Stenhouse in 2007, was Ganesh Sahathevan. With a background in law, journalism and taxation consultancy (having worked for KPMG and Price Waterhouse), Ganesh became a conduit of much information on Islam in Malaysia, Saudi Arabia and Iran. His investigation of financial trails for purportedly some Islamic charitable organisations in Australia led to interviews with the ABC and SBS, and to work with other like-minded groups.[5] He had contacts with intelligence gathering groups and was only too happy to share his findings with Fr Stenhouse. He was in awe at all the languages Fr Stenhouse knew and he felt understood when sharing his findings with him, giving eye-witness accounts of political situations in various countries. With regard to the drying up of Saudi oil wealth, he comments that "some princes now only fly in 747s, not in A380s." He relates that Fr Stenhouse was in Ethiopia in 2005 and saw Prince Al Waleed there (one of the nephews of the late Saudi king) with his retinue. From this he deduced that the Prince was seeking political favour in Ethiopia.

When Ganesh became disheartened at the lack of knowledge about Islam in Australia (having grown up in predominantly Muslim Malaysia), Fr Stenhouse encouraged him in his efforts to disseminate information and told him to keep trying, with the remark, "I have been at this for 30-40 years." Ganesh observed of his friend: "As a priest he had faculties and powers beyond his intellectual abilities … he embodied for me what Saint John Paul II understood by faith and reason." He was a spiritual advisor to Ganesh and in some sense still continues to be from beyond the horizons of this life: "I can confidently say he is overseeing my work."

Another student, Singaporean John Wong, was also a member of RACC, and had studied to be an architect. On graduation, he returned to Singapore, and having experienced the help of Father Stenhouse, left the line of earthly building for the more celestial building of God's kingdom on earth by becoming a Franciscan priest.

Then there was Alfred Wong from Hong Kong who became a long time friend. Alfred arrived in Australia in 1985 to undertake his HSC and then to study medicine at UNSW. A problem arose in the final stages of his medical studies for he had difficulties trying to obtain an internship here. Fr Stenhouse came to the rescue, for Alfred was one of many medical students with similar problems. On hearing of the internship difficulties, Fr Stenhouse managed some deft negotiations with university authorities. Need one ask the result? Alfred was given an internship at St Vincent's Hospital and graduated in 1994. He now practises medicine in Sydney and speaks warmly of his friendship with his priest friend – how they conversed, had meals at Eastgardens shopping centre and even watched 'Star Trek' at the Kensington Monastery.

When I rang Alfred he was seeing patients and said he would get back to me. He rang within minutes to talk about the priest for whom he had such a high regard and could not say enough to praise him. He related with some humour that Fr Stenhouse's Asian student friends were the first to get him a mobile phone in the early 1990s. It was one of those (by now) ancient big black Motorolas with an antenna. This was because the students had had some difficulties in contacting Fr Stenhouse in those pre-mobile days due to his busy life. So they rang him on his new Motorola which was later replaced by a smart phone. Alfred said that Fr Stenhouse "touched the hearts of many students", that he "lived for Christ" and "gave hope to others."

Quinney Chau, also from Hong Kong, sings the praises of Fr Stenhouse with evident emotion: "Father Paul ... he means so much to me and my husband. We all love Father Paul and should continue his spirit and passion within all of us." Quinney's husband David was prepared for Baptism by Fr Stenhouse, after the latter asked a simple question of him: "Why don't you become a Catholic, David?" David agreed to do so. This must be one of the easiest conversions to Catholicism on record.

As the Chaus worked in the garment industry, Quinney decided to donate gifts to Australian priests. She made many boxes of black shirts, in fact so many that they were given out to any priest who wanted them and were sent to seminaries. Like the loaves and fishes, they have not run out yet and there are still boxes in various places. While David has now passed away, Quinney braved the riots in Hong Kong, in true Stenhousian 'Indiana Jones' style, to attend the funeral of her great priest friend. I had the great privilege of conversing with her as I drove her back to her Sydney hotel, the day before she was due to fly back into rioting Hong Kong. She related her memories with tears in her eyes.

Many of Fr Stenhouse's students became friends and those who returned home became a focal point for many of Father Stenhouse's journeys to South East Asia, not to mention eyewitness sources of many articles in *Annals* on the state of the Catholic Church there. We have previously noted Fr Stenhouse's spiritual links with Lebanese politicians. Who knows what spiritual seeds were planted by Fr Stenhouse, and other MSC priests involved in many projects, as regards the fate of the developing world? While many in the West sought revolution, Fr Stenhouse moved quietly, mentoring young students, helping to build the future lives of key figures in their societies, always seeking ways to stability based on a well-informed, strong faith.. The inner power of such friendships can influence, indeed transform, the development of a country in the long term.

Visits, lifts, rosaries, helping the sick

Fr Stenhouse's help took myriad forms. From the very beginning, as Chris Lim says, Fr Stenhouse went the extra mile to help Asian students, visiting their homes, contacting their parents, reassuring them. Chris recalls Fr Stenhouse coming to say the rosary at his house with his family and other Malaysians in Randwick (and even further afield in Campbelltown) for decades. His children had a spiritual anchor growing up, absorbing the faith from a master teacher. And while some students rose to high positions in their fields, others came from poorer backgrounds and needed emotional and financial support. Chris said Fr Stenhouse "understood the poverty of the students" which he put down to Fr Stenhouse's own poverty in childhood, his mother having to raise two boys after the early death of her husband. Chris was deeply affected by this forevermore. This understanding heart of Fr Stenhouse was a talking point among the Malaysians.

Sometimes the Malaysian students were contacted regarding Asian students in need of help at Prince of Wales Hospital (POW) in Randwick. The MSC priests, Fr Stenhouse among them, were always willing to go there to give the Sacraments, consolation and whatever assistance they could. Sometimes the Malaysian students helped others outside their student group. Chris recounts that Fr Stenhouse helped a Chinese family whose daughter had severe Spina Bifida. No one could operate on her in China, but when she was brought to Sydney's POW Hospital, with the financial help of the Asian students in the RACC, Fr Stenhouse was on the scene to give much needed emotional, spiritual and practical support. The Malaysian community contacted a Mandarin-speaking professor of Chinese history to help boost the morale of the girl's father, Mr Chen. Mr Chen was a master in Qi Jong, a method of physical exercise, healing and meditation and held classes in Centennial Park for which people willingly paid. He taught some POW doctors his skills, at their request. In fact running these classes helped him raise much needed money. The operation on this occasion was successful. Against all odds, the family received permanent residency, after an application was made during Bob Hawke's time as Prime Minister.

Fr Stenhouse continued to help with various matters and arranged schooling for the son of Mr Chen at a Melbourne Catholic school.[6]

On another occasion, Chris told Fr Stenhouse that a group of Malaysians were concerned about a very sick boy in Malaysia. He had leukaemia and needed a bone marrow transplant but the Malaysian doctors did not hold out much hope. The boy's brother had suitable bone marrow and Australian doctors were willing to operate. The family was so poor, however, they could not afford the journey nor the treatment but with the help of the Australian Malaysian community and the RACC the boy was soon in POW Hospital. Chris called on his priest friend informing him, "Fr Stenhouse, there is a boy in hospital here ... he needs your help."[7] Fr Stenhouse responded immediately and gave whatever support he could to the family. While the operation was successful, however, the boy died afterwards from pneumonia. In the midst of the ensuing grief Fr Stenhouse consoled the family and friends, suggesting that "Something good will result from the death of this young boy." Chris says he was right. The money that the Malaysian community had raised for the medical costs (the doctors ended up waiving the medical costs) was given to the family who returned to Malaysia. With this money, the donor's brother had the chance to attend university which would have been previously impossible as the family was so poor. This altered their entire circumstances as the donor brother studied well, was able to come to Australia, attaining a high position in the financial world and was able to help many of his family and friends.

"Fr Stenhouse escaped from hospital to be with us"

Amid the countless stories, I was particularly struck by the one pertaining to an "early 85th" birthday party for Fr Stenhouse organised by his Malaysian friends in 2019. In fact, Fr Stenhouse had been in Kuala Lumpur five years previously at his 80th birthday party, as an honoured guest of RACC. There were celebrations

Fr Stenhouse with Quinney and David Chau in Hong Kong. Quinney made it through the Hong Kong riots to get to the funeral of Fr Stenhouse in Sydney. Fr Stenhouse influenced David to become a Catholic; Chris Lim (centre) with friends at the funeral of Fr Stenhouse at Our Lady of the Rosary Church in Kensington on 27 November 2019; Alfred Wong (back centre) with his family and Fr Stenhouse on his graduation day in 1994 as a medical doctor at the University of New South Wales; Fr Stenhouse helped him to obtain an internship at St Vincent's Hospital; with a young student Julian Leow, who later became a priest and is now Archbishop of Kuala Lumpur.

A few of the countless photos of graduations, marriage ceremonies, dinners, and various celebrations of many Asian students with Fr Stenhouse present; bottom left photo, with Archbishop Julian Leow in Kuala Lumpur. Archbishop Leow said Fr Stenhouse inspired him to become a priest; bottom right photo, Fr Stenhouse (centre back now) was invited to Malaysia for his 80th birthday by former students.

Blowing out the candles with some help from his friends; Fr Paul made a trip to the Liang family's hometown of Sarikei (Malaysia) having known the family since 1987. Belinda writes: "He had always heard of it and talked of it but had never visited. In January 2009, the family invited him to spend the Chinese New Year festival with them in Sarikei. This picture was taken after the Chinese New Year Mass at St Anthony's Church where he concelebrated with Fr Joseph. From left to right: Fr Paul, William (Roland's brother), Anna (William's wife), Emily (William's daughter), Fr Joseph (Parish priest), Timothy, Felix (William's son), Peter, Catherine (Roland's parents), Thomas, Belinda and Roland"; Fr Stenhouse with friends at his 'early' birthday party in July 2019. Chris Lim said he 'escaped' from hospital to be there. Fr Stenhouse was already very ill, a few months later he passed away; Belinda Yapp writes: "Fr Paul was our celebrant at our wedding at the monastery's chapel back in December 1997. In December 2017, we celebrated our 20th anniversary with a Mass at the Basilica di Santa Maria Maggiore in Rome. From left to right: Roland, Timothy, Fr Paul, Belinda and Thomas."

Fr Stenhouse, relaxing with friends in Bali; Mrs Han Fang Ryckmans at the funeral of Fr Stenhouse at Kensington, on 25 November 2019; Pierre Ryckmans, a longtime friend with whom Fr Stenhouse enjoyed much scholarly and witty conversation.

Jacob Majarian, photographer of Australian-Armenian background who accompanied Fr Stenhouse to his first trip to Armenia in 1991; Jacob being questioned by military police before entering a church for the installation of Karekin II, Supreme Patriarch and Catholicos of all Armenians. Fr Stenhouse then spoke to the military police, after which they allowed Jacob in; Armenians queuing for petrol with cans in 1991. There were many queues for essential supplies even after Soviet control ceased; Haghartsin Monastery in Armenia, dating from 1281. Jacob Majarian travelled throughout Armenia to photograph old churches and monasteries of the first country which converted to Christianity in 301 AD.

Jacob and Fr Stenhouse witnessed the ceremony to install Supreme Patriarch and Catholicos Karekin II in Yerevan, Armenia, in 1995. They took many photos. Jacob sent some to the Patriarch himself who was very pleased to receive them; Chai Changning, renowned flautist who played for the movie *Mao's Last Dancer*, cherished his friendship with Fr Stenhouse, who was instrumental in his conversion to Catholicism; Chai Changning playing 'The Mongolian Horseman' on the Chinese flute for his doctoral examination at the University of Sydney. He also played this with the group *Sirocco*.

and reunions with his loyal former students and friends, with Archbishop Leow present, with film clips made of this occasion, full of warmth and laughter. Seeing that Fr Stenhouse was very ill, Sunday, 29 July 2019, was set for an earlier celebration of his birthday (though the actual birthday was on 9 December). Chris and his wife Celine called at the MSC monastery to ask permission for the event. They then asked Fr Peter Hearn, the Randwick parish priest, to allow them to use Ventnor as a venue and he graciously agreed. However, the day before, 28 July, Fr Stenhouse was admitted to hospital and it looked like that was that. Chris cancelled the party realising how sick his priest friend was. But so determined was Fr Stenhouse to see his Malaysian friends, he discharged himself from hospital, explaining that he was coming to see them all.[8] Elated, Chris then rang the guests again – making 40 phone calls – and the celebration at Ventnor went ahead. Since then, Chris has declared far and wide that "Father Stenhouse escaped from hospital to be with us."

The RACC continues to be a close-knit group and Chris says that he receives about 20 emails a day from members informing him of their activities. He told me in one conversation that he had to leave as "[my] friend in Penang had a heart attack." He keeps in touch with wide networks of former students – the legacy of lifelong friendship and care continues ...

Vony Sugiarto: "He was always genuinely interested in our lives, our family, our culture"

Indonesian Vony Sugiarto was in tears at Fr Stenhouse's funeral. She remembers meeting her priest friend when she was a student, with her sister and another Indonesian friend. She had become a Catholic before coming to Australia (her parents were Buddhist) and was studying computer engineering at UNSW in 1990-1992. Her older sister, Merry, decided to convert in Australia and had instruction from Fr Stenhouse to prepare for her baptism in 1991. In a written account Vony recalled:

> He would drive to pick up another male university student and then pick up my sister and took them both to his office for catechism classes and then drove them back home again ... She was later baptized by Fr Paul along with two other young male Asian students. He gave a reference for my younger sister to study at St Vincent College and willingly became her guardian in high school.[9]

Vony says that after her sister was baptised, 'Fr Paul' continued to visit them and sometimes gave them transport to the airport. In 1992, when she was writing her engineering thesis, he spent time proofreading and correcting her written English. While Fr Stenhouse no doubt learned something of computer engineering, it turned out that he asked Vony for help with rendering Arabic translation to English, via a suitable font. She remembers:

> Fr Paul needed help with a problem he had while translating a book from Arabic to English. My friend, Gershwin Luhur, and myself helped him with creating a special font for MS Word for him. Gershwin and I spent quite some hours with him over many months.

She is sure that this contact strengthened the friendship between Fr Stenhouse and computer savvy friend Gershwin Luhur and his wife. The friendship extended beyond computer font in Arabic to many aspects of their life and culture:

> He ... came to the rescue with any help we needed. Even though he was extremely busy, he was always welcoming when we came to see him. He was very humble even though he was very intelligent and knowledgeable ...

There were many friends he visited, including Roland and

Belinda Liang, and Vony recalls him visiting her sick and elderly friends and relatives:

> I knew early on that Fr Paul was very apostolic. He was always running around from saying Mass at different Parishes all over Sydney to promoting Annals (back in the early 1990s), to visiting sick or elderly friends or relatives, or simply visiting someone in need of help. He seldom preached to us about the faith unless we asked him about it but his care and generosity for everyone and outlook in life was so attractive, that it gave witness to others. He respected everyone whatever their religions were. My parents are Buddhist and they could relate easily with Fr Paul. He seemed to know a lot about the Chinese rituals and when I had questions, he could explain a lot to me. During my time at University, I introduced some other university friends to him. I know a few of them that at the end became Catholic, including their whole family too.

Vony remembers Fr Stenhouse's journeys to Indonesia and his searches for gongs:

> ... He came to Indonesia a few times for both of my sisters' weddings and another time to attend the Annual Eucharistic procession in Ganjuran, Central Java (he wrote about this in *Annals*). In Jakarta, he saw that the Mass used a gong at the consecration instead of bells. He wanted to buy a gong so we took him to a street in Jakarta where many shops sell antiques and he was so happy when he finally found two antique gongs. My mum had to help bargain with the shop keeper. The gongs sat on his office for some time but I think it might be in use by the church in Randwick now (not so sure about this actually as this happened more than 20 years ago).

Of course, Fr Stenhouse often gave Vony and her friends copies of *Annals* to take home and he mentioned its current topics and his journeys. He often talked to them about the persecution of Christians in Indonesia and in Malaysia. Occasionally, when translating something from Arabic, Vony relates that Fr Stenhouse would give his Indonesian friends insights about Islam and the latest book he was working on. He gave Vony his 10-part series on Apologetics defending the Catholic Church. She says that he was "trying to help me as I was going out with a friend from University, Rudy, a zealous Presbyterian (as Fr Paul would describe him)." While Vony and Rudy left Australia for some years on graduation, they returned to Sydney and initiated preparation for marriage:

> Fr Paul helped prepare us for marriage and was the celebrant in our wedding (on 19 November 2000) and eventually also baptized all our children. My husband, Rudy, was a Presbyterian until about nine years ago, when he converted to Catholicism. Fr Paul never put pressure [on] him but always answered his questions about the faith. Over many years, he came to the city ... to have lunch with Rudy. From this genuine friendship and his example, among other graces from God, Rudy converted to Catholicism.

She recalls that "Fr Paul was like our own family" and that despite his many commitments, he travelled to their family home, 45 minutes drive from the monastery. He would celebrate birthdays of family members, welcome them at the monastery, help when they consulted him on choosing schools for their children and wrote references. If Fr Stenhouse found out that Vony and her family were catching a flight, "he would insist on us parking our car at the monastery and he would give us a ride to the airport." Vony cannot forget his cheerfulness and helpfulness:

> Fr Paul has given so much of his time for others all the time that he probably slept very little at night to do his important work with *Annals* and other projects. When he

drove us either to the airport or to have a meal somewhere, he was always finding routes that had the least ... traffic and traffic lights, even if that meant a longer distance, but would try to save time. We had the impression that he was always very efficient, if not in a hurry on the road as if trying to squeeze in more time. But when we talked to him, he never seemed to rush but gave us his full attention. He was always very cheerful and we never left without a good laugh with him. We really miss those conversations with him.

And conversations with Pierre Ryckmans ...

Another long-time friend of Fr Stenhouse was Pierre Ryckmans (1935-2014), widely known by his pen name Simon Leys but I will use his real name here. Ryckmans was a Belgian-Australian, a university professor of Chinese literature and language, a writer, essayist, literary critic, translator, art historian, calligrapher, and political commentator. He understood the various dimensions of Chinese culture and was one of the first intellectuals to denounce the Communist cultural revolution in China and the idolisation of Mao in the West in his trilogy: *Les Habits neufs du président Mao* (1971), *Ombres chinoises* (1974) and *Images brisées* (1976). He guest-edited a special China issue of *Quadrant* in 1978. Journalist Luke Slattery remarked that Pierre Ryckmans' adoption of a literary pseudonym, Simon Leys, was originally inspired by the novel *René Leys* (the name of its main character), set in Beijing towards the end of the Qing Dynasty. In addition to liking this character, Pierre's use of a pseudonym was a prudent measure for a young scholar hostile to the Communist Chinese regime. He won many awards including the Prix Renaudot, the Prix Mondial Cino Del Duca, the Prix Guizot and the Christina Stead Prize for fiction. In 1996 Ryckmans delivered the ABC's Boyer Lectures. A detailed outline of his life and work is given in Philippe Paquet's fascinating biography *Simon Leys: Navigator between Worlds* (2018).

Anne Elizabeth McLaren, Professor of Chinese Studies at the University of Melbourne and outspoken critic of distorted Western notions of China, said of Pierre:

> To ardent Maoists of the 1960s and 70s he was the bête-noire of sinology — one of the few China-watchers who turned his barbed wit and invective against the high tide of adulation for the Chinese leader that swept through leftist circles in the West.[10]

Pierre came from a large Belgian family and studied law and art history at the Université Catholique de Louvain [now the Katholieke Universiteit Leuven]. He studied law to follow a family tradition and art to pursue his personal interest.[11] A turning point came when he got the chance to visit China in 1955. In an 2011 interview with Daniel Sanderson, editor of the *Chinese Studies Association of Australia Newsletter*, Pierre recalled :

> The Chinese Government had invited a delegation of Belgian Youth (10 delegates – I was the youngest, age nineteen) to visit China for one month (May 1955). The voyage—smoothly organized – took us to the usual famous spots, climaxing in a one-hour private audience with Zhou Enlai. My overwhelming impression (a conclusion to which I remained faithful for the rest of my life) was that it would be inconceivable to live in this world, in our age, without a good knowledge of Chinese language and a direct access to Chinese culture.[12]

This conviction was to bear fruit within a very short time – via travels in Africa. The young Pierre went to the Congo to help his uncle, also named Pierre Ryckmans, who was a Governor General there from 1934 to 1946 and then delegate for Belgium to the

United Nations Trusteeship Council in 1946, helping negotiate with various nations in petitions, disputes and treaties. When the younger Pierre Ryckmans visited his uncle in Leopoldville for three months, in late 1955, his genuine fascination for all cultures grew to an ever greater consuming interest. Influenced by his uncle, Pierre's searching mind did not seek the merely exotic, but engaged with the heart and soul of any new culture. Another significant influence on the younger Pierre's life was his philologist uncle, Monsignor Gonzague Ryckmans, whose work fascinated Fr Stenhouse no end, and who wrote of him in *Annals*:

> Gonzague was a pioneer in the study of pre-Islamic Arabian ipgraphy of South Seminite inscriptions and especially of the ancient Sabaeo-Minaean language and culture that flourished in what was ancient Sheb – today call Yemen – from about 750BC to 115 BC.[13]

Young Pierre's cousin, Jacques Ryckmans, also became a scholar of ancient languages. With such an adventurous and scholarly pedigree, it is not entirely surprising that Pierre turned his mind to learning all he could about China, which had been his first inspiration in 1955. As he could not return to mainland China, now in the throes of revolution, he went to Taiwan to study Chinese and stayed there for twelve years. For his Ph.D, he did ground-breaking work on a treatise on painting by Shitao, a creative genius of the early eighteenth century.

When I spoke to Pierre's wife, Han Fang Chang (also known as Frances) Ryckmans, her memories ranged over such a panorama of the past century's dramatic events, that it was riveting to hear it from one who had experienced them.[14] Han Fang said she was born in China, that her mother was a Catholic and her father a Buddhist, a hydraulic engineer by profession.[15] A year before the Communist revolution in China, the family escaped to Taiwan where she grew up and later met and married Pierre in 1964. After spending time in Hong Kong and Singapore, in 1970 came a life-changing event. Pierre was offered a position at ANU, that of heading the Department of Chinese. This is what brought him to Canberra and suburban Garran:

> Professor Liu Ts'un-yan (Head of the Chinese department at ANU) came to see me in Hong Kong and invited me to join his department. Thus, with my wife and four (very young) children, we moved to Canberra for what was supposed to be a three-year stay, but turned out to become our final, permanent home.[16]

Pierre looked on the years at ANU as happy ones, having great admiration for professor Liu Ts'un-yan and was to give moving commemorative speeches extolling him later in 2009.[17] Later in 1987 he was invited to become head of Oriental Studies at the University of Sydney where he stayed till his retirement in 1993. Han Fang remarked that the students from Hong Kong and Singapore were amazed at their professor's "perfect Mandarin" and his profound knowledge of Chinese culture as well as Western literature, often expressing great gratitude to their teacher.

Then, came yet another fateful event, when Pierre met Father Stenhouse. As Han Fang recounts it, John and Judy Wheeldon, friends of Trish Kavanagh, Father Stenhouse's cousin, held a dinner one evening in 1986 to which they invited the Ryckmans. They also invited Fr Stenhouse, no doubt at the instigation of Trish Kavanagh. One can just imagine the resonance of minds, and the intellectual and personal friendship which lit up at that meeting, for Pierre was as fascinated with Fr Stenhouse's knowledge of Arabic (and all else) as Fr Stenhouse was with Pierre's expertise in Chinese culture (and all else). Han Fang tells us that this kind of conversation between like-minded intellectuals continued for the rest of their lives. They met at dinners, met in Europe, met at the Sacred Heart Monastery, attended art exhibitions and conferences. Many results of their discussions found their way into print. Pierre had a wide international scholarly network and he wrote for *Annals*.

Pierre Ryckmans deeply supported the thinking expounded by John Henry Newman in *The Idea of a University* (1852), and tried fervently to enable its true existence but he lamented the incursion of politically correct thinking into the universities. Han Fang said that her husband retired before his designated retirement age because of this. Anne McLaren writes that he was "sick at heart" with the increasing commercialisation of most universities. With sadness, he realised that tertiary education had become an export industry in which those running universities focused on business and acquired "the salaries and reputations of bank barons."[18] He saw them as:

> ...a bazaar where a thousand wares are spread haphazardly, while the scholars themselves are turned into peddlers, touts and pimps, desperately competing to hustle for a few more suckers.[19]

Like Fr Stenhouse, Pierre held to high standards of learning and was uncompromising on the role of scholarship and the true role of a university, which was not to be selling degrees, but to be a place where scholars' priority was the quest for truth and interior growth. When Campion College opened in 2006, the opening dinner was held at The Mint building in Macquarie Street, Sydney. As Karl Schmude related to me, it was Fr Stenhouse who suggested the Occasional Speaker, Pierre Ryckmans, later publishing Pierre's address in *Annals*.

It must have been a true relief for the two scholars to enjoy the depths of an intellectual and spiritual friendship, exchanging insightful, penetrating and scathing observations of the times. Each took a great interest in the other's work. What Phillipe Paquet said of Pierre Ryckmans, that he had a "daring, darting and capacious mind", can be equally applied to Fr Stenhouse.[20] The latter would have appreciated the aphorisms issuing from his friend, such as the one taken from 4th century BC Chinese philosopher Zhuang Zi: "Everyone knows the usefulness of what is useful, But few know the usefulness of what is useless."[21] Pierre saw in Fr Stenhouse a fellow mind which ranged over the whole world and he was quite happy to become chairman of the editorial board of *Annals*!

Fr Stenhouse regularly visited the Ryckmans' apartment in Darling Point and came to know his children, Etienne, Jeanne, Marc and Louis, officiating at the marriages of his daughters and baptising their children. In his *Annals* tribute, Fr Stenhouse called Pierre my "dear and valued friend." He spoke of a discussion on writing itself, with Pierre's comment on Wittgenstein's remark about Tolstoy: "There's a *real* man; who has a *right* to write", adding:

> Pierre and I discussed how our cyber generation would struggle to comprehend this [i.e. how to write], armed with its Apple or PC and spellcheck, and raised on a false belief in everyone's right to express their opinions no matter how wrong, bizarre or anti-social.[22]

Both men had delved long and deeply into literature, history and the human soul. Both had a sharp wit, constantly unmasking foolish claims and faulty scholarship. Their purview was the whole world and the human spirit.

And then there were Armenian journeys with Joseph Majarian

In Fr Stenhouse's office were papers with plans for a series of articles about Armenia for he had a great interest in this country. When the Armenian Patriarch, His Beatitude Nerses Peter XIX Tarmouni, visited Australia in 2001, to celebrate the 1700th anniversary of the conversion of Armenia to Catholicism, he led the long, colourful, heavily incensed procession into St Mary's Cathedral so he could say Mass with his Armenian brother priests behind him. Also in the procession was Fr Stenhouse and following it all was Jacob Majarian.

Jacob's family, of Armenian background, migrated to Australia via Lebanon. Jacob longed to visit Armenia which held a strong fascination for him. In particular he wanted to take photos of this country which was the very first to convert to Christianity (in 301 AD) and which had suffered greatly throughout history. It is well known that 1.5 million of the Armenian population were killed in what is known as the Armenian Genocide, and those who were able to escape became a wide diaspora in many countries around the world.[23] For a long time, many were afraid to return, or unable to do so under the Soviet regime under whose control Armenia fell. With the impending 'end' of the Soviet Union, Jacob set his sights on this persecuted country and so did Fr Stenhouse – even before they met! I was fortunate to meet Jacob and hear the story of his meeting with Fr Stenhouse and how they travelled together to Armenia at a pivotal point in its history.

Through the efforts of Armenian priest (later bishop) Anton Totonjian, Fr Stenhouse organised his first journey to Armenia in 1991.[24] As Fr Totonjian also knew Jacob, and knew of his passion for photography, he thought it a good idea that Fr Stenhouse and Jacob should meet and go together. The plan was that Fr Stenhouse would travel ahead to Paris to meet the Armenian Eparch, and Jacob would meet him there, in the airport lounge of Charles de Gaulle Airport, from where they would travel together to Armenia. Jacob flew to Paris and waited in the lounge to meet this mysterious person for the first time. Fr Stenhouse was dropped off at the Charles de Gaulle airport by Krikor Bedros XX Gabroyan himself, the Armenian Catholic Eparch and Bishop of France at the Éparchie Sainte-Croix-de-Paris des Arméniens.[25] Jacob had had a long wait in the airport lounge but did not dare put his baggage into a locker and go elsewhere, as his packed camera equipment was too valuable to risk. After several hours, he saw a tall priest walking towards him in the distance and recognised Fr Stenhouse's face immediately from the photos he had seen of him. It was July 1991. The Soviet Union had not yet released Armenia from its clutches – that was to come a few months later. In fact they were travelling at a rather dicey time.

The plane took off and arrived in Yerevan, the capital of Armenia, minus the luggage of Fr Stenhouse and Jacob – not a good start. Fortunately Jacob had his camera with him but not all the film he had packed and had hoped to use. Without their suitcases, they both went on to their booked hotel, one which had often been used by Communists. Meanwhile Jacob tried desperately to buy some film. Anyone who has tried these searches in Communist countries understands the angst involved. As it turned out, Fr Stenhouse came to his aid by giving him some East German rolls of film he happened to have with him, though where he got these is a mystery. Perhaps he had learned from his Dubrovnik days to be prepared for anything in Communist countries.

Fr Totonjian had organised for the pair to have meals in other people's houses as food was rather sparse at the hotel. So Jacob recalls an endless round of calling on various Armenian friends and having breakfasts there. To their great relief, their missing baggage arrived one week later. Jacob and Fr Stenhouse were able to visit and photograph old churches, many in a state of decay but in pristine, beautiful surroundings, for the landscapes in Armenia are breathtaking – the word Jacob used was "ethereal." From these photos, Jacob was to put together a book of stunning photographs called *Picture Armenia* (2009) for anyone interested in seeing this virtually unknown country. Though he was only there for a week on this occasion, Fr Stenhouse was very focused on getting to know the situation in Nagorno-Karabakh, next to Armenia, where war had broken out between the Armenians and Azerbaijanis. As some readers may recall, it was a hot item on the news for a while in the early 1990s (and sadly is again now, at time of writing). With the impending implosion of the Soviet Union, the Christian Armenian area of Nagorno-Karabakh wanted to secede from Muslim Azerbaijan, within which it forcibly lived, and from which many refugees had fled now that the dogs of war had been aroused. Fr Stenhouse managed to get to see where many refugees had escaped to within Armenia. He interviewed them with interpreters, obtaining first hand information about their plight. His reports would have doubtless reached Aid to the Church in Need, the Vatican and, of course, they reached *Annals*.

The second journey to Armenia with Father Stenhouse, which Jacob undertook in 1995, revealed even further the post-Soviet difficulties of the country. The 'end' of the Soviet Union did not bring the end to these difficulties – shortages, queues, pervasive military control. Jacob vividly recalled that one passenger had a full bottle of vodka and drank its entire contents during the Aeroflot flight to Yerevan. No doubt this was a strategy to steady the nerves. As he had boarded, Jacob noticed water drops falling from the ceiling of the plane. He also saw people boarding the plane, putting their knees over their voluminous baggage, evidently not trusting the process of booking their luggage through. When he and Fr Stenhouse reached Yerevan, they saw the queues for bread, water taps not working and little or no electricity, lingering evidence of past 'Soviet planning.' This time the pair stayed in the house of a friend of Fr Anton, an Armenian artist Vladimir Gregorian. The accommodation was quite cramped and Vladimir's wife left to stay with others. This was in order to prepare meals for Vladmir, Fr Stenhouse and Jacob who noticed they all wore many layers of jumpers to keep warm in the shivering cold. During this 1995 visit the new 'Catholicos' was elected, the head of the Armenian

Apostolic Church (Orthodox) and Jacob and Fr Stenhouse wanted to take photos. When Jacob tried to enter the church, guards were blocking his entrance and as he felt hesitant in such a situation, he did not argue the point. Fr Stenhouse, however, just told the guards "[he]e has to get in" and, whatever it was in his tone of voice, the guards immediately allowed them both in, enabling Jacob to take some hauntingly beautiful shots of the event, which he later sent to the new Catholicos himself who greatly appreciated them.

Jacob and Fr Stenhouse also visited Gumyri, where there was a small church where nuns looked after orphans. Jacob photographed location after location (he has now visited Armenia 29 times!) and Fr Stenhouse collected information and did interviews revealing this fascinating land to those interested. On this journey Fr Stenhouse came to know Vladimir Gregorian well. Vladimir later visited Australia with the help of Fr Stenhouse and exhibited his art there, also including it in *Annals*.

Jacob said his parents and brother Peter got to know Fr Stenhouse well over the years, with regular visits to their home, noting that Father Stenhouse treated him and his parents as family. As time went on, Jacob came to build bookshelves for the old office Fr Stenhouse used and also built the outstanding new ones in the more recent office, constructing a platform so it would be safe for his priest friend to ascend to the higher shelves, remarking with affection, "he is a person who truly deserves it." He also recalls that Fr Basil would ask Fr Stenhouse to the Armenian Catholic church in Lidcombe to say Mass when the priest had to be elsewhere. Fr Stenhouse always obliged.

In the latter months of 2019, Jacob, along with his brother Peter, has especially poignant memories of taking the ailing Fr Stenhouse to a hamburger shop in Gardeners Road one evening (391 Gardener's Road) where he claimed 'real' hamburgers were made (though Hungry Jacks might dispute this!). After their enjoyable hamburger, they asked Fr Stenhouse what he would like, which was a caramel milkshake, another favourite. The hamburger shop could not make it but Jacob and Peter made sure they found a place which sold them. This was just before Fr Stenhouse signed off on the last *Annals* and went into palliative care. When looking over more recent editions of *Annals*, shortly before Fr Stenhouse's death, Jacob recalls flicking the pages with him, and seeing a painting of a swagman, with Fr Stenhouse commenting, "this picture reminds me of myself", an enigmatic comment, perhaps thinking of himself as a spiritual pilgrim.

Looking wistfully ahead, Jacob said he was "a very simple" person who "never boasted" and never "behaved like an intellectual." He managed everything because he "was top of things, was organised." Jacob said of his unforgettable friend, "people look for someone like that", someone "who was authentic".

Chai Changning and meeting the messenger of the Living God

Many recall seeing the Oscar winning movies *The Last Emperor* (1987) and *Mao's Last Dancer* (2009) and might remember the haunting flute music in the background. The flautist who played in these movies was Chai Changning, who was also a friend of Father Stenhouse. Chai was born in China, in Sian (or Xi'an), the ancient capital of the Middle Kingdom capital of Shaanxi Province in northwest China. Interestingly, Sian, as one of the oldest cities in China, is the starting point of the Silk Road and home to the Terracotta Army of Emperor Qin Shi Huang (and yes, at some point Fr Stenhouse travelled the Silk Road).

When Chai was a young boy, his father introduced him to playing a Chinese bamboo flute which the boy took to playing with ease after a few lessons. Not long afterwards, his father bought him another flute as he was obviously musically gifted, indeed a child prodigy. At age nine, he was chosen to go where "millions of people want to go", to the prestigious Chinese Music Conservatory in Beijing. Here all gifted children reside and are treated with great largesse. Here Chai made rapid progress. He remarks that "we were privileged" but "the demands were great too." Practice was at least six hours a day but Chai says he was full of "determination" and went along with the abiding expectation of "Success, discipline, and obey the rules."[26]

As a young adult, Chai obtained a Professional Staff Scholarship, awarded by the NSW Conservatorium of Music, and came alone to Australia to further his experience. From this started a new chapter in his life involving performance, playing in films, concerts, performing with the group Sirocco, lecturing, completing a Doctorate at Sydney University and having the famous flute player James Galway call him a rare maestro. Amongst all these extraordinary experiences, he lived in a Clovelly apartment in eastern Sydney and practised the music of Western classical composers such as Mahler, Beethoven and Bach as well as classical bamboo flute music. He played the hauntingly beautiful 'Song for Mongolia' as part of his doctoral examinations at Sydney University.[27]

While most people would be content with such a brilliant flautist as their neighbour, one day a university student came knocking on Chai's door as he was playing a Mozart piece, saying she had an exam and asking if he could tone it down. She had no idea who Chai was. Nevertheless many did know, and he was invited to play in many places – including churches. Early in 1988, he found himself playing at the Church of Our Lady of the Sacred Heart in Randwick wheree he met Father Stenhouse. Though Chai was not a Catholic himself, nor did he have any inclination to become one, he recalls that day well: "I met Father Paul in March 1988 after I arrived from Beijing" and he continued to meet him at various churches. In one of their conversations, Fr Stenhouse said to him, of his flute playing that, "you are God's messenger" which gave Chai some pause for thought. As he continued to delight audiences with his music, Chai began to sense that the music he performed indeed came from God, but pondered who God was. Fr Stenhouse knew how to send out subtle messages, and such stirrings within the soul meant something. Chai had no idea where this would all lead.

In 2001 Chai returned to China to visit his family. He really wanted to find out more about his grandfather who had passed away and to visit his tomb. It must be remembered that many Chinese buildings and cemeteries had been destroyed in the enormous race for progress and all Chai could do, with his father and uncle nearby, was to stand on a roadside where the tomb had once been as the cemetery had been destroyed. Chai's father was a Party official and after questioning him, Chai was astounded to learn that his grandfather had been a Catholic, who previously lived in the city of Shin Dong. Not only that, but his grandfather had been very artistic and well-known for his art, and had been educated by Italian missionaries in the days when missionaries still lived in China, something too risky to mention under communism. As the mysterious pages of his family history unfurled, Chai learned that despite the Communist Party parameters of his life, the family had been largely Catholic. Afterwards, when the family lived in Sian, the grandfather, whose baptismal name was Joseph, took to preserving as much as he could of Chinese art, and was instrumental in saving the city walls and other parts of the city, including the bell tower, though much did go under the bulldozers.

Chai was astonished that his family had been Catholics. Now, with his interest well and truly aroused in his family's attempts at preservation of ancient buildings, he turned his thoughts to the Catholic dimension of his family history. He learned that Chinese excavators had sometimes unearthed crosses when they laid new foundations and people would remark that there had been a

Christian church there once. Chai kept unearthing his own complex and remarkable story.

On his return from China, Chai told Fr Stenhouse about the discovery of his family's Catholic background. Fr Stenhouse made another subtle comment to Chai, namely, "before I die, I hope you will come back to the family", a veiled encouragement to convert to the faith of his ancestors. For Chai, it was like the unfolding of an invisible, captivating world. In time, he came to understand that he wanted to be a Catholic so, about six months before Easter in 2016, he made the decision and put it to Fr Stenhouse who took on the preparation for his baptism. Chai relates that, "every week I came to Sacred Heart Monastery and studied the *Catholic Catechism* under the mentorship of Father Paul." This preparation culminated in the Chai's baptism, which he called "the greatest memory of my life":

> I was baptised at the Bishop Henri Verjus Chapel on Easter Sunday (on16 April 2016) at 1, Roma Avenue, Kensington, NSW. The attendees were my Mother , older sister, my late wife and friends of Mr Chen, Mr Carl Spain and Greg Spain, in a very small group. I was following the call of my "Living God" and finally back to the FAMILY. I was and have always remained so touched! It was an unforgettable experience and the greatest memory of my life! [28]

Chai greatly respected his new, knowledgeable friend and said that with all the joys and difficulties of his life, "Father Paul was always by my side to support me." While Fr Stenhouse had said Chai was "God's messenger", Chai came to understand that Fr Stenhouse was "the messenger of the Living God" in his life. When Chai speaks of this, the artist, poet, mystic and religious seeker within him all converge. He is deeply moved that his priest friend had brought his soul to understand who he truly was, and what eternity meant.

10

ANDIAMO! AND ON TO ETERNITY

Wings and Streams
Carrying me unto Thee,
The Sea of Goodness from whence they came.

'A Thanksgiving and Prayer for the Nation'
Thomas Traherne

Happy are those who die in the Lord! Happy
indeed the Spirit says: now they can rest
forever after their work, since their good deeds go with them.

Apocalypse 14:13

Fr Stenhouse was a puzzle to his doctor who said he was "the only man I know who has lived through four cancers" (as recounted to me by Peter Macinante, *Annals* office manager). Fr Stenhouse told me a few years before he died that a particular cancer had disappeared, and that in fact this had happened four times with malignant growths. Of course if he mentioned he were sick, people would immediately start praying. Who knows, Heaven may have been stormed by many earthly brigades of prayer, thus helping to give him extended tenure on earth. Such seemingly 'miraculous' cures aroused quiet amazement, but Fr Stenhouse just carried on as usual with his pastoral work, travelling and writing, even when he succumbed to a fifth cancer, letting people know about this in 2019, the year he died.

Fr Stenhouse, as do many writers, had diaries for each year, going back decades.[1] Such diaries are not collections of thoughts and feelings, rather appointment books with occasional observations. In his final diary of 2019, he had listed many names to ring, lunches to attend, people to see. For example, there are regular appointments with Peter Coleman who was very ill and then on 4 April 2019 he notes the funeral date. Throughout May 2019 he records times for meeting Piers Akerman, Tony Abbott, Fr Jim Littleton, Jamie Stenhouse as well as Jim and Irene Franklin. He mentions meeting Joseph and Angela Assaf on 30 May at 6pm and notes in this final diary that he is to say Mass for the Brown Nurses in Coogee, which he did throughout that year, not to mention his constant attendance at medical appointments, scans, blood tests and discussion of his condition.[2]

On 16 August 2019 he writes that Karl Schmude will come to see him and has a quotation nearby, perhaps given to him by Karl or gleaned from elsewhere – "the fanatic is always concealing a secret doubt" – and informs us that this comes from George Smiley in John le Carré's spy novel *Tinker, Tailor, Soldier, Spy*, a significant comment as Fr Stenhouse abhorred fanaticism. He was an inveterate collector of sayings, aphorisms, and *bon mots* which he may have found useful. He also owned a book which I saw in his office labelled 'Bedside Notes' in which he had some jottings, doubtless not to lose any good ideas that floated by at night and to remind himself of appointments. On Saturday, 14 September, among other appointments, he noted that he is to meet his friends from Trinidad and Tobago. In fact, the appointments with various groups and people go well beyond the day he died.

When told he did not have long to live, sometime during 2019, those who knew Fr Stenhouse recall that he was busy getting things organised before departing this earth, though no one knew when this would happen and many hoped it would be postponed or simply would not happen. He managed to get the final edition of *Annals* completed at the beginning of November that year. He had given a lecture at his beloved Campion College on 19 October 2019 when he spoke of John Farrell and his reformist ideas. I met him after this lecture and he was filled with joy at the interest people had shown in what he said.

Throughout the year he had regularly gone out to have coffee with Fr Stidwill, Fr Austin and Bishop Moore at a local cafe.[3] While there, Fr Austin speaks of people coming up to Fr Stenhouse in the shopping centre and having a chat. Cafe owners, fruiterers and others at the mall knew him – all wanted to chat. Given the length and breadth of his contacts, one could say this was likely to happen anywhere Fr Stenhouse went.

As his cancer was progressing, Fr Stenhouse drove one day to visit Agnes Nguyen, the sister of the Vietnamese Cardinal Francis-Xavier Nguyễn Văn Thuận (now Venerable), who suffered imprisonment under the Communist regime for 13 years (died on 16 September 2002) and whose cause for beatification is in progress. Agnes, as it happens, is the Cardinal's only living sibling and resides not far from the monastery. I had met her by chance outside a church in Maroubra one day, and spoke to her with a view of writing an article about her memories of her saintly brother. Agnes graciously agreed and in the course of our interview, I learned that she had not yet met Fr Stenhouse. I became the go-between and drove her to meet him at the monastery soon afterwards with each delighted to meet the other. Then, as his health worsened, Agnes related that Fr Stenhouse came to visit her in quest of a relic of her brother Cardinal which Agnes gladly gave him. Doubtless this relic gave great consolation and helped Fr Stenhouse complete his mission on earth. For he still had the last edition of *Annals* to complete – which he did, no doubt with the help of Venerable Xavier Nguyễn Văn Thuận and other saints whose help he had sought. Agnes told me, "I am so glad I met him."

At one stage, not long before his death, he had a visit from Tony Abbott with whom he had had an enduring friendship. He told me, "I first met Fr Paul in the late 80s, I think, at a lunch organised by the late John Wheeldon and also attended by Joseph Assaf. That was the start of a friendship of over 30 years."[4] Although there were sometimes no more than a few meetings per year, he remarked that "Paul was one of those people who would resume a conversation where it had left off, even if that was months or years earlier!" When he heard from Dennis Shanahan that his priest-friend was terminally ill he went to visit him reflecting that he was "frail but still extremely lucid." After the usual pleasantries and reflections on the state of the world, Fr Stenhouse, after some questioning from Tony, spoke on the nature of the separation of the body and soul after death, how we are more than our bodies, that our souls will be with other souls. I doubt that there are many who could speak like this near death. Abbott had asked several priests and ministers the same question, and considered Fr Stenhouse's answer to be more lucid than any he had previously received – even as his friend's life was ebbing to its close:

> Fr Paul's response is the most thoughtful I've yet heard and entirely typical of a man who was both highly intellectual and deeply spiritual.

Abbott spent over an hour with him at the Sacred Heart Monastery, and was to write in a future *Spectator* review of Fr Stenhouse's final book:

> Writers die, but their writings never do; and while they continue to be read the writer lives on, at least in spirit. After three decades of friendship, I owed him this review; to encourage others to get to know, albeit posthumously, a wonderful man, a fine teacher, and a friend of *The Spectator Australia*.[5]

During these last months before his death, Fr Stenhouse told many *Annals* writers and friends, one by one, including myself, "I have terminal cancer", leaving a few seconds of silence to elapse, then proceeding to talk about work, articles, by-lines, dates, and other matters, as if there were years of work ahead. When I was with him, he spoke with enthusiasm of the last edition of *Annals*, declaring he wanted the journal to "go out with a bang". In other words, he wanted to include as much as possible that was typically *Annals,* to make it memorable. He was totally driven to complete his mission but determination did not entail any dramatics, simply a quiet zeal and persistence. According to reports, those who went past his office at night, saw him at his desk, sometimes bent over, transfixed in severe pain, pausing for a few seconds, and then continuing to type, forging ahead through sheer willpower. As previously mentioned, Dr Alfred Wong thinks that perhaps Fr Stenhouse did not take all the pain killers people in his condition would usually take, in order to keep clarity of mind for his final tasks.

About six weeks before he died, Fr Stenhouse began to be assisted at the monastery by the competent nursing skills of Therese Compton, wife of UNSW University Professor Paul Compton (who had also written for *Annals*). She accompanied him sometimes to buy ice cream, remembering that he always liked a double scoop and enjoyed observing people. She recalls that he was "extraordinarily peaceful." Therese also came with him on a final visit with Armenian friend Jacob Majarian (and his brother Peter) to the shop at the Rocks which sold caramel milkshakes. Jacob recalls that they all sat near the water and enjoyed looking at the scenery together. Therese's care was key in helping him deal with his pain and complete his final edition of *Annals*. No sooner had he finished it than he was medically advised that it was time to investigate his pain management, as his pain levels had begun to spiral out of control. Therese told me that he even expected to return after a stay in hospital, but this was not to be. When he left the Sacred Heart Monastery, after living there for 53 years, he was never to return.

Queues at the hospice

If anyone is under the impression that Fr Stenhouse spent quiet days in the hospice, it is interesting that while they were quiet in one way, they were 'busy' in another. According to Peter Macinante and MSC Superior Father Kelliher, more than 60 (others estimate over 80) people visited him, myself being part of this endless stream. Therese Compton was there outside his room, keeping an eye on him, allowing Fr Stenhouse's friends in for a few minutes at a time. Her quiet, compassionate care truly eased his suffering and kept friends informed of the 'stage' he was at, and what to expect. Superior of the MSC Monastery in Kensington, Fr Kelliher, called to give his brother priest the Last Sacraments. Archbishop Fisher visited him, as did Bishop Desmond Moore, Fr Pat Austin and Fr Stidwill, among others, all praying with him in his final days.

Many were already asking Fr Stenhouse to pray for them in the next world, among them Peter Macinante who was convinced that this holy soul would have considerable clout in high places. So he entered the next world laden with spiritual requests.

Among the many visitors was Chinese flautist Chai Changning, mentioned in the previous chapter, who had played in the movie *Mao's Last Dancer* and now came to play the flute around the bed of his dying priest friend. He gently walked around his bed (I saw this on a youtube film clip) and played Christmas carols, rendering the notes of 'The First Noel' in haunting lyricism as he bowed over the bedside of his friend with affection and gratitude.[6] As previously noted, he had called Fr Stenhouse "a messenger from the living God" in his life and was now serenading his beloved messenger of holy and eternal things on his final journey.

Agnes Nguyen, sister of Venerable Cardinal Francis-Xavier Nguyễn Văn Thuận, in Fr Stenhouse's office. Agnes gave Fr Stenhouse a relic of her brother; a photo of Fr Stenhouse within a cedar of Lebanon frame a gift of the Lebanese community in Sydney; Fr Peter Guy MSC (right) stands with Fr Matthew Attia from the Coptic Orthodox Church, at the funeral of Fr Stenhouse. The Orthodox church always stocked *Annals*; 30 priests processed into the church for the funeral.

Archbishop Anthony Fisher prays over the coffin of Fr Stenhouse; carrying out the coffin – left to right: Jamie Stenhouse, Peter Macinante, Richard Stenhouse; Paul and Therese Compton, friends of Fr Stenhouse. Therese gave much needed nursing care to Fr Stenhouse in the last weeks of his life; Peter Rosengren, editor of the *Catholic Weekly* with journalist Monica Doumit, at the funeral.

Douglas Park, final resting place at the MSC cemetery. Chris Lim, longtime friend of Fr Stenhouse, throwing some soil on the lowered coffin; members of the Stenhouse family at Douglas Park, after the burial.

Some of Fr Stenhouse's friends present for his burial at Douglas Park; more friends at the final *Annals* lunch on 29 November and, below, also at the lunch, Fr Kelliher holds the microphone with Fr Malone on the right.

My first impression of seeing Fr Stenhouse in his hospice bed was that he looked even taller than usual, thin and gaunt, like a noble king, spiritually at peace, ready to meet God. There was his breviary, a statue of Saint Joseph with the infant Jesus near him and pictures of Our Lady and some saints. As I stood there, he said 'hello' and I related that I had recently spoken about *Annals* to a group. As if it were 'work as usual', Fr Stenhouse suddenly opened his eyes and told me to find out the surname of a particular person I had mentioned, implying he would get back to him. As I stood there somewhat bamboozled at this show of energy, he just closed his eyes again and drifted off under sedation. Then a minute later, he woke up to speak of the *Annals* lunch planned for 29 November, suggesting somehow that he could leave the Hospice and make it. Again he wafted off. He had escaped from a hospital months before to attend a function with his Malaysian friends and perhaps thought there was a chance he might do so again. The next day I heard that the amount of his pain killing medication was increased, and like many others, I was so grateful to have seen him before this happened.

Another person who would have come if he could have, was Cardinal George Pell, but the Cardinal was imprisoned at the time for charges which were later found to be totally baseless. Of this, journalist Zoe Zaczek wrote in the *Daily Mail*:

> Pell's biggest regret about his time spent inside was the effect it had on his family and friends, such as Father Paul Stenhouse, who he was unable to visit when he lay dying of cancer in November 2019.[7]

The Cardinal and Father Stenhouse had shared a long friendship, as previously described, and without doubt Fr Stenhouse would have rejoiced from above on hearing that the Cardinal was finally released on 7 April 2020, in a 7-0 ruling of the High Court of Australia, where all judges found him to be innocent of the charges against him. Fr Stenhouse had been his unceasing supporter.

The time came ...

After the farewells, the music and continual prayers, Father Stenhouse went to eternal life early in the afternoon (around 2pm) on 19 November 2019. After a lifetime of prayer and service to others, he was now in the presence of the One to whom he had devoted his life. There would be no more phone calls, emails or conversations about the situation in Yerevan, Beirut or Damascus. The journeys to the earthly kingdoms had ceased and earthly conversations had faded into silence ...

When the news of Fr Stenhouse's death filtered through to his family, priests and friends, the finality left them stunned for it seemed inconceivable that he was no longer here. A memorial evening was organised at the chapel of the Monastery of the Sacred Heart on 24 November 2019. It was moving to see fellow MSC priests and friends sing Fr Stenhouse into eternity.

> Let there be music and let there be song
> for the triumph that your life has been
> Hear how God's angels and saints in their joy
> Join with us as we sing
> Welcome home.

(From the hymn "Welcome Home", Frank Anderson MSC).

People gave individual testimonies at this memorial night of their priest friend's care for them and their families. Some young Lebanese men carried in a piece of a cedar of Lebanon, onto which was affixed a youthful photo of Fr Stenhouse. Some wept remembering what he had done for them, others quietly came up and touched his coffin, lost in thought. As much as there was a need to say good-bye, there was a need to remember it all, and from this arose the idea of sharing written testimonials of this holy, faithful priest – and may there be many.

The funeral was held on 25 November 2019 at the Church of Our Lady of the Rosary, Kensington, near the monastery. There was a natural beauty to the day, totally out of kilter with the sadness and numbness of loss, the spring sunlight framing all mourners as they arrived. Archbishop Fisher, bishops, priests, and many friends, filled the church, all united in the profusion of memories of Fr Stenhouse's words, prayers, kindnesses, his witness to Christ and intelligent defence of the Church. While there was an almost palpable air of disbelief, there simultaneously unfolded a new legacy, a golden alliance of friendship among those left behind which shows no sign of passing away.

Thirty priests walked in procession, including Fr Stenhouse's friend, Orthodox Fr Matthew Attia, from the nearby Coptic Church of St George in Kensington and many unable to come were there in spirit. The church was filled to capacity and brother priests spoke of him with genuine friendship and affection. From Fr Jim Littleton, "Paul Stenhouse knew much more about Middle Eastern religions and politics than the average journalist, he was a great searcher for the truth and proclaimed it fearlessly"; and from Father Michael Fallon, "Till we meet again, dear friend, in the mystery of God's love, we bid you farewell and thank you for the gift and inspiration you have been to us all. Thank you for your love."

Archbishop Fisher said that with the death of Fr Paul Stenhouse, "a light has been extinguished in our world, even if for him it has merely been a change of address in our Church", adding that "Paul was undoubtedly one of the sharpest intellects among the Australian clergy ... a man of deep faith, humanity, keen observer of culture and society, a prolific writer and editor, an editor and linguist", subsuming all of these qualities with the comment that Fr Stenhouse was, "above all a loyal son of the Church and a friend to many."[8]

Deputy Vice-Chancellor at the ACU (Australian Catholic University), Professor Hayden Ramsay was to speak of Fr Stenhouse as a great treasure in the Church, an "ornament" to his Order, a rare authority on languages of the Middle East and a public intellectual, who confronted the anti-Christian animus of the day. It was ACU which had awarded Fr Stenhouse its highest honour, Doctor of the University (*honoris causa*) in 2015, "in recognition of his significant contributions to knowledge and the life of learning in Australia and internationally, to higher education, to journalism and Catholic culture, and to priestly service and pastoral care of the Catholic community."[9] Professor Ramsay noted of Fr Stenhouse that he was very much a man of his time in that "[he] could speak with authority on the terrible persecution of Christians in the 21st century", that most current issue of our times, adding that "[he] was sweet and kind" and that this is what was shared in the memories of his many friends.[10]

After the funeral liturgy, people walked out into the sharp, almost painful sunlight, doubtless sensing the passing of a magnificent era in which they had all participated. Then came the inevitable journey to the burial place at Douglas Park, in a funeral car with many others following. At Douglas Park, time seemed to stand even stiller. It was not just that we were all suddenly aware of statues of angels there, not to mention the rich history shown in the tombstones of Fr Tréand, Archbishop De Boismenu, Bishop Gsell, Fr 'Doc' Rumble, Fr Paddy Ryan, Fr John King and many MSCs amidst the gum trees, magpies and flowers. It was that finally we understood Fr Stenhouse had gone to eternity, pointing out the pathway of life beyond earthly horizons by the life he had lived. While he had a new world of heavenly contacts, as a Catholic journalist might say, his earthbound friends, though bereft, had myriad contacts with each other forevermore. The coffin was lowered in a cloud of incense, solemn prayers were said. The history of his spiritual and scholarly legacy had begun.

After the funeral

A few days later at the *Annals* farewell lunch (on 29 November 2019) at the Sacred Heart Monastery in Kensington, there was an atmosphere of warmth and camaraderie. There were many exchanges of stories, reunions of old friends, an empty chair for Cardinal Pell and, of course, one for Fr Stenhouse. Several priests gave speeches, as did Fr Chris McPhee, MSC Provincial, and Professor Michael Wilding, Emeritus Professor of English from the University of Sydney. There was an emotional address from Peter Macinante who recalled that Fr Stenhouse had told him not long before he died that, according to the doctors, the only organ still working in him was his heart. In youth Fr Stenhouse had had problems with an enlarged heart. Now, with the passing years, it came easily for Peter to say, "Father Stenhouse, you are all heart," with tears in his eyes.

A modern day St Paul

Who could really summarise this priest-scholar who seemed an enigma? He was a priest whose knowledge seemed greater than that of other mortals, yet could speak with everyday ease, who dazzled with his insights yet never sought the limelight, who seemed both extrovert and introvert, who was genial yet razor-sharp in his perceptions, who demolished certain ideas but never people, who was serious yet had a continual eye for ironic humour, who lived several lives, each one to the full, who was understated and yet heroic in his efforts to reach out to individuals who suffered. There was a unity underlying these 'Stenhousian' qualities and paradoxes. That unity arose from what can be put simply as – a heart on fire with love for Christ, on fire to spread the Gospel and to effect it in any way he could. This fine balance constantly impelled the tasks of his everyday life, whether he was driving students to the airport, preparing souls for Baptism, writing sermons, books and articles, travelling by train to Ekaterinburg, studying in Topkapi Palace in Istanbul or climbing mountains in Kashmir.

One could quote many pointed verses of Scripture. Fr Stenhouse could truly be numbered among the "blessed ... who find wisdom, those who gain understanding" (Proverbs 3:13) and shared this wisdom and understanding with all he met. He knew that, "[a] gentle answer turns away wrath (Prov 15:1): that the "quiet words of the wise are more to be heeded than the shouting of a ruler" (Ecc 9:17); and that "I have the strength for everything through him who empowers me" (Phil 4:13). His life resonated unceasingly with St Paul's exhortation to the first Christians: "let us fix our eyes on Jesus, the origin and crown of all faith, who to win his prize of blessedness endured the cross and made light of its shame, Jesus, who now sits on the right of God's throne" (Heb 12:2).

There was that deep-seated humility so many noted of him. There were deep wells of thought issuing from faraway places within his soul. Fr Stenhouse could be described by words he had used of his great-grandfather John Farrell: "he was a mystery, even to his friends ... he never sought the glare of footlights ..." Similarly, the words he used in his obituary of Richard Hughes in 2018 point to his own deep reflection on the nature of mystery itself:

> Richard's life, like the lives of us all, was a mystery ... Mysteries are not things to be analysed or picked at, grappled with or stripped down like an old car, to find out what makes it work. Mysteries are not meant to be solved or 'explained' away.... Mysteries are meant to be revelled in – appreciated, and loved. A mystery is something that we should be in awe of, ecstatic about, swept off our feet by, completely astonished and enthralled by ...[11]

One could say that Fr Stenhouse saw and was continually

enthralled by the mysteries which permeate our lives on earth. Gravitas and joy, deep focus and wonder accompanied his long working days. Similarly there was something mysterious in the way Fr Stenhouse shared some things in conversation, though at some deeper level he seemed to keep his own counsel, propelled by a unique internal rhythm and constant poise. It was as if he were equanimity itself, acting on his interior vision and understanding of the eternal ordering of things.

He exemplified the true MSC spirit in action. While some see him as an Indiana Jones or others a secret spy for the Vatican – perhaps the notion of a priest in the Diplomatic Service for God's heart comes more easily. Many have noted his gifts for restraint and inner balance, his psychological insight, a quick, supple perceptiveness of what is going on under the surface of things. He was not easily fooled, and often more than ten steps ahead of others in his comprehension of geopolitical situations and of people's spiritual needs. Of his trip to the Middle East, previously referred to, where he chartered a boat from Cyprus to deliver pharmaceuticals to the victims of the Lebanese war, he was as far away from mere hand-wringing as you could get. As Professor Marek Chodakiewicz remarked:

> Unauthorized and unorthodox, the mission was a success and a prime example of what the Missionaries of the Sacred Heart could accomplish. Before this audacious stunt, virtually all aid moving through the so-called proper channels had fallen into the hands of thugs and militias. Our priest figured out a way to outsmart them as well as the dead hand of international bureaucracy.[12]

While people complained, he planned and acted. No doubt his wide circle of friends and contacts helped. They had perceived his goodness long ago and willingly helped him in whatever he did as they knew he was on the side of the angels. He acted quickly as he saw through the webs of deception around him. One tribute referred to "his scepticism of so many false idols, his calling-out of sham posturing or pretence in politics and public life or treachery and deceit in international affairs." [13]

The young trainee journalist from Camden who became a priest, writer, pioneering scholar, and adventurous problem solver, was at the same time sensitive to the small, the unnoticed, the vulnerable, the suffering. He drew many souls to the light of faith from all kinds of starting points and his converts around the world are evidence of this. Perhaps Pope Emeritus Benedict XVI's words on St Augustine are apt here:

> Augustine fixed his gaze on this mystery and in it he found the Truth he was so ardently seeking. Jesus Christ, the Incarnate Word, the Sacrificed and Risen Lamb, is the Face of God-Love for every human being on his journey along the paths of time towards eternity.[14]

Fr Stenhouse reflected this God-love "*along the paths of time towards eternity.*" His gifts were held together in a unique wisdom and compassion, his focus continually on what is holy, drawing us to the eternal light threading our days. He inspired us, he influenced his order, and he became part of the history of his country as a journalist and moral force. He ceaselessly pointed us all to the higher things despite our current morally inverted era. Now we are left looking back at the lighted path this priest carved out, reflecting on his great legacy of witness to Christ, in hushed amazement at all he said and did. A rare soul indeed has passed from our midst.

Vale Fr Stenhouse – till we all meet again!
(Photo taken at Campion College during a lecture in 2011).

Endnotes

Chapter 1

[1] Taken from an interview with Richard Stenhouse on January 31, 2020. Much detail in this chapter is taken from the author's transcript of this interview.

[2] From an interview with Margaret Fisher on July 16, 2020. Fr Stenhouse told her that his father had gone to Casino to work as a journalist.

[3] Paul Stenhouse, "Random Memories", *Annals Australasia; Journal of Australian Catholic Culture,* November/December 2019, 40-43. Much of the account in this chapter has been taken from this autobiographical account included in the last edition of *Annals* itself. Fr Stenhouse was not one for seeking limelight, nor for writing an autobiography, but similarly, always seeking facts, he would have baulked at inaccuracies which might be written about his life and family. Perhaps this account was written to stave off any such inventions.

[4] Paul Stenhouse, *John Farrell: Poet, Journalist and Social Reformer, 1851-1904* (Victoria: Australian Scholarly Publishing, 2018). This was presented by Fr Stenhouse to the University of New England for a Master of Arts Degree (Honours) and subsequently made into a book.

[5] Paul Stenhouse, "Memories 'R' us", *Annals Australasia,* July 2014, 5.

[6] A comprehensive list names can be found at: The Australian ex Prisoners of War Memorial: https://www.powmemorialballarat.com.au/world-war-2-s-v.php

[7] From an official Camden website entitled 'Roll of Honour'. http://www.camdenremembers.com.au/crwwII.html

[8] Manuscript of this account among papers of Father Stenhouse in his old office at Kensington. On this account is written: DOC NAME MRS S2. 2MRSS. 13 pages long. Copy in possession of the author.

[9] Manuscript MRS S2. 2MRSS. From pages 1-2.

[10] Paul Stenhouse, "Random Memories", 40.

[11] From the eulogy of Father Michael Fallon, delivered at the funeral of Fr Paul Stenhouse, on November 19, 2019. Personal copy of the author.

[12] Paul Stenhouse, "Random Memories", 40.

[13] Ibid., 40.

[14] Ibid., 40.

[15] Ibid., 41.

[16] Online entry on the school entitled 'St Paul's Camden.' https://www.spcdow.catholic.edu.au/index.php?option=com_content&view=category&layout=blog&id=76&Itemid=486

[17] Ibid.

[18] Paul Stenhouse, "Random Memories", 41.

[19] Ibid.

[20] "Children's Page", *Catholic Weekly*, 5 December 1946, 22. https://trove.nla.gov.au/newspaper/article/146614255

[21] Paul Stenhouse, "Random Memories", 42.

[22] Ibid., 42-43.

Chapter 2

[1] Paul Stenhouse, "The Annals of *The Annals*: 'Within a Shining Pool,'" *The Australasian Catholic Record*, July 1994, 274.

[2] Anthony Caruana, MSC, *Monastery on the Hill: A History of the Sacred Heart Monastery Kensington: 1907-1997* (Sydney: Nelen Yubu Missiological Unit, Chevalier Resource Centre: 2000), 231.

[3] Taken from author's notes of conversation with Fr Jim Littleton MSC, 17 February 2020.

[4] See the Entry on 'St Mary's Towers Retreat Centre'. Author's name not given. https://www.towersretreat.org.au/history/st-mary-s-towers-msc-training-centre-1904-2004

[5] The history of the purchase of Douglas Park is of considerable interest. Here is a part entry on its website: 'Fifty years after our foundation in France and twenty after our arrival in Sydney to care for the Pacific missions entrusted to us, the Missionaries of the Sacred Heart (MSC) took possession of this rural property. It would be at various times a training centre for our Australian

Endnotes

members through school, novitiate and seminary, a farm, parish centre, and retreat centre and renewal centre.' (No author given) More detail given on: https://www.towersretreat.org.au/history/st-mary-s-towers-msc-training-centre-1904-2004

[6] Entry on 'St Mary's Towers Retreat Centre' provided by the MSC order: https://www.towersretreat.org.au/history/st-mary-s-towers-msc-training-centre-1904-2004

[7] From the record of interview with Richard Stenhouse on 31 January 2020.

[8] St Thomas Aquinas and St Pio of Pietrelcina attended such minor seminaries. There are about many minor seminaries still extant in the world, with *Agenzia Fides* reporting 101, 616 minor seminarians in the world: 'Vatican – Catholic Church statistics: 2018'. http://www.fides.org/en/news/64944-VATICAN_CATHOLIC_CHURCH_STATISTICS_2018

[9] As personally related to me by Robert Brian in Sydney on 5 May 2020.

[10] As personally related to me by Richard Stenhouse on 31 January 2020. From author's notes taken from this meeting.

[11] "Town Talk", *Camden News*, 16 December 1954, 7. There was a similar item of news given in the previous year's "Town Talk."

[12] As personally related to me by Rob Marden on 6 February 2020. From author's notes.

[13] More detail on the history of the purchase of Douglas Park is given here: https://www.towersretreat.org.au/history/st-mary-s-towers-msc-training-centre-1904-2004

[14] Entry on 'St Mary's Towers Retreat Centre'. Author's name not given. https://www.towersretreat.org.au/history/st-mary-s-towers-msc-training-centre-1904-2004

[15] Regina Gantner makes this point throughout much of her writing. For a discussion of European missionaries in Australia, see her work: *The Contest for Aboriginal Souls: European Agendas in Australia* (Canberra: ANU Press and Aboriginal History, 2018), an excerpt of which can be found here: https://press-files.anu.edu.au/downloads/press/n4239/html/ch01.xhtml?referer=&page=4#

[16] Ibid. This site gives interesting historical detail, well worth reading in full for those seeking some of the context as well as history and aims of the MSC order. Here is an excerpt describing early attempts on the part of the MSCs to

come to the Antipodes: 'A multinational MSC contingent arrived at Thursday Island in October 1884 (Fr. Louis-André Navarre, Fr. Ferdinand Hartzer, and Br. Giuseppe de Santis and three young Italian Brothers, Mariano Travaglini, Nicola Marconi and Salvador Gasbarra). They purchased land at the first land sale on the island in January 1885, and erected a church and dwelling. Their congregation consisted mostly of Filipinos participating in the pearling industry. A Sisters' convent was added and the first three French Sisters arrived in January 1886, opened a school 1887 (which also taught the children of government resident John Douglas), established the first hospital in Torres Strait and a charitable children's asylum serving New Guinea and New Britain. The Sisters therefore entrenched the MSC in the leadership of an emerging community. During this period (1884-1889) Thursday Island served as the point of departure for all Catholic missionaries to British New Guinea and New Britain. Setting up a base on Thursday Island mirrored the London Missionary Society (LMS) strategy since 1871 of establishing stepping stones across the Torres Strait and New Guinea.'

[17] 'Missionaries of the Sacred Heart', *Catholic Encyclopedia*. http://www.newadvent.org/cathen/13306a.htm

[18] From the website of the Daughters of Our Lady of the Sacred Heart. https://www.olshaustralia.org.au/about-us/our-history.html

[19] Ibid.

[20] While berating some past Christian missions, the ABC wrote favourably of Sister Anne Gardiner's work as a missionary nun on 26 January 2016.

[21] Paul Stenhouse, "New Name for Old Confraternity", *Annals Australasia*, September 1983.

[22] Fr P. Fleming, "Eastern Papua Mission Club", *The Annals of Our Lady of the Sacred Heart*, February 1936.

[23] See the following for more detail: J. Franklin, "Catholic missions to Aboriginal Australia: an evaluation of their overall effect", *Journal of the Australian Catholic Historical Society*, Vol. 37-1, 2016, 45-68. A comprehensive bibliography pertaining to the Catholic missions in Australia is appended to this work (citing work by Fr Peter Hearn, Anne Haebich, Osmund Thorpe, Eugene Stockton, Peter Sutton and John Pye, among many other researchers in this area).

[24] "Missionaries of the Sacred Heart Australia". 16 July 2013. https://misacor.org.au/index.php/what-we-do

Endnotes

25 For further details read the interesting story of this priest's life: 'Frank Flynn Biography', entry on the following MSC website. The name of the author is not given. https://www.misacor.org.au/index.php/emagazine/current-news/1495-msc-history-fr-frank-flynn

26 "Missionaries of the Sacred Heart", 18 February 2015. No author given. https://misacor.org.au/index.php/emagazine/current-news/307-the-bishop-with-150-wives

27 Ibid.

28 J. Franklin, "Catholic missions to Aboriginal Australia: an evaluation of their overall effect", op. cit., 48-49.

29 Website of 'Missionaries of the Sacred Heart'. April 16, 2013. No author given. https://www.misacor.org.au/index.php/what-we-do

30 Taken from notes of an interview with Father Pat Austin on 9 June 2020.

31 Paul Stenhouse, "Reflections on the Catholic Church", *Annals Australasia: Journal of Australian Catholic Culture*, Vol. 8, 2016, 3, 5.

32 The cause of beatification and canonisation of the Servant of God Jules Chevalier was established on December 8, 2013, in France. More about the spirituality of the MSC order can be found on: http://www.sacredheart.org.au/nationalshrineOLSH/Chevalier%20and%20Family.htm#spitiualityoffatherfounder

33 John F. McMahon, M.S.C., B.A. (Syd.), B.Litt. (Oxon.), "About the Editor": https://web.archive.org/web/20150907150040/http://jloughnan.tripod.com/author.htm

34 Quoted in Paul Senz, "Journalist Peter Seewald: Pope Benedict is one of the most misunderstood personalities of our time", *Catholic World Report*, 12 January 2017. http://www.catholicworldreport.com/Item/5342/journalist_peter_seewald_pope_benedict_is_one_of_the_most_misunderstood_personalities_of_our_time.aspx

35 From record of conversation on August 20, 2020 with Jim Giltinan from Coogee Real Estate, who regularly advertised in *Annals* for many years . He told me he would meet Fr Stenhouse for lunch and lively discussions always ensued.

36 Paul Stenhouse, "Emeritus Professor Alan David Crown, AM 1932 – 2010". https://learning.mandelbaum.usyd.edu.au/about-us/alan-crown/.

[37] As related in the account of fellow MSC, John F. McMahon, "About the Editor", May 2014. https://misacor.org.au/index.php/emagazine/current-news/1129-from-the-annals-archive-fr-paul-stenhouse-msc

[38] Taken from the written record of an interview with Rob Marden on 6 and 7 February 2020. The following details of their meetings are taken from these accounts.

[39] Related to me by Joseph Assaf, Fr Stenhouse's cousin Trish Kavanagh and several other friends.

[40] Paul Stenhouse, "Illyria/Albania", *Annals Australasia: Journal of Australian Catholic Culture*, vol 8, 2010, 3.

[41] Ibid.

[42] This was related to me on 16 December 2019 by Joseph Assaf and Marko Franovic.

[43] From an email sent to me by Robert Stove, dated 23 November 2019.

[44] Personal account sent to the author by John Madden, on 16 March 2020.

[45] According to the archives of the University of Sydney, Fr Stenhouse obtained his B.A. in 1973 and his PhD in 1982.

[46] Entry in Mandelbaum Publishing appears on its website as follows. 'Father Dr Paul Stenhouse: Mandelbaum Studies in Judaica 1, The Kitab al Tarikh of Abu'l-Fath: The Chronicle of Abu'l-Fath'. https://learning.mandelbaum.usyd.edu.au/mandelbaum-publishing/father-dr-paul-stenhouse/

[47] As personally related to me by Richard Stenhouse on 31 January 2020. From author's notes taken from meeting.

[48] Professor Alan D. Crown, "The Dead Sea Scrolls Part I", *Annals Australasia*, April, 1990; "The Dead Sea Scrolls – Part 2", *Annals Australasia*, June-July, 1990; "God's word or the word of the bible translators? Which Bible Do You Read?", *Annals Australasia*, July 1997; "Eyes, Teeth and Tunnels in the Bible", *Annals Australasia*, Jan/Feb. 1999. This is just a small selection of Professor Crown's articles – many others are to be readily found on the *Annals* Archive website. https://web.archive.org/web/20151013181726/http://jloughnan.tripod.com/portal.htm#112. A selection of Professor Crown's other work can be found on: https://learning.mandelbaum.usyd.edu.au/mandelbaum-publishing/professor-alan-crown/

[49] As personally related to me by Joseph Assaf on 31 January 2020. From author's notes taken from meeting.

Endnotes

⁵⁰ John F. McMahon MSC, "About the Editor". On the MSC website: https://www.misacor.org.au/index.php/who-we-are/join-us/msc-life-stories/1275-life-story-paul-stenhouse-msc

⁵¹ Steven Dives, "RIP Paul Stenhouse MSC", 19 November 2019. MSC Website: https://www.misacor.org.au/index.php/e-magazine/latest-news/3154-rip-paul-stenhouse-msc/

Chapter 3

¹ Paul Stenhouse, "The *Annals*, 1889-2019", *Annals Australasia*, November-December, 2019, 11.

² Paul Stenhouse's earlier memoir of *Annals* is entitled: "The Annals of *The Annals*: 'Within a Shining Pool'", *The Australasian Catholic Record*, July 1994, 273. Much factual material in this chapter draws from this source.

³ Paul Stenhouse, "The Annals of *The Annals*: 'Within a Shining Pool'": 271-281.

⁴ Ibid., 272.

⁵ Ibid., 272.

⁶ Paul Stenhouse, *John Farrell: Poet, Journalist and Social Reformer, 1851-1904* (Victoria: Australian Scholarly Publishing, 2018).

⁷ Written account sent to the author by Michael Wilding on 15 March 2020.

⁸ Anthony Caruana, MSC, *Monastery on the Hill: A History of the Sacred Heart Monastery Kensington: 1907-1997* (Sydney: Nelen Yubu Missiological Unit, Chevalier Resource Centre: 2000), 104.

⁹ Paul Stenhouse, "The Annals of *The Annals*: 'Within a Shining Pool'", 273. Fr John McMahon writes of this early period: "The first issue of *Annals* appeared in December 1889. The driving force behind it was a pioneer Missionary of the Sacred Heart, *Emile Merg*, who came to Sydney in 1887 and was appointed as curate to Randwick Parish until he left in 1909. Being a French-speaking priest he depended very heavily on the gifted volunteer teacher in the Randwick parish school, Mary Agnes Finn. It was Miss Finn who translated into English much of the early material in *Annals* and who wrote many a short story and the longer serial stories for so many years to come. Her brothers were also well-known commercial printers in the city of Sydney and became before long the early printers of *Annals*." John McMahon MSC, "Editors of the Annals", *Annals Australasia*, November 1989.

[10] Fr Edward McGrath MSC was appointed as first Priest in charge of Coogee parish by Provincial Fr Peter Tréand MSC. Fr McGrath was to play a pivotal role in the life of Eileen O'Connor.

[11] John McMahon MSC, "Editors of the *Annals*", *Annals Australasia*, November 1989. https://web.archive.org/web/20150907135243/http://jloughnan.tripod.com/annalseds.htm

[12] Paul Stenhouse, "New Name for an Old Fraternity", *Annals*, September, 1983. https://web.archive.org/web/20150907113547/http://jloughnan.tripod.com/confrashat.htm

[13] Ibid., 272.

[14] James McAuley, "Poems of Papua", *Annals*, March 1956, 36. McAuley then worked in the Australian School of Pacific Administration in Mosman, Sydney, making several trips to Papua. The poems were written and published on the occasion of Archbishop De Boismenu's death. The latter was declared Venerable in 2014 after Pope Francis confirmed he lived a life of heroic virtue.

[15] Many of 'Doc' Rumble's answers to specific questions can be found on the following *Annals* site: https://web.archive.org/web/20150907144449/http://jloughnan.tripod.com/indexx.htm

[16] *The Australian Dictionary of Biography*. Entry on 'Rumble, Leslie Audoen'. http://adb.anu.edu.au/biography/rumble-leslie-audoen-11584

[17] "Santa Sabina Guild," *The Catholic Press*, 18 November 1937, 30. Author's name not given. *The Catholic Press* was a Sydney-based newspaper first published on 9 November 1895, running until 26 February 1942, after which it amalgamated with the Catholic *Freeman's Journal* and was reborn as *The Catholic Weekly*.

[18] James Franklin, "Catholic Thought and Catholic Action: Dr Paddy Ryan MSC", *Journal of the Australian Catholic Historical Society* 17 (1996), 44-55:44.

[19] P. Ryan, "Question Box", *Catholic Freeman's Journal*, 3/7/1941, 8.

[20] Fr P. J. Ryan, MSC., D.D., PhD. In *Dean Hewlett's Sixth Socialist of the World*, 1942; 3-4. http://digital.slv.vic.gov.au/view/action/singleViewer.do?dvs=1596965523466~540&locale=en_US&metadata_object_ratio=10&show_metadata=true&VIEWER_URL=/view/action/singleViewer.do?&preferred_usage_type=VIEW_MAIN&DELIVERY_RULE_ID=10&frameId=1&usePid1=true&usePid2=true

Endnotes

21 This article was the text of a speech by Fr Ryan, broadcast on the Macquarie Radio Network (these are the only details given) on 3 January 1956. It was published in *Annals* as: Rev. P. Dr. P.J. Ryan, MSC., DD, "Is Peace Possible", *Annals*, March 1956.

22 Rev. J. J. McMahon, "Golden Jubilee of Our Lady's Nurses for the Poor", *The Annals*, August 1963, 228 ff.

23 From the 2019 Diary of Fr Stenhouse held within the *Annals* Office. Each week for a large part of the year, he had an entry for them.

24 John McMahon, "About the Editor" on the following site: https://www.misacor.org.au/index.php/who-we-are/join-us/msc-life-stories/1275-life-story-paul-stenhouse-msc

25 John McMahon MSC, "Editors of the Annals", *Annals Australasia*, November 1989.

26 Joyce Milton, *The Road to Malpsychia: Humanistic Psychology and Our Discontents* (USA: Encounter, 2003). One of the best accounts of the 1960s era and its effects.

27 Taken from notes of a personal interview with Cardinal Pell on 31 July 2020.

28 Paul Stenhouse, Editorial, *Annals*, September 1966.

29 A Reflection By Father Peter Malone MSC: Service Before The Interment Of Father Paul Stenhouse MSC Saint Mary's Towers, Douglas Park, 2:30 PM, Wednesday, 27 November 2019. From author's copy of the text.

30 Stenhouse, "The Annals of the *Annals*: 'Within a Shining Pool'", 276.

31 Ibid.

32 Taken from personal notes of a conversation with Fr Pat Austin on 8 June 2020.

33 Frank Fletcher MSC., "Understanding a Teenager", *Annals*, September 1963.

34 Paul Stenhouse, "New Name for old Confraternity", *Annals Australasia*, September 1983.

35 Karl Schmude, "Paul Stenhouse (1935-2019): Catholic Editor Extraordinaire", *Catholic Herald*, 11 December 2019. https://catholicherald.co.uk/commentandblogs/2019/12/11/fr-paul-stenhouse-msc-1935-2019-catholic-editor-extraordinaire/

36 Paul Stenhouse, "Alister Kershaw, 1921-1995", *Annals Australia*, June 1995, 44.

[37] Ibid., 45.

[38] Ibid.

[39] Ibid.

[40] Taken from Fr Stenhouse's obituary on his friend entitled: "James Waldersee (1926-1988).". In the papers of Fr Stenhouse. Author's copy.

[41] Quotations are from a written communication received from James Franklin on 16 June 2020.

[42] Ibid.

[43] As noted in a Polish article written on the Polish website "Puls Polonii": Andrzej Siedlecki, "Wspomnienie o Henryku Skrzyńskim", *Puls Polonii*, 10 March 2009. http://www.zrobtosam.com/PulsPol/Puls3/index.php?sekcja=5&arty_id=7037

[44] Quoted from personal correspondence from both Matthias and Joseph Skyrzyńsky, 1 July 2020.

[45] Ibid.

[46] Ibid.

[47] Ibid.

[48] Paul Stenhouse, "A True Friend of "The Little People": Unexpected death of a well-known artist" *Annals Australia*, July 1986, 34-35.

[49] Ibid.

[50] Ibid.

[51] Ibid.

[52] Paul Stenhouse, "Kevin Drumm (1943-2006)", *Annals Australasia*, November/December 2006. All subsequent quotations about Kevin Drumm are taken from this article.

[53] John Colborne-Veel, "*Annals* History of Carols", *Annals Australasia*, 2002, 9/10, 27ff.

[54] Ibid.

[55] R J Stove's story can be found on the *Why I'm Catholic* site under the title "Atheist Convert: RJ Stove": http://whyimcatholic.com/index.php/conversion-stories/atheist-converts/item/96-atheist-convert-rj-stove Accessed (7 July 2013). A similar account of Robert's conversion to Catholicism can be found in the book: Wanda Skowronska, *Catholic Converts from Down Under and All Over*, (Melbourne: Connor Court Press, 2015), Chapter 2.

⁵⁶ The text of a lecture given by Robert Stove, sent in an email dated 19/10/2019 in the possession of the author.

⁵⁷ Robert J. Stove, "The Ghost of Madness", *Annals Australasia*, September 2001. https://web.archive.org/web/20150907144229/http://jloughnan.tripod.com/madness.htm

⁵⁸ These quotations are taken from several letters in the preserved correspondence of Fr Stenhouse, which I was privileged to read in early 2020 at the Monastery of the Sacred Heart, Kensington.

⁵⁹ Karl Schmude, "Fr Paul Stenhouse MSC (1935-2019) – Catholic Editor Extraordinaire", *Catholic Herald*, 11 December 2019. https://catholicherald.co.uk/fr-paul-stenhouse-msc-1935-2019-catholic-editor-extraordinaire-2/

⁶⁰ This quotation comes within an article about Kashmir: Paul Stenhouse "Remembering Barambulla", *Annals Australasia*, March 2010. The comment comes from *"Teenage Magnanimity and the Beautiful"* by Douglas McManaman, past president of the Canadian Fellowship of Catholic Scholars. (No other reference given)

Chapter 4

¹ John McMahon, "Life Story: Paul Stenhouse MSC". https://www.misacor.org.au/index.php/join-us/msc-life-stories/1275-life-story-paul-stenhouse-msc

² Michael Novak, "The Truth About Religious Freedom", *First Things*, March 2006. https://www.firstthings.com/article/2006/03/the-truth-about-religious-freedom

³ Marek Jan Chodakiewicz, "Fr Paul Stenhouse, R.I.P.", *Crisis Magazine*, 21 January. https://www.crisismagazine.com/2020/fr-paul-stenhouse-r-i-p

⁴ Fr Paul Stenhouse, "Cambridge Spies and Post-modernist lies." *Annals Australasia*, March 2003. The best known of these spies are Kim Philby, Douglas Maclean, Guy Burgess, Anthony Blunt and John Cairncross. They all rose to high positions in English society and passed valuable information to the Soviet which resulted in the deaths of many western intelligence officers.

⁵ Fr Stenhouse quotes copiously from: Michael Straight, *After Long Silence* (UK: Norton, 1983).

⁶ Fr Paul Stenhouse, "Cambridge Spies and Post-modernist lies."

⁷ From notes taken in a personal interview with Cardinal Pell on 31 July 2020.

⁸ Pope Benedict XVI, "Christmas Greetings to the Roman Curia", 21 December

2012. http://www.vatican.va/content/benedict-xvi/en/speeches/2012/december/documents/hf_ben-xvi_spe_20121221_auguri-curia.html

[9] Quoted in: Paul Stenhouse, *Islam: Context and Complexity*, (Melbourne: Scholarly Press, 2019), 101. Taken from Pope John Paul II, *Ecclesia in Europa* (2003).

[10] Paul Stenhouse, "Why do Catholics ... Give Saints' Names to their Children at Baptism?", *Annals Australia: Journal of Catholic Culture*, July 1997.

[11] Ibid.

[12] Ibid.

[13] Ibid.

[14] These are included in the *Annals* Archive which can be found at: https://web.archive.org/web/20151013181726/http://jloughnan.tripod.com/portal.htm

[15] Fr Paul Stenhouse, *Whatever Happened to the Relics of the True Cross?* (Sydney: Chevalier Press, 1996); *Whatever Happened to the Twelve Apostles* (Sydney: Chevalier Press, 2006). These give an excellent history of the issues in a synthesised form. They would be good on secondary school and tertiary course reading lists.

[16] Walter McEntee, C.P., B.A. (Hons.), "The Blood of the Martyrs Is the Seed of the Church – Tertullian", *Annals Australasia*, March, 1983.

[17] Currently there are 2,400 articles on the *Annals* Archive which can be found at: https://web.archive.org/web/20151013181726/http://jloughnan.tripod.com/portal.htm Within this Archive is a course on Catholic belief by 'Doc' Rumble, divided into clear, separate topics. https://web.archive.org/web/20150907134638/http://jloughnan.tripod.com/cathinstrcrs.htm

[18] McEntee, op.cit.

[19] Ibid.

[20] Ibid.

[21] Paul Stenhouse, "Lest we Forget", *Annals Australasia*, July 1990. https://web.archive.org/web/20150907145939/http://jloughnan.tripod.com/lestforget.htm

[22] Ibid.

[23] Paul Stenhouse, "CHRIST IS TRULY RISEN: *The return of Great Archbishop Cardinal Myroslav Lubachivskyj to his faithful Byzantine-Rite Catholics*", Easter

1991, *Annals Australasia*, May 1991. One of the most extraordinary articles written about the return of Cardinal Lubachivskyj to his people, after years of Soviet suffering. https://web.archive.org/web/20150907152852/http://jloughnan.tripod.com/ukraineb.htm

[24] Reprinted from Aid to the Church in Need newsletter, no author given, "Heroic Nuns murdered in the Congo", *Annals Australia: Journal of Catholic Culture*, vol 8, 1998: 16-17: Paul Stenhouse, "Illyria/Albania", *Annals Australia: Journal of Catholic Culture*, vol 8, 2010: 3-6.

[25] Taken from a personal account of Stuart Rowland, sent to the author.

[26] Paul Stenhouse MSC, Ph.D. *Catholic Answers to 'Bible' Christians: A Light on Biblical Fundamentalism* (Sydney: Chevalier Press, 1988), 1. Further references to this issue are taken from this book. These booklets are still available from the Sacred Heart Monastery.

[27] Ibid.

[28] Ibid.

[29] Ibid., vii ff.

[30] Ibid., 2.

[31] Ibid.

[32] Ibid., 5.

[33] Ibid.

[34] Ibid.

[35] Ibid.

[36] Ibid.,10.

[37] Ibid.

[38] Paul Stenhouse MSC, Ph.D, *"Catholic Answers to 'Bible' Christians: A Light on Biblical Fundamentalism"*, 12

[39] Paul Stenhouse, "The Tragedy of Marcel Lefebvre", *Annals Australia*, July 1988.

[40] Ibid.

[41] Ibid.

[42] Bob Gould, "My Enemy is Dead and I Mourn him", 4 February 2008. On the Marxists' website: https://www.marxists.org/archive/gould/2008/20080204a.htm

⁴³ Rupert Lockwood, "Gorbachev's Russia", *Annals Australia*, January/February 1990, 13.

⁴⁴ Rupert Lockwood, "Can the Robespierre Fever Strike Again", *Annals Australasia*, April/May 1993. https://web.archive.org/web/20150907131808/http://jloughnan.tripod.com/robesfever.htm

⁴⁵ Ibid.

⁴⁶ Comment made by Father John George about *Annals Australasia* on October, 2014, quoted the online journal *Eureka Street* which was lamenting the closure of some Catholic press. https://www.eurekastreet.com.au/article/catholic-press-struggles-to-earn-trust

Chapter 5

¹ The *Annals* Archive section on articles on Islam can be located here: https://web.archive.org/web/20150907143102/http://jloughnan.tripod.com/portislam.htm

² Paul Stenhouse, *Islam: Context and Complexity* (Melbourne: Scholarly Press, 2019). Henceforth referred to as Stenhouse, ICC. Fr Stenhouse addressed similar issues in *Quadrant* articles: e.g. Paul Stenhouse, "Ignoring signposts on the road: Da`wa: Jihad with a velvet glove," *Quadrant Magazine*, 1 June 2007; "Partisans of Allah", *Quadrant*, 1 May 2009; https://quadrant.org.au/magazine/2009/05/partisans-of-allah-jihad-in-south-asia-by-ayesha-jalal/; "What is going on in Syria", *Quadrant*, 1 April 2012. https://quadrant.org.au/magazine/2012/04/what-is-going-on-in-syria/.

³ Stenhouse, ICC. The brief biography comes on the first page which is unnumbered. Fr Stenhouse's articles on various topic related to Islam appeared in a wide range of scholarly journals and mainstream media.

⁴ As John F. McMahon MSC says in: "Life Story: Paul Stenhouse MSC", September 2014. https://www.misacor.org.au/index.php/join-us/msc-life-stories/1275-life-story-paul-stenhouse-msc

⁵ Marek Jan Chodakiewicz, "Fr Paul Stenhouse, R.I.P.", *Crisis Magazine*, 21 January 2020. https://www.crisismagazine.com/2020/fr-paul-stenhouse-r-i-p

⁶ The original hand-written diary was on Fr Stenhouse's desk in the office of Fr Stenhouse at the Monastery of the Sacred Heart in Kensington, Sydney. I express great gratitude to Fr Chris McPhee for permission given to Peter

Endnotes

Macinante, James Franklin (editor of the *Journal of Australian Catholic History*) and myself to see Fr Stenhouse's general papers early in 2020. I am indebted to Peter Macinante for locating the passport of Fr Stenhouse which matched his travel dates to the diary dates. The diary records entries from 16-24 April. Henceforth this diary will be referred to as *Stenhouse Diary Middle East*.

[7] *Stenhouse Diary Middle East*. Most likely the date is Thursday 17 April the day of arrival in Cyprus, though this is not stated. Fr Stenhouse's flight left on 16 April.

[8] *Stenhouse Diary Middle East*, 20 April.

[9] Ibid.

[10] *Stenhouse Diary Middle East*, 21 April.

[11] Ibid., 20 April.

[12] Samir Geagea (Ja'ja) was the executive chairman of the Lebanese Forces, a Christian political party in Lebanon. After the civil war in Lebanon, he was accused of four assassinations and placed in solitary confinement for 11 years. He denied all charges. After his release, and after being restored to health, he began to take part in political life again. A 2019 news article stated: "The head of the Lebanese Forces Party Samir Geagea said in a televised speech late on Saturday that the challenges facing the country are unprecedented."We have not seen any serious intention by the Lebanese officials to address the crises," Geagea said. Geagea announced the resignation of the Lebanese Forces Party's four ministers from Saad Hariri's government ... Lebanon cannot be as effective and strong as a state as long as Hezbollah continues to be armed." From: "Samir Geagea announces resignation of his ministers from Hariri cabinet," *Al Arabiya*, 20 October 2019. https://english.alarabiya.net/en/News/middle-east/2019/10/20/Samir-Geagea-

[13] Ibid.

[14] Ibid.

[15] Elie Karami (Karameh) was a successor to Pierre Gemayel, the senior Christian political figure who helped found the Phalangists or Kataib (Kataeb), a Christian democratic political party in Lebanon which played a major role in the Lebanese Civil War (1975-1990).

[16] John Kifner of the *New York Times*, wrote on 30 August 1984: "Pierre Gemayel had recently announced that he had chosen his physician, Dr. Elie Karameh,

as his successor as leader of the Phalangist Party. He said he had been "grooming him for the last four years". https://www.nytimes.com/1984/08/30/world/leader-of-lebanese-christians-dies-adding-to-unrest.html

[17] Suleiman Bey Kabalan Frangieh, last name also spelled *Frangié*, *Franjieh*, or *Franjiyeh* (1910-1992), was a Lebanese Maronite politician who was President of Lebanon from 1970 to 1976.

[18] It is Geagea's grandson in the article photo. From *Reuters*, 15 November 2018. https://www.reuters.com/article/us-lebanon-politics-christians/lebanese-christian-civil-war-foes-shake-hands-make-up-after-40-years-idUSKCN1NJ253

[19] Stenhouse, ICC, 159.

[20] Kahlil Gibran, *The Collected Works*. (New York: Alfred A. Knopf, 2007), 878.

[21] In addition to his scholarly articles which had an international reach, Australian writers have referred to him in an authoritative way, for example, in the following article: John Stone, "The Muslim Problem and What to Do about It, " *Quadrant*, vol. 50, No. 9, September 2006. https://search.informit.com.au/documentSummary;dn=176058240842618;res=IELIAC

[22] Paul Stenhouse, "Islamic Law: questions no one will ask", *Annals Australia*, October 1989. https://web.archive.org/web/20150907195957/http://jloughnan.tripod.com/islaw.htm. Fr Stenhouse used the spelling 'Koran' more in his early work, as it was a more familiar spelling for readers, and used 'Qur'an' in his later writings, as this had become more widely used .

[23] Paul Stenhouse, "Understanding, Islam I", *Annals Australasia*, March 2015, 9. Much of this is based on his *Annals* article: "Christians in pre-Islamic Arabia", *Annals Australasia*, March 2015. This is turn relies on the source: Ibn Ishaq. in the edition of ibn Hisham: As-Sira an-Nabawiyyah. Dar Ehia al-Tourath al-Arabi. Rue Dakkkache. Beirut. Lebanon, vol. 3, 5ff

[24] While the oldest known extant copy of the whole Bible translated into Arabic – the Mt Sinai Arabic Codex 151 – dates from 867 when it is written it was 'done' – the word 'done' can referred to being copied or translated. So there could well have been earlier copies.

[25] Stenhouse, ICC, 2.

[26] "Christians in pre-Islamic Arabia", *Annals Australasia*, March 2015. Comprehensive sources are cited in the body of the article and in the footnotes.

[27] Ibid.

²⁸ Stenhouse, ICC, 28.

²⁹ op. cit., 112.

³⁰ op. cit., 46.

³¹ Paul Stenhouse, "INDIFFERENTISM and ISLAM", *Annals Australasia*, November/December 2011. https://web.archive.org/web/20150912134212/http://jloughnan.tripod.com/compendislam.htm

³² Ibid.

³³ Stenhouse, ICC, 48.

³⁴ A comprehensive account of this is given in: Stenhouse, 1CC, 50ff. This payment of the jizya tax is also focused on by Mark Durie's excellent account of Islamic principles in his book: *The Third Choice: Islam, Dhimmitude and Freedom* (US: Deror Books, 2010). Fr Stenhouse knew Mark Durie and published some of his articles in *Annals*.

³⁵ Stenhouse, 1CC, 50-51.

³⁶ Ibid., 113.

³⁷ Ibid., 53.

³⁸ Paul Stenhouse, "The Crusades And The Spin Doctors", *Annals Australasia*, October 2007. https://web.archive.org/web/20150912071620/http://jloughnan.tripod.com/crusspin.htm

³⁹ Ibid., 67.

⁴⁰ Ibid., 69.

⁴¹ Stenhouse, ICC, 77.

⁴² Ibid., 78.

⁴³ Paul Stenhouse, "The Crusades And The Spin Doctors".

⁴⁴ Paul Stenhouse, ICC, 120.

⁴⁵ Ibid., 102.

⁴⁶ Paul Stenhouse, "Islamic Fundamentalism", *Annals Australasia*, August 2002. https://web.archive.org/web/20150912073124/http://jloughnan.tripod.com/isfundy.htm

⁴⁷ Paul Stenhouse, "Dialogue with Islam: Planning to Fail?", *Annals Australasia*, March 2008. Italics are in the original text of his article. https://web.archive.org/web/20150912075027/http://jloughnan.tripod.com/isdialogue.htm

⁴⁸ Paul Stenhouse, "Dialogue with Islam: Planning to Fail?"

[49] Ibid.

[50] Paul Stenhouse, "Militant Islam: A Wake-Up Call For Catholics And The West", *Annals Australasia*, October 2004. https://web.archive.org/web/20150912071711/http://jloughnan.tripod.com/miliscall.htm

[51] Fr Stenhouse was one of the few to publicly do so.

[52] Jill Rowbotham, "Catholic hits Islamic Chair", *The Australian*, 16 January 2008. http://www.theaustralian.news.com.au/story/0,25197,23058343-12332,00.html

[53] Ibid.

[54] Sureyya Nur Cicek, Doctoral thesis entitled: "The Gülen/ Hizmet Movement in Melbourne and Sydney and its development of social capital in dialogical engagement with non-Muslim communities," 2016, Monash University. The comments were brief and did not address the issues Fr Stenhouse presented.

[55] Paul Stenhouse, ICC, 124-5.

[56] Stenhouse, op. cit., 125.

[57] Paul Stenhouse, "Dialogue with Islam: Planning to Fail?"

[58] Stenhouse, ICC, 146.

[59] Ibid., 90.

[60] Fr Samir Khalil Samir SJ, "Benedict XVI and Islam", *Annals Australasia*, September 2006. https://web.archive.org/web/20150912075555/http://jloughnan.tripod.com/benedislam.htm

[61] Ibid.

[62] Ibid.

[63] Ibid. Fr Samir adds in the same article. "*It is worth recalling that already as far back as 1999, Cardinal Ratzinger took part in an encounter with Prince Hassan of Jordan, Metropolitan Damaskinos of Geneva, Prince Sadruddin Aga Khan, deceased in 2003, and the Grand Rabbi of France René Samuel Sirat. Muslims, Jews and Christians were invited by a foundation for inter-religious and inter-cultural dialogue to create among them a pole for cultural dialogue.*" In the same article, Fr Samir lays emphasis on the words of then Pope Benedict XVI: "*It has been said that we must not speak of God in the European Constitution, because we must not offend Muslims and the faithful of other religions.*" The opposite is true. As Ratzinger points out, "*What offends Muslims and the faithful of other religions is not talking about God or our Christian roots, but rather the disdain for God and the sacred, that separates us from other cultures and does not create the opportunity for encounter, but expresses the arrogance*

of diminished, reduced reason, which provokes fundamentalist reactions." Also see: "When Civilisations Meet: How Joseph Ratzinger sees Islam." https://www.metransparent.com/old/texts/samir_khalil_samir_how_joseph_ratzinger_sees_islam.htm

[64] Stenhouse, ICC, 162.

Chapter 6

[1] Norbertines are also known as the Premonstratensians, The Order of Canons Regular of Prémontré, and, in Britain and Ireland, are known as the White Canons. They are a religious order of Canons regular of the Catholic Church founded in Prémontré near Laon in 1120 by Norbert of Xanten. It is one of the oldest religious orders in the world. More information can be found on: https://norbertines.org/vocations/norbertine-formation-program/faq/#1

[2] From a personal account by Phillip Collignon, sent to the author on 12 September 2020.

[3] A good account of the development and growth of this organisation can be found in: Joanna Bogle, *Father Werenfried: A Life* (UK: Gracewing, 2001).

[4] From a personal account by Phillip Collignon, sent to the author on 12 September 2020.

[5] Ibid.

[6] Conversation between Phillip Collignon and myself on 14 January 2020 in Sydney. The travel details are taken from this exchange.

[7] Ibid.

[8] Taken from a copy of the original itinerary in a filing cabinet in his old office. This cabinet was filled with the ticket vouchers of each journey he had done.

[9] Miranda Devine, *The Daily Telegraph*, 2 November 2011. https://www.dailytelegraph.com.au/blogs/miranda-devine/our-scorn-for-the-truly-deserving/news-story/849ece7ede014cb8528859dc56ca48d3

[10] These reports, excellent factual accounts of the state of Christian persecution, can be accessed on the ACN website. https://www.aidtochurch.org/reports

[11] The Radio Interview (interviewer name not given) in which the article of the UN Declaration of Human Rights is referred to by Fr Stenhouse, among several points. The interview is available on the following MP3 link. https://www.misacor.org.au/images/rer_20141112_1745.mp3

[12] From a personal account by Phillip Collignon, sent to the author on 12 September 2020.

[13] From personal correspondence with Karl Schmude concerning his friendship and work with Fr Stenhouse. Dated 1 April 2020.

[14] Ibid.

[15] Ibid.

[16] Ibid.

[17] Ibid.

[18] Ibid.

[19] The lecture was entitled: "John Farrell – Australian Social Reformer" and can be found on the following website: http://chestertonaustralia.com/media.php

[20] The interview with Cardinal Pell took place on 31 July 2020 in Sydney. References and quotations in this section are taken from a transcript of a recording of this meeting.

Chapter 7

[1] The account of her youth in Cobbitty, by May Stenhouse, was previously mentioned in Chapter 1. I saw the typed manuscript is at the Monastery of the Sacred Heart Kensington. It was labelled Manuscript MRS S2. 2MRSS. I have a copy of this manuscript. The descriptions come from pages 1-2. May Stenhouse also kept notebooks of sayings of writers.

[2] There were many pages of genealogical diagrams in the office of Fr Stenhouse, much of it related to his work on John Farrell, his great grandfather.

[3] Taken from an interview with Richard Stenhouse on 31 January 2020. Much detail has been taken from the author's own transcript of this interview.

[4] Homily by Father Jim Littleton MSC. Requiem Mass for Father Paul Stenhouse MSC. Our Lady of the Rosary Parish Kensington, 10.00am Wednesday, 27 November 2019. Author's personal copy of the text.

[5] From a personal interview with Fr Littleton on 17 February 2020. Taken from personal notes of the author.

[6] Ibid.

[7] In conversation with the author at the MSC monastery.

Endnotes

[8] Related to me in a personal conversation with Sister Mary Ruth on 28 February 2020.

[9] As related to me in an interview with Fr Stidwill on 28 May 2020.

[10] From notes taken of an interview with Fr Pat Austin on 10 June 2020.

[11] Taken from the eulogy of Father Michael Fallon, delivered at the funeral of Fr Paul Stenhouse, 27 November 2019. Personal copy of the author.

[12] Ibid.

[13] From the obituary of Fr Peter Malone given on 19 November 2019.

[14] As related to me in a personal conversation with Fr Peter Guy on 28 February 2020.

[15] As related to me in a personal communication with Fr Matthew Attia on 1 June 2020.

[16] This quotation and other material in this section is taken from the author's notes of an interview with Trish Kavanagh in Sydney on 2 January 2020.

[17] Ibid.

[18] Whether this was a one-off occasion or whether he did this more than once, it is not clear. Others who recount a similar story say Fr Stenhouse went to Cyprus and took a boat from there. Perhaps there were several such missions to Lebanon. Joseph Assaf's recollection was that Fr Stenhouse went to Lebanon 29 times.

[19] Author's notes of an interview with Trish Kavanagh in Sydney on 2 January 2020.

[20] From the speech (author's personal copy) given by Peter Macinante at the final *Annals* lunch on 29 December 2019.

[21] Taken from private notes of an interview with Greg Quinn on 15 April 2020. Most of this section on Greg Quinn is taken from this interview.

[22] Ibid.

[23] Ibid.

[24] Ibid.

[25] Private correspondence with Hendrikus Wong, dated 22 April 2020.

[26] Ibid.

[27] Ibid.

[28] Ibid.

[29] Written account of memoirs sent to the author by Giles Auty on 17 March 2020. Most of the material from this section is taken from this and from some recent conversations.

[30] Written account of memoirs sent to the author by Giles Auty on 17 March 2020.

[31] Ibid.

[32] Ibid.

[33] Taken from personal notes of an interview with James Murray on 30 April 2020. Most quotations are taken from this conversation.

[34] James Murray, "The Passion of the Christ", *Annals Australasia*, March 2004. https://web.archive.org/web/20150907134756/http://jloughnan.tripod.com/passmurray.htm

[35] Taken from an article (no author given) posted on the MSC website: "REMEMBERING 130 YEARS OF ANNALS – A COMMEMORATIVE LUNCH", published: Friday, 13 December 2019, on the following site: https://www.misacor.org.au/index.php/e-magazine/latest-news/3175-remembering-130-years-of-annals-a-commemorative-lunch

Chapter 8

[1] I was able to meet some of these friends before Fr Stenhouse died, but many more of them after he died, friends with many recollections of his kindnesses and spiritual example.

[2] Written on a small card, found among other mementoes in the office of Father Stenhouse.

[3] Paul Stenhouse's moving tribute to his mentor and friend appears on a University of Sydney website: "Emeritus Professor Alan David Crown, AM 1932-2010." https://learning.mandelbaum.usyd.edu.au/about-us/alan-crown/

[4] From a written account of Stuart Rowland's personal memoirs given to the author.

[5] Paul Stenhouse, "For democracy to thrive, Bashar al -Assad needs a chance", *The Australian*, 12 October 2011. https://www.theaustralian.com.au/news/world/for-democracy-to-thrive-bashar-al-assad-needs-a-chance/news-story/6a62f9627853f2918e0307af679c4276

Endnotes

⁶ The interview with Joseph Assaf took place in Leichardt, Sydney, on 16 December 2019. Quotations are taken from the author's recordings and written transcripts of this interview.

⁷ Ibid.

⁸ Ibid.

⁹ Samar Kadi, *The Arab Weekly*, 24 June 2018. https://thearabweekly.com/lebanons-Hardine-treasure-trove-beaten-track

¹⁰ Paul Stenhouse, "Beatification of Nimatullah Yussef Kassab As-Hardini", *Annals Australasia: Journal of Catholic Culture*, June 1998, 10ff. https://web.archive.org/web/20150907135521/http://jloughnan.tripod.com/yussef.htm

¹¹ Paul Stenhouse, "Beatification of Nimatullah Yussef Kassab As-Hardini".

¹² "Nimatullah al Hardini", Maronite Heritage website. https://www.maronite-heritage.com/Saint%20Nimitullah%20Hardini.php

¹³ "Interview of General Michel Aoun for *Annals* by Paul Stenhouse, Marseille, 19 November 1992", *Annals Australasia: Journal of Catholic Culture*, Jan-Feb, Vol. 1, 1993. https://web.archive.org/web/20150907120113/http://jloughnan.tripod.com/aounsten.htm

¹⁴ Ibid.

¹⁵ A brief account of this can be found on: https://www.europeanforum.net/countries/lebanon

¹⁶ Paul Stenhouse, "Lebanese Elections: Tinkering with the Truth, Caught in the Cross-Fire", *Annals Australasia*, 2009.

¹⁷ Ibid.

¹⁸ Ibid. All quotations are taken from this personal memoir written by John Madden.

¹⁹ Ibid.

²⁰ Ibid.

²¹ Ibid.

²² Ibid.

²³ Written personal account of Stuart Rowland in possession of the author, sent 22 January 2020.

²⁴ Ibid.

[25] Taken from notes of a personal conversation with Margaret Fisher on 3 July 2020.

[26] From a personal tribute sent to the author on 15 June 2020.

Chapter 9

[1] From the record of an interview with Chris Lim on 5 March 2020. Most of the material in this section is taken from this interview.

[2] Carole Egan, "35th Anniversary of the Randwick Asian Catholic Community", *St Margaret Mary's Randwick North, Our Lady of the Sacred Heart Randwick*, September 2015. This is the local Parish Magazine.

[3] Ibid.

[4] From the record of an interview with Chris Lim on 5 March 2020.

[5] As related to me in a personal conversation/interview with Ganesh Sahathevan on 10 September 2020.

[6] Ibid.

[7] Ibid.

[8] Having seen some of the diary accounts and medical reports among the papers of Fr Stenhouse, he was very ill with multiple complications. But no doubt he did not literally 'escape' but discharged himself temporarily.

[9] Written account of memories sent to the author by Vony Sugiarto on 26 March 2020.

[10] Anne Elizabeth McLaren, "Simon Leys, navigator between worlds, unique Australian intellectual", *The Conversation*, No 13, 2017.

[11] See: Daniel Sanderson, "An Interview with Pierre Ryckmans", *China Heritage Quarterly*, 26 June 2011. http://www.chinaheritagequarterly.org/tien-hsia.php?searchterm=026_ryckmans.inc&issue=026

[12] Ibid.

[13] Fr Paul Stenhouse, "Pierre Ryckmans", *Annals Australasia*, September 2014.

[14] Taken from notes of a conversation with Han Fang (Frances) Ryckmans in Sydney on 13 March 2020. Details of the life of Pierre Ryckmans are taken from this.

[15] From the conversation in Sydney on 13 March 2020.

[16] Daniel Sanderson, "An Interview with Pierre Ryckmans", op cit.

Endnotes

17 The speeches made by Pierre Ryckmans and John Minford at the commemorative service held for Professor Liu at ANU on 24 August 2009 can be found here: http://www.chinaheritagequarterly.org/features.php?searchterm=019_vale_liu.inc&issue=019

18 Ibid.

19 Anne Elizabeth McLaren "Simon Leys, navigator between worlds, unique Australian intellectual", *The Conversation,* No 13, 2017.

20 Comment made in the Introduction of Philippe Paquet's biography of Pierre Ryckmans: Philippe Paquet, *Simon Leys: Navigator between Worlds.* Translated from the original French by Julie Rose (Melbourne: La Trobe University Press, in conjunction with Black Inc., 2018).

21 Quoted in: Luke Slattery, Pierre Ryckmans: "Distinguished Australian intellectual was a figure of world renown", *Sydney Morning Herald,* 22 August 2014. https://www.smh.com.au/national/pierre-ryckmans-distinguished-australian-intellectual-was-a-figure-of-world-renown-20140822-1073br.html

22 Fr Paul Stenhouse, "Pierre Ryckmans", *Annals Australasia,* September 2014.

23 General information on the Armenian Genocide can be found on this site: https://www.history.com/topics/world-war-i/armenian-genocide

24 The details of this journey and Jacob's friendship with Father Stenhouse are taken from a written account of a meeting with Jacob on 19 March 2020. Fr Stenhouse's friend, Father Tontonjian, wrote about the situation of the Armenians in Australia in Annals. One such article is: https://web.archive.org/web/20150907123141/http://jloughnan.tripod.com/armenschool.htm. Fr Anton Tontonjian, "First School for Armenian Catholics in Australia", *Annals Australia,* November/December 1984.

25 Krikor Bedros XX Gabroyan was born in Syria. He studied at the Gregorian University in Rome prior to becoming Armenian Eparch.

26 These quotations and recollections are taken from notes made during a conversation with Chai Changning on 20 April 2020.

27 Chai's playing on the occasion of his examination is well worth listening to and can be seen and heard on the following site: https://www.youtube.com/watch?v=IA3yz08WxLY

28 Taken from the author's notes made during a conversation with Chai Changning on 20 April 2020.

Chapter 10

[1] I was able to read these diaries and some correspondence. My unending gratitude is due to Fr Chris McPhee and Peter Macinante for being able to see these books and papers during February and March 2020.

[2] Ibid.

[3] As related to me by Father Pat Austin on 9 June 2020.

[4] As told to me by Tony Abbott on 29 October 2020. Most quotations are from this reflection sent to me.

[5] Tony Abbott, "Religion of Peace?", *The Spectator*, 21 December 2019. https://www.spectator.co.uk/2019/12/religion-of-peace/

[6] The film clip was taken down from the internet after a week and is in the private possession of the flautist. I saw it – Chai bowed and almost lightly danced around the room while playing for Fr Stenhouse who lay on his Hospice bed.

[7] Zoe Zaczek, "The old friend who kept him 'sane', working for $10 a week and his biggest regret: Cardinal George Pell's handwritten diary reveals how he endured 13 months behind bars", *Daily Mail*, 14 April 2020. https://www.dailymail.co.uk/news/article-8215445/George-Pells-handwritten-diary-reveals-spent-time-bars.html

[8] Quoted in: Marilyn Rodrigues, "Hundreds Farewell Father Paul Stenhouse", *Catholic Weekly*, 29 November 2019. https://www.catholicweekly.com.au/humble-intellectual-fr-paul-stenhouse-farewelled/

[9] "Defender of the Faith: Fr Paul Stenhouse MSC", *Catholic Weekly*, 5 December 2019. Author not given. https://www.catholicweekly.com.au/defender-of-the-faith-fr-paul-stenhouse-msc/

[10] Ibid.

[11] The description of Farrell came from his lecture was entitled "John Farrell – Australian Social Reformer" which can be found on the following website: http://chestertonaustralia.com/media.php. The words about Richard Hughes (1931-2018) came from Fr Stenhouse's pagegyric on his friend, given at his Requiem Mass. Copy in possession of the author.

[12] Marek Jan Chodakiewicz, "Fr Paul Stenhouse, R.I.P.", *Crisis Magazine*, 21 January. https://www.crisismagazine.com/2020/fr-paul-stenhouse-r-i-p

[13] "Defender of the Faith: Fr Paul Stenhouse MSC", *Catholic Weekly*.

Endnotes

[14] Homily of His Holiness Benedict XVI, Basilica of St Pietro in Ciel d'Oro, Pavia Third Sunday of Easter, 22 April, 2007. http://www.vatican.va/content/benedict-xvi/en/homilies/2007/documents/hf_ben-xvi_hom_20070422_vespri-pavia.html

www.ingramcontent.com/pod-product-compliance
Lightning Source LLC
Chambersburg PA
CBHW071401300426
44114CB00016B/2146